01655701

73/3998

942.081 BUR
BURTON
73/3998

DISCARD

D1349619

B.C.H.E. - LIBRARY

00120523

*The Early Victorians
at Home*

The Early Victorians at Home
1837 - 1861

ELIZABETH BURTON

illustrated by
FELIX KELLY

LONGMAN

LONGMAN GROUP LIMITED
London
*Associated companies, branches and representatives
throughout the world*

Text © Elizabeth Burton 1972

Illustrations © Felix Kelly 1972

All rights reserved. No part of this publication may be reproduced, stored in a retrieval system, or transmitted in any form or by any means, electronic, mechanical, photocopying, recording, or otherwise, without the prior permission of the Copyright owner.

First published 1972

I S B N 0 582 10810 1

In series with this volume
by Elizabeth Burton illustrated by Felix Kelly

THE ELIZABETHANS AT HOME

THE JACOBEANS AT HOME

THE GEORGIANS AT HOME

NEWTON PARK

COLLEGE

BATH

LIBRARY

DISCARD

CLASS NO. 942.081 BUR

ACC. NO. 73/3998

*Printed in Great Britain by
Clarke, Doble & Brendon, Ltd., Plymouth*

'This is a new reign,' said Egremont,
'perhaps it is a new era.'
'I think so,' said the young stranger.

BENJAMIN DISRAELI
Sybil, or the Two Nations

To the memory of my father
Richard Burton

CONTENTS

Acknowledgements   viii

  I   Early Victorian England   1

  II   Buildings   45

  III   Interiors   84

  IV   Food   128

  V   Medicine   172

  VI   Recreations   213

  VII   Gardens   266

  VIII   'Der Tod das ist die kühle Nacht'   300

Bibliography   315

Sources   319

Index   327

ACKNOWLEDGEMENTS

I am much indebted to His Grace the Duke of Devonshire for allowing me to make use of information about Sir Joseph Paxton, and to Mr T. S. Wragg, M.B.E., T.D., Librarian and Keeper of the Devonshire Collections, who has for so many years given me his unstinted help and advice.

Without the kindness of Dr Mark Girouard, who knows everything there is to know about Victorian houses and who loaned me a rare book on Scarisbrick Hall, I should have been completely lost. Mr Felix Kelly has also contributed more than his enchanting illustrations; his help with Chapter II was invaluable, as was his encouragement throughout the whole of the book. Mr David Green, Blenheim's historian, has also given me the benefit of his wide knowledge and understanding and whenever I have been in doubt on a point connected with gardens or architects I have gone to him for help and advice.

I am most grateful to Dr Margaret B. Noble, M.R.C.O.G., for reading Chapter V for me and also to Mr R. G. Goodes who first drew my attention to the fact that the custom of exhibiting grottoes on St James's Day had not died out in the eighteenth century but had persisted throughout the nineteenth century and well on into our own. For the most generous assistance in tracing and confirming this point I have various officials of the London Borough of Tower Hamlets to thank: Mr J. Wolkind, Chief Clerk; Mr J. Sudell, Public Relations Officer and Mr Herbert Ward, F.L.A., Borough Librarian, who spent much time in tracing and verifying this and thus considerably lightened my work.

Mr L. R. Whiter of the Spode Works was of great assistance on certain aspects of Victorian china and Mr J. R. Mitchell, managing director of Thurston and Co. Ltd, was most helpful in supplying me with biographical details of John Thurston as well as with information on the development of billiards.

Acknowledgements

As usual I am vastly indebted to the librarians of the Bodleian Library, the library of the Radcliffe Infirmary, the London Library and the Witney branch of the Oxfordshire County Library, all of whom I have depended on for help and guidance.

I have visited so many museums, great and small, that it is impossible to list them all, but I would like to take this opportunity to thank all the curators and attendants who have so freely given me their time and attention.

To many friends and acquaintances who have patiently answered my questions about their great-great-grandparents and who have allowed me to examine their possessions I am truly grateful. All that remains to be said is that with so much help and advice given me by experts in their own lines, any errors of fact, any mistakes of judgement, are entirely my own.

Hailey, Oxon   E.B.

May 1971

CHAPTER ONE

Early Victorian England

It was a curious party which set out from Amorbach in the spring of 1819. The hired, ancient coach, drawn by two dray horses, carried a pregnant woman, her daughter by a previous marriage, a qualified midwife, a lady's maid, two insufferable lap-dogs and several cages of canaries. On the box of this lumbering vehicle sat an odd-looking driver, a big pop-eyed man of fifty-four wearing an ulster and a private's forage cap over what remained of his dyed hair. Yet he handled reins and whip in masterly fashion, which was just as well as the road from Amorbach to Calais, where the party were to take ship for England, was rutted, pot-holed and treacherous.

Thus, after a rough voyage by land and sea, the future Queen Victoria arrived in her native land in mid-April and *in utero*. The coachman, her father Edward Augustus Duke of Kent, fourth son of King George III, was determined that his child should be born on English soil. Further, there were to be no accusations of a 'warming pan' baby levelled at him. On May 24th 1819 at Kensington Palace, in the presence of the Home Secretary, George Canning; the Archbishop of Canterbury, Manners-Sutton; and the Master-General of the Ordnance, the Duke of Wellington, the Duchess of Kent gave birth to a girl, Alexandrina Victoria.

Shortly afterwards the 'midwife', Fräulein Dr Marianne Siebold, obstetrician to the Saxe-Saalfeld-Coburg families, hurried back to the Rosenau to deliver the second child of the young ill-fated Duchess of Saxe-Saalfeld-Coburg. Her husband, brother to

Kensington Palace, Princess Victoria's birthplace

the Duchess of Kent, was busy falling out of love with his wife. Nevertheless, the child, born at six o'clock on the morning of August 26th, was his. The boy was christened Albert Francis Charles Augustus Emmanuel.

On January 23rd 1820 the Duke of Kent, unexpectedly, died leaving his infant daughter to the sole care of her mother. In lieu of a father was her mother's other brother, Prince Leopold of Saxe-Coburg (later King of the Belgians), who became the princess's favourite uncle and adviser. When, in March 1821, the four months old daughter of King William IV and Queen Adelaide died, 'in a convulsive fit', due to an 'entanglement of the bowels',[1] Princess 'Drina' became heiress presumptive to the throne.

On May 24th 1837 Princess Victoria attained her majority.* Uncle William gave a ball for her at St James's Palace and, as a special present, a grand pianoforte which, considering he was the only tone-deaf member of an extremely musical if unharmonious family, was thoughtful and kind. Their Majesties both loved the Princess but they had been permitted to see very little of her as the arrogant, tactless, ill-mannered Duchess of Kent, over-conscious of her daughter's destiny and of her own importance as probable Regent, did not wish her daughter to play with the King's grandchildren, the offspring of the ten royal bastard FitzClarences. Doubtless, too, she feared that, as her daughter grew older, the Duke of Cambridge's boy Prince George, whom Queen Adelaide had virtually adopted, and the Princess might fall in love. This certainly would not have suited the ambition of the Coburg clan, headed by brother Leopold, who by the death of Princess Charlotte, only daughter of George IV, had been prevented from setting up a Coburg dynasty in England, and had long had his nephew, the beautiful and very shy Prince Albert, in view as a suitable match for Drina. Since death had decreed that it could not be Charlotte and Leopold, Leopold and his sister agreed that it should be Victoria and Albert. This tacit agreement had been made when the children were about five.

The Duchess herself disliked King George IV and King William IV, a dislike which was so heartily reciprocated that William, who detested the Coburgs, was openly rude to the Duchess. But she continued with her own little private court, ably assisted by the Comptroller of her Household, Sir John Conroy. She took her daughter on royal progresses and wished to receive loyal addresses to herself (as future Regent) until prohibited by the sovereign. In fact she, the mother of the future Queen, was going to keep herself and her daughter well in the

---

* By Act of Parliament heirs apparent or presumptive came of age at eighteen.

The Rosenau, Prince Albert's birthplace

public eye. She was also going to keep her daughter well under that dominating Coburg thumb.

It was a grief to the old King that he could not attend the coming of age party himself but he was not well. Since February when his asthma had become worse, the seventy-two-year-old monarch had been ailing, intermittently. Although it was well known that he was subject to attacks of a mysterious, recurring illness,

4

such attacks had never been very severe nor had they lasted long. But this year it was obvious to those about him that the King was a very sick man. He was also a very obstinate man. He refused to see doctors and continued doggedly and dutifully to transact state business. Equally stubbornly, he refused to allow bulletins to be issued on his health. From time to time he rallied and the Queen was hopeful, but the fact was the Reform King was dying and he knew it. All he had wanted to do was to live long enough to be sure his niece would ascend the throne untrammelled by her mother. This he had done.

To this bluff, genial, warm-hearted, blundering, eccentric man there may also have been some muddled feeling of poetic or historic justice in this. A sense of rightness that he, the last of the male Hanoverian sovereigns of England, should be succeeded by a woman, for as he once remarked angrily to the Duke of Cumberland who had been tactless enough to toast a male heir when there was already a female one, 'My crown came with a lass, my crown will go to a lass'.[*2]

It was not in his nature to take death lying down. He was finally forced to lay down the burdens of state; but he would die sitting upright, just as he had sat upright night after night at the beginning of his reign conscientiously signing, with gouty, aching hand, the thousands of state papers his brother could not be bothered with.

William the 'Sailor King' was not brilliant. He knew little of politics and had had no training in kingship, but he had the sense to know that he did not know and was willing to take advice from those he learned to trust. Because of this willingness, William IV survived one of the most troubled political periods in our history. The monarchy, under the tenure of George IV, both as Regent and King, had become so discredited that many feared or favoured its abolition. This the King knew. He knew a

* By the Act of Settlement (1701) the Protestant succession was fixed on the House of Hanover. When Queen Anne, last of the House of Stuart, died (1714) the Elector of Hanover, great grandson of James VI and I became King George I King of England and Elector of Hanover. Thus the two countries were united under one crown until the death of William IV.

good deal more about ordinary folk than any of his brothers, and prided himself on it. Queen Adelaide by kindness, devotion, tact and subtle management had reformed William. He drank little, he kept clear of debt, loved his wife and was, perhaps for the first time in his life, settled and happy. Further, the Queen had set an example for good behaviour at court. It was she, not Queen Victoria, who first cleaned it up, got rid of the gamblers, drinkers, parasites and raffish crew so favoured by George IV. It may be an exaggeration to say that King William preserved the monarchy but it rather looks as if he helped to do so, for certainly this underrated monarch did much to 'soften the disgust for royalty'[3] which had become so visibly evident and vocal during the previous thirty years.

The King's approaching death caused small concern in capital 'S' society. In such circles he was considered negligible, with a pious prude for a wife. A contemporary diarist observes : 'If he had been born in a private station, [he] would have passed through life like millions of other men, looked upon as possessing a good-natured and affectionate disposition, but without elevation of mind or brightness of intellect.'[4]

Perhaps this is why he and the Queen gained the affection of ordinary folk. The King was often, though not always, cheered when he appeared in public, whereas his brother had not dared to show his face in public towards the end of his life for the hisses and boos with which he was received. He also liked to walk unattended through the streets of London and to talk to people; and he was probably the first British monarch who prided himself on being an ordinary man first, a king second. He opened the hitherto exclusive royal parks to the public, had not a trace of a German accent, which all other members of the Royal Family had; had travelled about the world more than any other monarch and knew a vast number of people of all classes. He saved the country money when he could.

His brief reign was far from uneventful. In 1832, after much personal distress and vacillation which caused the resignation of the cabinet, he agreed to create, if necessary, sufficient sympathetic

Whig peers to make certain that Earl Grey's great Reform Bill would not again be thrown out by the Lords. His reign also saw the abolition of slavery, a new Factory Act to limit the working hours of children in all textile mills (other than silk); the establishment of the British Association for the Advancement of Science, the beginning of the Oxford Movement and, unhappily, the Tolpuddle Martyrs. It saw the introduction of the hansom cab into London and the first railway line to reach the capital— the London and Greenwich (1836)—for which a new engine *Royal William* was built. Even earlier (1833) another *Royal William*, a steam-boat built in Quebec had made the Atlantic crossing in about three weeks under steam. This delighted the King, who had long been ridiculed for advocating steam for the Royal Navy. His love for the Navy never lessened. His genuine interest in and concern for naval men of all ranks persisted to the end.

And so this obstinate, contradictory, kindly man, whom Nelson had loved, died in his chair at twenty minutes after two o'clock on the morning of June 20th 1837, and his eighteen-year-old niece became Queen Regnant.

The accession of a sovereign always inspires poets, professional or non-professional, to celebrate the event in verse of absymal quality. Thus, from her darkened room, thirty-one-year-old Miss Elizabeth Barrett delivered herself of the following :

> Oh ! maiden heir of Kings,
> A King has left his place;
> The majesty of death has swept
> All other from his face.
> And thou upon thy mother's breast
> No longer lean thee down,
> But take the glory of the rest,
> And rule the land that lives the best.
> The maiden wept,
> She wept to wear a crown.

Miss Barrett seems to have known peculiarly little about the new monarch, that barely five foot tall eighteen-year-old, obstinate, rather stupid, self-possessed girl with the slightly protuberant Hanoverian eyes, fine skin, prominent front teeth, lovely voice and a tendency to run to fat. The young Queen had no intention whatsoever of leaning on her mother's breast. She had not done so for a long time. Mother and daughter had not been on good terms for some years and one of her first personal acts on the day of her accession—busy though she was—was to have her bed removed from the Duchess's bedroom into a room of her own. She forbade the Duchess to attend any of the meetings on that day or at any other time in the future. She would be quite alone and preferred to remain so. She also immediately dismissed the hated Sir John Conroy, Comptroller of the Duchess's household (1786–1854), from her own household although she could not dismiss him from her mother's. This subsequently led to the rumour that Sir John and the Duchess had long been lovers and the Queen knew it.

As for weeping? The maiden did, indeed, weep but not because she wore a crown. Her brief tears were for the dead King, Uncle William, whom she had not been able to see—he had always been so affectionate and kind (no matter what he had been to the Duchess). Her thought, too, was for gentle Aunt Adelaide to whom she immediately wrote a letter of condolence and sent it to Windsor by Lord Conyngham. She addressed the letter to 'The Queen of England' and when it was pointed out to her that she, herself, was Queen, she replied that she was well aware of it but would not be the first to remind the Queen Dowager of her altered position. 'The Crown', Greville writes, 'has been transferred to the head of the new Queen with a tranquillity which is curious and edifying.'

The young Queen carried out her state duties with a modesty, self-possession and charm which impressed her ministers. Now that she was no longer a penurious princess, she paid off her father's debts and also entertained at court with a certain degree of success. 'I find Queen Victoria perfect in manner, dignity and grace, with great youthfulness and joyousness,' writes a guest, then adds, 'I find dinner at court very curious to see, but my bad nature prevailed, and I got so impatient towards eleven that I could hardly bear it . . . she [the Queen] talked almost entirely to the men, but very graciously and kindly to us.' Still, the Duchess of Kent, even while playing whist looked 'careworn, but all seems smooth'.[5]

All was not smooth between mother and daughter, while obviously some were already bored by court parties and by evenings at court which were to grow even more boring over the years. Yet a joyous Queen talking almost entirely to the men is a picture of which one entirely approves. The young Victoria was, for a time, gay, and as glad to be able to be gay as she was self-willed. She could stay up until the early hours of the morning dancing and be perfectly fresh next morning for the day's work. The Queen was also in love, in love with being Queen, being free from her dominating mother, and also with her Prime Minister, Lord Melbourne. This ageing statesman (he was fifty-six) was sophisticated, amusing, witty, intelligent, idle and a product of the eighteenth century. He saw the Queen every day. He sat next to her at dinner. He was her counsellor, her friend, and introduced her into the mysteries of politics—Whig politics. Melbourne was a man of the world and she had never met one before. He fascinated and charmed her. He salted all his lectures on politics, the duties of a constitutional monarch, foreign affairs, finance, clothes, personal appearance, with wit and amusing sayings. He had the ability to make things look not so bad as they were—a dubious accomplishment in an adviser but one which he shared with most of the Queen's ministers. He praised her, encouraged her and gave her self-confidence. Yet Lord Melbourne was a reactionary. Perhaps the Queen was too young and inexperienced to be aware of this, but he did not care a jot what hours children worked, how beastly we were to the Irish, or about the conditions of the poor; he seems to have been against the abolition of any inhumane law or the introduction of any humane measures. It is fortunate that the Queen herself was thoughtful and warm-hearted.

The Queen was also very interested in making sure, since she had to make speeches, that her accent and pronunciation were correct. Her charming voice would hardly be thought charming if she spoke the guttural English of her mother or Baroness Lehzen, or if she pronounced certain words in the old-fashioned way as Lord Melbourne and his generation did. We learn from Lady Lyttelton that 'The Queen says *gold*, open, not *goold*; also *Rome*, open, not *Room*. . . . When she became Queen, being very anxious to pronounce right, she asked the Ministers about a word and they decided in my way. . . . She is particularly pleased at being reckoned an authority about accent, and takes great pains about it.'[6]

Her accent may have been perfect but her disposition was not. Soon the enclosed world in which she lived, bounded at one end by Lord Melbourne and at the other by her ex-governess Baroness Lehzen, bored her. Her temper became short, she shouted at her maids, worried about her health, became almost morbid about the weight she was putting on, did not like her eyebrows and was, by 1839, generally miserable, confessed to feeling 'unworthy' and also to unutterable boredom. She may have ruled the land that lived the best, but she was not enjoying the job.

That we lived the best, if by best material prosperity is meant, was undoubtedly true. 'Between 1815 and 1830 the purchasing capacity of the classes above wage-earning level was all but doubled—and the Victorian belief in progress was bottomed on the complacency which comes of steadily-rising incomes and steadily improving security.'[7] Here the key-words are 'above the wage-earning level'. This prosperity was built largely on new, costly machinery, new factories and mills, booming trade and a labour force of underpaid men, women and children. An age of production, of export, of enormous prosperity for many was one of wretched poverty for many more. It was the age of the newly harnessed giant, steam. Steam solved many problems, but it created new ones which could not be solved and which are still with us today.

The growth of industry, the dramatic spurt in the growth of population, the building boom, and the coming of the railways changed the whole character of the country in too short a time. The change could not be digested and assimilated; indeed it was barely understood at the time. Small towns were buried and overlaid by expanding industries and became a new kind of town, vast, sprawling, uncoordinated. New railway towns such as Crewe and Swindon came into being. Much of the rural population became urbanized by railways and even where untouched by them, country people and agricultural labourers drifted into the towns to seek work. By 1850 half the people of a country recently predominantly rural were huddled into cities. Urbanization too often spelt degradation and brutalization.

Many employers when they made money, moved away from the sources of their fortunes, bought country estates, which gave them the privileges only land could confer, and hoped to become landed gentry. Sometimes they succeeded. Their managers ringed the industrial towns with handsome new villas and created new and prosperous suburbs. Skilled workmen lived in or at the edge of the town in new houses built in new streets, but millions of workers lived in slums, or packed into long-vacated old, upper- and middle-class houses which had fallen into desuetude and decay. They lived without sanitation or adequate water-supply; without paved streets or lighting, without benefit of law or order. They lived without schools, decent food or clothing and without hope.

Cottage industry, now all but dead, no matter what its evils, had meant that people at least worked at home. Even if home had been an overcrowded cottage, it had not been a squalid tenement. Now, with the huge new mills and the multiplying mines, many had to walk miles to work—the bicycle had not been invented. Even with the various Factory Acts* hours for women and

---

* The ten hours' Bill was not passed until 1847 and was easily evaded, though as early as 1842 people had been shocked to learn from a report on mines that, children commonly became mine workers at six or seven. In many mines they began at five or six, and in one a child of three was employed. Sometimes babies were taken into mines to keep the rats off their fathers' food. In long, low, narrow passages children and women were employed instead of pit ponies.

11

children were never less than ten a day. In winter on the scantiest of breakfasts—if any—men, women and children left their terrible slums with hours of darkness and the prospect of freezing before them, as work usually began at 5.30 a.m. Ill-fed, ill-clad, ill-paid and often in very ill health, thousands upon thousands of workers lived lives of abject misery, anguish and despair. It is not surprising that drunkenness became the chronic disease of the time and that opium taking was commonplace. The one brings insensibility, the other relieves hunger pains.

The heat of summer brought its own wretchedness and 'the imagination can hardly apprehend the horror in which thousands of families . . . were born, dragged out their ghastly lives and died; the drinking water brown with faecal particles, the corpses kept unburied for a fortnight in a festering London August; mortified limbs quivering with maggots; courts where not a weed would grow and sleeping dens afloat with sewage'.[8]

What was true of London was no less true of other cities now linked and drawn together by the railways, and the railway (our gift to the world) was ironically the chief factor in our new prosperity. New factories and large-scale production require a wide market; and to command a wide market, organization and transportation are needed. Railways with their greater speed and capacity superseded canals and horsedrawn wagons, and in a sense, created or made possible a greatly increased export trade (our chief exports were cotton, coal and pig-iron). They delivered the goods in quantity, quickly and relatively cheaply to our ships of which we had more than any other country. Railways had become the largest single employer of labour in the country. Labour to construct the new lines, to blast tunnels and dig embankments, was cheap and there was plenty of cheap labour to be had as industry and the mines could not employ all the able-bodied. There were also the impoverished, and hated, Irish, who flocked over to work as they had done when the canals were built. The Irish would work for less than the English, they lived in unutterable squalor and were a threat to wages.

Railways probably did more to transform England than any

12

Railways prosper, canals decay

other single factor, and in diverse ways. They helped level out food prices. They affected government as, for better or for worse, members of parliament were now only a few hours instead of several days away from their constituencies. They also brought mobility to millions who had never in their lives travelled further than the next village.

Sitting bolt upright in a first-class carriage, designed like a horse-drawn coach, without heat save for a foot warmer and with light supplied at night by an evil-smelling and dripping oil lamp fixed in the roof; without being able to communicate with the next carriage or the guard, the strong-stomached (for travel sickness was always a risk) and well-to-do travelled in the utmost discomfort. Nevertheless, one passenger returning to Birmingham from London in 1838 is enthusiastic about this new form of transportation. 'This morning I set out per railroad,' he writes. 'Of six whom the coach contained I knew three. We talked Magnetism and I read III of Nicholas Nickleby, very amusing and in one part powerfully written. I think railroads will go far towards making us a more social people. There is more chance of meeting gentlefolks than in the old coach system.'[9]

Gentlefolk were not to be found in the roofed but open-sided second-class carriages. Nor in third-class carriages—where provided. These were merely trucks, often unroofed, equally often, without seats, where passengers were choked and blinded by smoke and blistered by sparks, particularly when going through tunnels. This deplorable state of affairs lasted until 1846, when a law was passed compelling all railways to roof third-class carriages and to provide at least one train each weekday for third-class passengers, the train to stop at every station on the line.

Many were opposed to railways, some landowners were afraid of them. The Duke of Wellington was against them because they would encourage the lower classes to move about. The Headmaster of Eton believed they would distract the boys—from what, it is difficult to say—and the vice-Chancellor of Cambridge was sure God would be displeased. Nevertheless, it is the railway cutting across the land which completely severs the Victorian era from all previous eras. It was the symbol of progress. A progress of hitherto unknown rapidity. The railway station, not the church, the town hall or the Corn Exchange, became the most important and significant building of the early Victorian era, just as the cinema became the characteristic building of the between-the-wars period of our own century.

But if the countryside was made smelly and noisy by trains which, it was thought by many a landowner, would, by rushing through fields, scare cattle to death, set fire to corn, cause cows to abort and frighten horses to madness, Victorian city dwellers had their own complacent picture of what rural life was like. A picture to which Mrs Hemans (1793–1835) had contributed with her popular poem *The Homes of England*, backed by Miss Mitford (1787–1855) with her literary sketches *Our Village*, and charmingly painted by the expurgating brush and eye of Myles Birket Foster (1825–99). Foster, in particular, brought home to them, 'the rural beauties of English country life, beauties not only of hedgerow and woodland, meadow, stream and lane, but of the rustic childhood fitted into all its appropriate surroundings, of the innocent play and simple duties of humble cottage life'.[10]

This is all very pretty and comfortable but it is a largely untrue picture. 'The cottage homes of England/By thousands on the plains'[11] were not, in the main, the idealized and sentimentalized cottages set in a pastoral or rural landscape as painted by Birket Foster. The enclosure of open fields and common, together with new agricultural machinery and farming methods had turned agriculture into a more efficient industry which spelt prosperity for rich landowners and big farmers. But enclosures and machinery had dispossessed the smallholders who became landless agricultural labourers (or who drifted into the towns) while cottagers who had lost their own common rights lived as best they could—which usually meant a hand-to-mouth existence. In North Hampshire, William Cobbett (1763–1835) tells us, 'there is one farmer . . . who has nearly eight thousand acres of land in his hands; who grows fourteen hundred acres of wheat and two thousand acres of barley! He occupies what was formerly 40 farms! Is it any wonder that *paupers increase*? And is there not here cause enough for the increase of *poor* . . . ?'[12]

In addition to dispossession, by the end of the eighteenth century rural housing was fast deteriorating. With increasing population and little new building in the early decades of the nineteenth century, existing cottages became seriously overcrowded and decayed still further. Many cottages were picturesque enough to look at—old Tudor cottages of stone, herring-bone brick, wattle and daub, with thatched roofs, but inside walls were crumbling and green with mould, roofs let in the daylight and the rain, earthen floors were slippery with damp, rotting doors swung on rusty hinges, broken windows were stopped with paper or rags.

But not all Victorians complacently accepted the Foster–Mitford–Hemans picture. Some saw conditions as they really were and were shocked and horrified. Hence in 1848 *The Society for Improving the Conditions of the Labouring Classes*, long promoted by Lord Shaftesbury was founded. This was a year of revolution on the continent which brought the French King Louis Philippe and his family as penniless exiles to England. It was the year in which the Chartist movement, bred of simmering political and social unrest and the underlying general poverty of the people, held its monster meeting on Kennington Common and purposed to march on Westminster to deliver its great petition with its millions of signatures.

Only a dozen years before, in 1836, the movement had begun when William Lovett (1800–77) founded the London Working Men's Association. In 1838 he and Francis Place (1771–1854) had drawn up a People's Charter calling for universal male suffrage, abolition of property qualifications for M.P.s, the secret ballot, equal electoral districts, payment of M.P.s and annual parliaments. The Association was soon joined by like-minded but separate groups of radicals and socialists which already existed all over the country and Chartism, thus expanded, became the first national working-class movement in Great Britain. The People's Charter had been presented to, and rejected by, Parliament in 1839 and again in 1842. Rejections were followed by strikes and riots which caused great fear and alarm among the governing and manufacturing classes. But, due to government and police interference, the monster march from Kennington did not take place and Chartism, as a force, ended in the fiasco of April 10th 1848.

16

Back in 1839 when the Chartists had first presented their petition, a bored, disconsolate and fretful nineteen-year-old Queen ran into trouble. The tragic affair of Lady Flora Hastings which blew up into a particularly nasty scandal, thanks to court gossip, brought censure upon Her Majesty who, unfortunately, deserved it. Lady Flora, a friend of Conroy, and one of the Duchess of Kent's ladies, was suspected by Lady Portman and Lady Tavistock of being pregnant. They voiced their suspicions to the Queen who agreed. She, too, had observed. Her own eyes, which never missed a thing, had told her that Lady Flora's figure had changed. Further, Lady Flora was seeing Sir James Clark, physician to the Duchess, twice a week for some complaint or another. The Queen and the two gossipy ladies concluded that Lady Flora was either secretly married or an immoral woman. To cut a long, complicated and unhappy story short, the Queen did not inform her mother of her suspicions, although she should have done as Lady Flora was one of the Duchess's ladies, but, via an intermediary, asked Sir James Clark to make a medical examination. Lady Flora was stunned but agreed, provided another physician, Sir Charles Mansfield Clarke, who had known her from childhood, was present. To Sir James this sounded as if Lady Flora wanted the examination put off and it seems that the Queen shared Sir James's view. Accordingly, she sent a message to Lady Flora that she must not appear until her character had been cleared by a medical examination. Sir James then informed the astounded Duchess that Lady Flora was pregnant. Shortly afterwards the medical examination was carried out by Sir James and Sir Charles and showed that no pregnancy existed or ever had existed. The Duchess dismissed Sir James. The Queen apologized to Lady Flora with tears in her over-observant eyes. It was too late. The scandal had already got abroad. It created a hubbub not only in England but in Europe as well. The Queen and her ladies were attacked in newspapers, journals and broadsheets. The prestige of the court had not been lower since the days of George IV, and 'the whole proceeding was looked on by society at large as to the last degree disgusting and disgraceful . . .

17

it is inconceivable how Melbourne can have permitted this disgraceful and mischievous scandal, which cannot fail to lower the character of the Court in the eyes of the world'.[13]

Lady Flora escaped on July 5th when, as a post mortem showed, she died of a growth on the liver. The Queen had gossiped and listened to gossip. She had behaved stupidly, unjustly and without dignity or compassion. Many of her subjects knew this and hissed her when she appeared in public.

During this imbroglio came 'the Bedchamber Crisis'. Melbourne's government resigned early in May over the Jamaican Constitution Bill. The Queen was in a 'dreadful state of grief' over this. It meant losing her dear Melbourne. Melbourne advised her to send for the Duke of Wellington to form a government. The Duke, pleading age and deafness, refused and advised her to send for Sir Robert Peel, whom she disliked. She thought him gauche and restless which was almost as bad as being a Tory; further he was neither distinguished looking nor handsome. He was cold, odd, his manner stiff and unattractive. That he was highly intelligent* and well-balanced she was too young to see. What she did see was that he wanted her to get rid of some of her ladies of the Household, all of whom were Whigs chosen by Melbourne, and to replace them with Tories. The Queen was insulted and said so. Peel pressed the point. Melbourne, with whom she was in communication and should not have been, urged her not to give way. She did not. Even the Iron Duke when called in to try to solve the problem could not bend that iron will. Peel, rightly, taking this as a sign of lack of confidence, resigned. Melbourne returned. 'It is a high trial to our institutions', Greville writes, 'when a Princess of nineteen can overturn a great Ministerial combination, and when the most momentous matters of Government and legislation are influenced by her pleasure about her Ladies of the Bedchamber.'[14]

It turned out to be a trial to the Queen too. She was met with

---

* Later he became Prince Albert's friend and admirer. He had sense enough to recognize the Prince's excellent qualities and abilities and to make use of them. The Queen also learned to like and admire Sir Robert.

ancient Romans. The figures were just under a foot high. At the feet of the Prince lay a dog, symbol of fidelity; at the Queen's feet lay a pair of turtle doves, symbol of conjugal felicity. Nearby, a Cupid busily wrote the date of the marriage in a book whilst assorted Cupids gaily disported themselves elsewhere. The cake was also dotted with small bouquets of white flowers tied with white ribbon in a true lovers' knot. These were favours for the guests.

At four o'clock the Queen and Prince set out for Windsor, 'in one of the old travelling coaches, the postilions in undress livery',[19] instead of in a handsome new coach or carriage like most rich newly married couples. Cheering crowds followed, in carriages or on horseback and on foot and all the way to Windsor. The cheering and excited crowds were so great along the route that the couple did not arrive until eight o'clock. The Queen was popular again; she also had a raging headache.

On May 1st of that same year there was 'great bustle at the Stamp Office'[20] when, after a four years' struggle, Mr Rowland Hill's postage stamps—not valid until the 6th—went on sale in London for the first time. It was, in fact, the first time these small, adhesive labels, invented by Hill, were used anywhere in the world and they were valid only within the British Isles. Rowland Hill (1795–1879) had had the greatest difficulty in persuading the government to see the advantage of cheap, prepaid postage as opposed to postage rates calculated according to distance and payable by the addressee. He felt that a low single rate would increase volume enormously and so increase revenue, while the poorer people—those who could write—would be given a benefit now enjoyed only by the well-to-do. The Postmaster General had other views, and thought the idea the most extraordinary of all wild and visionary schemes he had ever heard. John Wilson Croker (1780–1857), best remembered for his blistering review of Keats's *Endymion* and a one-time opponent of the Reform Bill, held that cheap postage would make sedition easier. But the Cabinet, with rare good sense, accepted Hill's scheme in 1839 and in 1840 the penny post was established by Parliament. The

Architectural splendour in new railway stations, *circa* 1845

now famous 'penny black', familiarly known as 'The Queen's Head'—and the twopenny blue, also bearing the sovereign's head, were the first stamps to be issued. The Queen must have liked the head for she remained plump and young on all stamps until 1900. These were individual stamps for individual letters and packets, but in addition there were covers to be had, designed by William Mulready, R.A. (1786–1863). Mulready's terms of reference were to produce something beautiful to improve and educate public taste, yet so elaborate that forgery would be impossible.

The second of these requirements Mulready most certainly fulfilled. At top centre Britannia sits on a rock which resembles a pork pie, an elderly comatose lion at her feet. Behind, three sailing ships seem in imminent danger of dashing themselves to pieces on a rocky, mountainous shore while an ill-defined body rides, presumably over the same ocean, in a sleigh drawn at great speed by a single reindeer. On Britannia's right in the top corner is an American scene with someone in a Pilgrim Father's hat shaking hands with a feathered Red Indian, while several slaves appear to be making a barrel. In the opposite corner two elephants and two camels overtop figures in a variety of Eastern costumes. Towards these two groups angels, as heavenly postmen, wing their way.* Unfortunately, one angel lacks a leg. The lower corners are equally decorated. In one, a mother and two happy children read a letter, presumably from papa. In the other, some unfortunate person obviously *in extremis* is having a letter read to him by brother, cousin, vicar or friend.

Mulready's artistic efforts and the avowed intention to improve public taste did not have the desired effect. An unaesthetic and unappreciative public greeted the one-legged angel with howls of delighted and derisive laughter. In general the envelopes came in for a good deal of criticism and caricature. Said one-year-old *Punch* in 1842 :

Hail ! O Mulready ! Thou etcher of penny *envellopes* !
How can we praise the ethereal air of the garment
That hangs down behind from the shoulder of Mrs Britannia?
What is the thing that is perched on the top of her helmet?
Is it a wasp with its head cut off, stuck on its tail there?

Ridicule kills more swiftly than anything else. The 'Mulreadies', as they were called, were withdrawn and a large number

* Sir John Henniker Heaton (1848–1914) postal reformer and M.P., won imperial penny postage in 1898; Anglo-American in 1908.

were burned. However, this first illustrated cover soon gave rise to the 'picture' envelopes which became enormously popular for private use and also for advertising and propaganda purposes. Yet low postage and increased volume did not increase revenue. Revenue in 1839 had been above £1,200,000 and although the number of postal packets had shot up from 82 million to 106 million in 1840, revenue dropped to £500,000. Hill had been wrong on this. Croker, on the other hand, was right—that is if one considered the Anti-Corn Law League seditious, and many people certainly did.

Agitation for the repeal of the Corn Laws had been going on ever since their imposition in 1815 when the government, to assist the landed interests which were suffering because of the disastrous fall in the price of corn after the Napoleonic wars, prohibited the importation of corn from Europe until the price of home-grown wheat reached eighty shillings a quarter. This caused great hardship to the poor. There was sporadic agitation; sporadic because if harvests were good, bread was cheap and agitation died down until the next bad harvest. During seasons of bad harvest working men had to spend their money on dear bread and the bare necessities of life; this did not suit the manufacturers, who did not like to see money spent on bread alone with the consequent contraction of the home market for manufactured goods. Further, as other countries sent us food in exchange for coal and manufactured goods, import restrictions and high duties on corn (a sliding scale had been introduced in 1828) curtailed and damaged export trade. 'Free Trade in Corn' soon became the rallying cry of the manufacturing and middle classes—and free trade was violently opposed by the landowners. Since most M.P.s and all members of the House of Lords were of the land-owning class, Parliament, for the most part, was strongly Protectionist.

The late thirties saw a series of bad harvests, and in October 1838 a handful of Manchester business men formed the Anti-Corn Law Association, later known as the Anti-Corn Law League. Under the leadership of men like John Bright (1811–99) and in particular Richard Cobden (1804–65), the League became the most important political pressure group in the country. The year 1839 also saw the beginning of what became known as 'the hungry forties', and a severe trade depression did nothing to alleviate the want created by bad harvests. Dear bread and widespread unemployment were allies of the League.

The year 1840, as we know, saw the introduction of the penny post and for the first time in our history there was a means of reaching many more people than by the traditional mass meetings, public oratory, or through the newspapers. The League was quick to seize on this brand-new service for propaganda purposes. Although Croker might have called it seditious, information was disseminated in the form of pamphlets, leaflets and reprints of speeches via the new postal service. That the League would have won, in time, is undeniable as it now had large middle-class and commercial support. But it might not have won so quickly had it not been for this cheap new means of communication.

In 1845 there was a very bad harvest and in Ireland a hitherto unknown blight ruined the potato crop. As potatoes were to Ireland what rice is to India, terrible famine ensued which, together with typhus, killed thousands. What was needed, unless the Irish were to suffer and die in even greater numbers, was corn in vast quantities and we had barely enough in England. Corn had to be imported, and cheaply; accordingly on May 26th 1846 Sir Robert Peel repealed the Corn Laws. This measure was, in the words of G. M. Trevelyan, 'the most important political event between the First and Second Reform Bills'.[21] It was the first major victory of the middle classes over the gentry and their landed interests; the first victory of industrial interests over agriculture, but it cost Peel his political life.

The Whigs, now led by Lord John Russell, were jubilant. The Queen was not. 'I have to thank you for your kind letter', she writes to her Uncle Leopold. 'It arrived yesterday, which was a very hard day for me. I had to part with Sir R. Peel and Lord Aberdeen, who are irreparable losses to us and the Country; they were both so much overcome that it quite overset me, and we have lost in them two devoted friends. We felt so safe with them. Never during the five years that they were with me, did they *ever* recommend a *person* or a thing which was not for my or the Country's best, and never for the Party's advantage only; and the contrast *now* is very striking; there is much less respect and much less high and pure feeling. . . . Then the discretion of Peel, I believe, is unexampled . . . the Corn Law Agitation was such that if Peel had not wisely made this change (for which the *whole* Country blesses him) a convulsion would shortly have taken place, and we should have been *forced* to yield what has been granted as a boon.'[22]

One can hardly believe that this 'Sir R. Peel' is the same man the young Whig Queen had so detested only seven years before. But all his ability and his soundness might have gone unrecognized by the Queen had not Prince Albert seen and admired his qualities, just as Sir Robert saw and admired those of the Prince.

Unfortunately, a bad year followed. 'The price of bread is of unparalleled height,' wrote the Queen, 'we have been obliged to reduce everyone to a pound a day and only secondary flour to be used in the Royal kitchen.'[23] But a good harvest that summer and the following made it clear that neither the country nor agriculture had been ruined by the abolition of the Corn Laws, and by 1850 when Peel died we had moved into a period of unprecedented production and prosperity epitomized for all to see in the huge glass showcase of the Great International Exhibition of 1851. From then well on into the 1860s we were on a splendid high plateau from which we could view the past with relief and satisfaction and the future in the confident hope of even better things to come. It was a period of material and moral optimism.

London, the seat of government, the home of the sovereign, the centre of the legal profession, the heart of the literary and scientific world was the largest city in the world. It was also very dirty and smoke-begrimed, and had filthy streets where crossing-sweepers fully earned their miserable pennies. The Thames, once the great highway of London, was now little better than a common sewer. London, although it had not increased in industrial importance to the same extent as provincial towns and cities such as Manchester, Birmingham, Liverpool, Leeds, Bolton, had become a great commercial city and a world financial centre. As a port and great warehouse it was unrivalled.

London in 1850, was very different from the London of the beginning of the century. Then there had been no hansom cabs, omnibuses, railways or stations. No gas-lit streets, steam vessels on the Thames, nor electric telegraph connecting it to all parts of the country, and not an inch of plate glass anywhere in private houses or in shops. Now many new shops—a sign of prosperity —had opened; among them Swan & Edgar in Piccadilly, Benjamin Harvey at Knightsbridge, Henry Heath and Peter Robinson in Oxford Street, Lilley & Skinner at Paddington Green, Daniel Neal the shoemaker on the Portman estate, the Scotch House, Aldgate, and a brand-new grocer in the Brompton Road, Henry Charles Harrod. There was the new, quick way of making pictures, photogenic drawings, as photographs were then called, first produced in England by Fox Talbot (1800–77). Mr Beard was the first person to use this commercially in a 'studio' on the corner of Parliament Street and King William Street. He became very successful after Prince Albert sat for his likeness on March 21st 1841. But gone were the old days when the area around Trafalgar Square had been known as Porridge Island and there had been outraged cries in the Press while the square, and the National Gallery, were being built on the site of the old Royal Mews. Nelson's Column had been erected in 1840 and the figure of the Admiral added in 1843.

The new Palace of Westminster replacing the ramshackle old palace destroyed by fire in 1834 was nearly completed and the vast new building by Charles Barry (1795–1860) and A. W. N. Pugin (1812–52), ornate and very different, was not to everyone's taste. The House of Lords had not been completed until 1847 and the Commons though usable was still not quite finished. The new buildings had already taken nearly twenty years of the century and, worse, had cost £2 million instead of £800,000. But the buildings were very fine and before they were finished the public had been admitted to Westminster Hall, on payment of a shilling, to see the 140 paintings submitted in a competition to provide frescoes for Westminster Palace. *Caesar's First Invasion of Britain by* Edwin Armitage (1817–96), *Caractacus Led in Triumph through the Streets of Rome* by G. F. Watts (1817–1904), and *First Trial by Jury* by C. W. Cope (1811–90) had each won a first prize of £300.

Despite new-built streets and old houses torn down to give better access to different parts of London, traffic was still as appalling as ever. New money had brought many people more fine houses, more elaborate and expensive furniture, more servants, splendid clothes and more carriages—a steady stream of them. One could barely get down the Strand or Bond Street. Oxford Street, in spite of its relatively new paving with wooden blocks bonded together with boiling tar was as jammed and noisy as Piccadilly. New Oxford Street, opened for carriages in 1844 to connect Oxford Street and Holborn, was just as bad. Shopkeepers no longer took their goods out to the 'carriage trade', the occupants of carriages for the most part condescended and went into the shops.

There were countless bright new carriages. But the lumbering old family coach came out, chiefly by night if a family were going to a ball or the opera and taking the daughters of the house with them. These, dressed in delicate white net evening gowns, with flounces edged in pink or blue, over white satin, worn with embroidered or fringed merino cloaks, would have found a small equipage too damaging for their vast crinolines. Closed broughams had come in in 1838 and were now rivalled by phaetons of different designs. The fast phaeton, fancied by young men, had light steel shafts and was stripped down to a bare minimum. Others were the park phaeton, the light and graceful swan-necked phaeton and the nautilus-shell phaeton. These, beautifully painted and with silver or brass mountings and velvet or heavy silk linings, were for the rich. Still others were functional, unpretentious and even dowdy—these were in the majority. There were open and closed carriages, light two-wheeled gigs, victorias, barouches and open sociables, as well as the relatively new pilentum, larger than most carriages and with an ample folding roof—an excellent carriage for travelling as well as for town. Then there were hansom cabs by the hundred, plying for hire. There were carts from the country, horse-drawn omnibuses, innumerable wagons of different kinds carrying goods from one part of the city to another, and (until 1856) cattle driven through the streets to Smithfield market.

But if many private carriages were colourful and the footmen in their liveries even more so, men's dress in general had sobered down considerably by mid-century. It is true men wore their perfumed hair moderately long, waved and curled, and in the mid-fifties made lustrous with scented macassar oil, under a top hat of silk plush or beaver in white, fawn, grey or black. The top hat was to the whole of the nineteenth century what the tricorne had been to the eighteenth. But now the top hat had straight sides, whereas in the forties sides had been curved. Prince Albert had made the black silk top hat popular and black silk was always worn on formal occasions.

Men in the 1850s were ceasing to be clean-shaven. They wanted luxurious hair on the head and also on the face. Moustaches, favoured by the army, were now cultivated by civilians, so were side-whiskers which, as they descended to the chin, were allowed to grow so long that the hair fell below the jawbone although the chin was left clean-shaven. As the decade progressed so did the whiskers and gained the name of 'mutton chops' or 'dundrearys' and, later, 'Piccadilly weepers'.

Clothes were becoming sadly stereotyped and settling down into a long, dull period never before known and which is only now beginning to end. By the fifties colours had become very sombre indeed; gone were the brightly coloured and lavishly embroidered waistcoats of silk and satin, to be replaced by white or light-coloured plain cloth ones worn under a braid-trimmed tailcoat or frockcoat. Waistcoats were festooned with massive gold watch-chains but little jewellery was now worn by men; rings, cuff-links, studs of pearl, sometimes of exquisite enamel and gold, were permitted. Monocles, unrimmed, were popular. Snuff boxes were still used, although cigars were rapidly ousting snuff, and cigar holders and cases rivalled snuff boxes in ornateness.

New to the fifties was the cutaway (also a tailcoat), which for the really well-dressed man replaced the tailcoat. Our morning-coats are the direct descendant of the cutaway. Jackets or the 'full suit' came in for sport, country or seaside wear. Full suits—and here is where we get our word, suit, for men's wear—were usually in a rather dreary brown tweed with a long jacket, narrow collar and undistinguished trousers of the same colour and material as the jacket. Coat colours in the fifties were black, navy and dark grey; these had, unhappily, replaced the blues, wine colours and dark greens of the forties.

No fashion-plate was the Poet Laureate when he attended the Manchester Art Treasures Exhibition, opened by Prince Albert on May 5th 1857. He was, an American observer records, the 'most picturesque figure without affectation that I ever saw; of middle size rather slouching, dressed entirely in black, and with nothing white about him except the collar of his shirt, which methought might have been clean the day before. He had on a black wide-awake hat with a round crown and wide, irregular brim, beneath which came down his long black hair, looking terribly tangled; he had a long pointed beard too, a little browner than his hair, and not so abundant as to encumber any of the expressions of his face. His frock coat was buttoned across his breast.' He also moved with 'short irregular steps—a very queer gait as if he were walking in slippers too loose for him'.[24] Tennyson as Poet Laureate could dress as he pleased; others were more conventional.

Women's clothes—and Paris was the centre for women's fashions just as ever since the Napoleonic wars London had been for men's—made up in colour and design what men's lacked. The most noticeable feature of women's dress was that the low-necked dress for day or promenade, which had been popular for three centuries, disappeared completely during the 1840s and women covered themselves from neck to floor and to the wrist.

Nothing was exposed during the day but head and hands. Hands were gloved and the head was concealed in a bonnet which grew deeper and deeper so that ultimately it stuck out beyond the cheeks. A corset shaped like an outsize hour-glass provided for a smooth, rounded but uncloven bosom like the stern end of a coal scuttle, a V-shaped waist allowed a vast crinoline to burgeon over satin, kid or leather and cloth heelless shoes, or over boots with cloth tops laced with coloured laces. Later, boots dispensed with laces in favour of elastic sides. A mantlet or cloak or three-quarter length coat was worn, depending on the weather. So dressed a woman was ready to take what sun and air she could get. Fabrics for day wear were satin, silk, brocade, velvet, taffeta, tarlatan, muslin, gauze, lawn, moiré, gingham, poplin, serge, soft wool, merino and worsted. The plain, serviceable stuffs were used for promenade or walking dress, the more elaborate were for home wear and morning-dress—one paid morning calls until four in the afternoon. The weight and kind of fabric varied with the season.

In the evening, save for the décolletage, which allowed a woman to expose her shoulders and chest, styles followed day wear rather closely. Fashionable evening fabrics were very much lighter in weight and in colour than those for day wear. Nothing could be more chaste, feminine or innocent for unmarried women of all ages than rosebuds, singly or in knots caught up in satin ribbon looped round a gauzy crinoline. Lace and embroidery in black and white, silver or gold, fur fringe, velvet fringe, braid and appliqué work were generously applied and greatly favoured by matrons; over-ornamentation in dress as in everything else was a sign of the prosperous times. Unfortunately, in the late fifties older women were unbecomingly upholstered in purples, strong blues, plum, bright green and magenta. Still, against the plain dark clothes of the men such colours stood out, albeit more than a trifle harshly.

'The Englishman', says Emerson, 'wears a sensible buttoned coat to the chin . . . of solid lasting texture. If he is a lord he dresses a little worse than a commoner. They (the English) have diffused the taste for plain substantial hats, shoes, and coats through Europe. They think him the best dressed man whose dress is so fit for his use that you cannot notice or remember to describe it.' But he also has this to say : 'There is no country in which so absolute a homage is paid to wealth . . . the Englishman has pure pride in his wealth, and esteems it the final certificate. A coarse logic runs through all English souls—if you have merit, can you not show it by your good clothes and coach and horses? How can a man be a gentleman without a pipe of wine? . . . There is a mixture of religion in it. They are under the Jewish law, and read with sonorous emphasis that their days shall be long in the land, they shall have sons and daughters, flocks and herds, wine and oil. In exact proportion is the reproach of poverty. They do not wish to be represented except by opulent men. An Englishman who has lost his fortune is said to have died of a broken heart.'[25]

The opulent, well-dressed, well-housed family, safe and secure in mid-century could not but feel :

> God hath been gracious to our isles,
> Largely His gifts are poured,
> Freedom, and wealth, and influence—
> Be then His name adored![26]

That wealth and influence were the rewards of virtue, few doubted, and without wealth and influence freedom would be sadly curtailed. Prosperity was a signal mark of God's favour which showed itself in man's character by an enviable self-confidence and an unenviable arrogance, smugness and complacency. For there is not much doubt that the Victorians believed themselves to be the chosen people and held that material prosperity was the result of goodness—or godliness. No self-respecting or God-fearing family ever did without family prayers. Some had them every day, some only on Sunday but every member of the family attended, including the servants.

Although wealth and religion were serious matters, a genuine religious faith played a great and motivating part in many lives, as did an equally genuine and humanitarian concern for the poor, the unfortunate, the wretched. Pride in material progress was enormous but, for many, horror at social conditions and concern with how to solve social problems far outweighed pride in wealth. That the Victorians were, on the whole, materialistic and complacent is undeniable, but it would be both unjust and unfair to see them only as that.

As for the church where formal worship took place—and religious observance and faith, within and without the church, are at the heart of the Victorian picture—the church now had so many aspects and encompassed so many beliefs that it could, with some justice, claim to be really national. The Established Church had developed three definite wings—high, broad and low. The low or Evangelical wing did not hold with ritual or apostolic succession, but based itself on Bible reading, particularly at home, and on sermonizing. Within this wing there was little prejudice against Dissenters, Methodists, Quakers, Presbyterians and other sects, but there was dissension as to how far Evangelicalism should go. It could be and often was dull, dreary and ridiculously strict, particularly over Sunday observance, but it was out to help the less fortunate at home and abroad. It was much given to zeal and self-improvement. In politics it favoured the Liberal and even the Radical cause, but the Evangelicals were, on the whole, unpopular within the church. They were derided and disliked by the more conventional and it was nearly impossible for an Evangelical clergyman to secure any preferment in the church.

The high church, an offshoot of the *Oxford Movement* and the *Tractarian Society* of the 1830s, was rigidly orthodox in doctrine and dogma and believed 'apostolical descent' to be the basis for the church's authority. It did not approve of Liberal tendencies within the church or Liberal leanings without. It disliked dissenters, opposed reforms and was, generally speaking, Tory. Its opponents thought the beliefs and ritual of the high church little better than Roman Catholicism not very well disguised.

But there were many who were neither high nor low. These belonged to the broad or Latitudinarian wing of the church and when there was too much theological banging about, too much dispute over the sung or spoken Eucharist, too lengthy and too deadly sermons by those too inwardly convinced, many more sought refuge and comfort under the shelter of the broad wing.

Both the Queen and Prince Albert (once a Lutheran) were 'broad'; both were deeply religious, but to the Queen religion did not mean gloom and doom. It may have meant Heaven in the world to come, but Hell did not enter into her calculations as it did into so many people's. No child of hers was going to be frightened of God or threatened with a God who turned Moloch at any petty offence. 'I am quite clear', she writes in a memorandum concerning the eight-year-old Princess Royal, 'that she should be taught to have a great reverence for God, for religion, but that she should have the feeling of devotion and love which our Heavenly Father encourages His earthly children to have for Him, and not out of fear and trembling; that the thoughts of death and an after life should not be represented in an alarming and forbidding view, and that she should be made to know *as yet* no difference of creeds, and not to think she can only pray on her knees, or that those who do not kneel are less fervid and devout in their prayers.'[27] Here the Queen sounds as if she verged on Christian Socialism.* With her strong disapproval of fear and trembling and her dislike of a forbidding or alarming view of the after life she might have been a follower of F. D. Maurice.

Frederick Denison Maurice (1805–72) who with Charles Kingsley (1819–75) was a founder of Christian Socialism, had had the bad taste and effrontery to deny in his *Theological Essays* the belief in everlasting damnation and thus he came into violent conflict with Dr Pusey. For this view Maurice was damned by being asked to resign his Professorship of History at King's College, London. The founders of the 'Christian Socialists' were broad churchmen. Although Maurice at one time had flirted with

* The term in this context in the nineteenth century denoted opposition to *laissez faire* individualism and was a Christian demand for some form of political or economic action in the interests of all the people. Common ownership was not demanded nor was control of the means of production and exchange.

the Tractarians he had been put off by Pusey's Tract on Baptism which he found 'represented everything he did not think and did not believe . . . and represented the parting point between him and the Oxford School'.[28]

The aims of the 'Christian Socialists' were to vindicate the Kingdom of Christ and its authority over industry and trade. Charles Kingsley, best remembered for *The Water Babies* and *Westward Ho!*, even had a touching belief that science and religion could be reconciled. But these men were greatly stirred by the sufferings of the poor and they criticized conservative Christianity with force and energy. They stood for self-sacrifice and cooperation as against self-interest and competition. In effect, this meant that their chief concern was with day-to-day problems and they directed much of their zeal toward social and material betterment. They sponsored adult schools, working men's colleges, campaigned for the better education of women and tried to Christianize education. The church, they believed, should be a living church in every respect and in all its aspects. In many ways Christian Socialism was unpractical, and it lived only a decade. Its immediate influence was, unfortunately, limited but its influence on the future of the church was more creative than either the Evangelical or Oxford Movements.

By 1860 the 'Christian Socialists' movement was over. So were a good many other things. That ill-timed, ill-considered and unnecessary venture into the Crimea had ended four years before. Its horrors and the negligence and incompetence of the War Office had been exposed, largely due to the efforts of William Russell, war correspondent of *The Times*, while for the first time in history because of the new medium, photography, people at home had been able to see in plain, unglamorized and unvarnished detail just what war really looked like. 'John Bull', says Hawthorne at the beginning of the war, 'is going with his whole heart into this Turkish war. He is a great fool.'[29] People in general were delighted, excited and gaily belligerent about this new adventure. Peace was a bit boring. This made a change. We would win, of course, and it would be a quick win. When

Photographer's wet-plate outfit, *circa* 1850

the war went badly one result was that the pacific government of Lord Aberdeen (1784–1860) fell and Lord Palmerston's reign began.

Prince Albert, never popular, had his own difficulties at this time. 'Prince Albert is far from being liked by those who come into personal relations with him', Hawthorne was told by an Englishman, and adds, 'This seems to be on account of his German character—cold, slow, heavy, undemonstrative, proud and stiff. He snubs the high nobility of England. There appeared to be a kindly feeling for him among the people at large when I first came here; but I now think it has passed into indifference.'[30]

Indifference is hardly the word as, for some unknown reason, just before the war the Prince was thought to be pro-Russian and was harassed and execrated by certain sections of the press. He was even denounced as a Russian (or Austrian) spy and rumour ran that he was confined to the Tower on a charge of high treason. He was also accused of having unconstitutional in-

38

fluence in state affairs. Rumour went even further and whispered that the Queen had also been arrested and thousands turned out to see her pass through the Traitors' Gate. They were disappointed.

Albert had seen the war coming. 'We are getting nearer and nearer war,' he writes to that pedantic busybody, Stockmar, 'and I entertain little hope of its being averted. The Emperor of Russia is manifestly quite mad . . . God be merciful to the world if it comes to this.'[31] Of the accusations against him he says: 'The increasing attacks upon me in the press here . . . have really reached an incredible height',[32] but he felt he could bear it with tranquillity and calmness. He could not. It wore him down. He became miserable and melancholy. It must have been hard for a man who had an obsessive sense of duty, who had worked incessantly for the country's good, and who had no illusions whatsoever about Russia and her policy of expansion or about war, to bear these calumnies. And although both Lord Aberdeen and Lord John Russell made statements in Parliament on the unimpeachable loyalty of the Prince, his services to the Queen and to the country, that the Prince had been badly wounded is as unquestionable as the fact that he hid the wound.

It was, however, peace not war which provided the general environment of England. No European war had disturbed the country since 1815—nor would again until 1914. True there had been bothers in Afghanistan, and the shocking Indian Mutiny (1857–58) and the Chinese wars, but these had been at a distance. The long peace had brought a settled prosperity and a stability to the country and, save for the Crimea which was hardly Europe, we had avoided all involvements on the Continent even in that year of revolution 1848 when many a European monarch had feared to lose his crown if not his head.

The continent, a political nuisance, nevertheless had its uses—apart from being our biggest customer. It was a good place in which to travel, to live in cheaply if creditors pressed or one was on half-pay; to take the waters or one's mistress, or a holiday. Travelling there was much easier now that most continental countries had, at last, got railways. The Queen visited France, Coburg, Germany and Belgium, but her favourite holiday resort was Balmoral.

In 1847, on the death of Sir Robert Gordon, brother to Lord Aberdeen, Albert had acquired the reversion of the lease of Balmoral and later became the owner, bequeathing it to the Queen. He and the Queen arrived at the small castle of Farquharson on the estate in September 1848. It was, 'a pretty little castle in the old Scottish style. . . . There is a nice little hall, with a billiard-room; next to it is the dining-room. Upstairs (ascending by a broad staircase) immediately to the right, and above the dining-room is our sitting-room . . . a fine large room —next to which is our bedroom, opening into a little dressing-room which is Albert's.'[33] But the pretty little castle soon became too small and additions to it could not keep pace with additions to the family so the new Balmoral was designed, chiefly by Prince Albert with William Smith of Aberdeen as architect. Balmoral is in the Baronial-Schloss style and the Queen was ecstatic. 'Every year my heart becomes more fixed in this dear Paradise', she writes, surrounded by antlers and plaid, 'and so much more so now, that *all* has become my dearest Albert's *own* creation, own work, own building, own laying out as at *Osborne*; and his great taste, and impress of his dear hand, have been stamped everywhere'.[34]

The Prince had fallen in love with Scotland at first sight in 1842 and it was a love affair which grew, 'many of the people' looked 'like Germans',[35] the countryside was 'extremely picturesque', and, writes the Queen, 'Albert says very German-looking',[36] while Perth reminded him of Basle. It seems obvious that, for Albert, Scotland was a substitute homeland and filled him with both romantic nostalgia and satisfaction. Also, he soon knew he was unpopular in England and, one feels, this sensitive man who was a compulsive worker felt less of an alien in Scotland and among its people.

For Albert when he married had laid down strict rules of conduct for himself from which he never deviated; had he done so he might have been thought less German, rigid, prudish and boring. He 'denied himself the pleasures—which to one so fond as he was of watching and inspecting every improvement that was in progress, would have been very great—of walking at will about the town. Wherever he went, whether in a carriage or on horseback, he was accompanied by his equerry. He paid no visits in general society. His visits were to the studio of the artist, to museums of art and science, to institutions for good or benevolent purposes. Wherever a visit from him, or his presence, could tend to advance the real good of the people, there his horse might have been seen waiting; never at the door of mere fashion. Scandal itself could take no liberty with his name. He loved to ride through all the districts of London when buildings or improvements were in progress, more especially when they were such as would conduce to the health or recreation of the working class.'[37]

This is admirable and true even if it is an eulogy officially approved by the Queen. Unfortunately, it makes Albert sound totally unhuman. A dislike of Germanic thoroughness (as displayed by the Prince) is part of the Englishness of the English. For if, and when, we are thorough we are at some pains to disguise it. Thoroughness, like professionalism, has always been considered rather shameful or ridiculous.

The Prince alienated the aristocracy because he did not visit. This was probably not a question of snubbing them or of snobbery but of a certain rectitude. Pledged politically to one or other of the two political parties as most of the great houses were, to be on intimate terms with any noble household might be thought to indicate political bias. For their part the aristocracy found him too intellectual, too serious-minded, while the severe moral tone and the apparent domestic happiness at the palace were considered—not without reason—boring, middle-class and dowdy. Perhaps the only real friend Albert ever had in England was Sir Robert Peel, and he wept like a child at Peel's death.

But his greatest service to the country, for which he got small credit, was to bring the Queen to see that the crown must be above politics. He saw that the influence of the crown should be a non-partisan agency in domestic affairs. In foreign affairs he wished to see the Foreign Office supremely well-informed. With all the royal connections which he and the Queen had on the continent, they were in a position to know more about foreign affairs by private intelligence, than the Foreign Office and could, therefore, supply that office with advice and information which would not be available otherwise. In time Albert had become the Queen's private secretary and confidential adviser, saw that she did not make decisions based on self-will, and worked indefatigably and tirelessly to help her. In so doing, he made her nearly as hard-working as himself.

As for his prudishness, Albert was undoubtedly a prude but this, one feels, sprang from his own knowledge of the terrible unhappiness immorality had caused in his own family, and was founded on fear. His elder brother Ernest, a womanizer like his father, had twice contracted a venereal disease. This distressed Albert greatly, not only because of the moral implications but because he feared Ernest would not have healthy children. Then, too, it would not have escaped his notice that the English court (and the Queen's uncles and father) had enjoyed a very unsavoury reputation during George IV's tenure as king. The court must be made spotless and remain spotless. No man or woman whose moral character was not unimpeachable from birth should move in court circles. This was a trifle limiting and often unkind. When Lord St Leonards (1781–1875), the distinguished law reformer, became Lord Chancellor for a brief spell in 1852, his wife was not received at court because she had eloped with him whilst he was still at school and had lived with him for a few years prior to their marriage in 1808. She was now nearly seventy and he seventy-one. Although the Prime Minister, Lord Derby (1799–1869), asked to have the ban repealed, the Queen refused. Albert had done his work too well.

He was also said to be devoid of a sense of humour and in public that was so. In private it was not. Albert was no romp, it is true, but one has a glimpse of him at twenty-one showing guests at Windsor Castle some caricatures and 'running from one to another and standing over us to see how we laughed, and laughing so loud himself as to be quite noisy and boyish'.[38] He soon lost his boyishness, but he was a devoted father, played games with his children, made funny faces for them (and was an over-strict supervisor of their education). He amused the Queen with mimicry and he was at least not sufficiently Germanic to go in for practical jokes. One of his notes to the Queen—who hated his being away—written when he went to lay the foundation stone for the new Grimsby docks is not very heavy-handed. He writes :

'Your faithful husband agreeable to your wishes reports :
1. That he is still alive.
2. That he has discovered the North Pole from Lincoln Cathedral, but without finding Captain Ross or Sir John Franklin.
3. That he arrived at Brockelbury (where he was the guest of Lord Yarborough) and received the address.
4. That he subsequently rode out, and got home quite covered with snow, and with icicles on his nose.
5. The messenger is waiting to carry off this letter which you will have at Windsor by morning.
6. Last and not least (in the Dinner-speech's phrase) that he loves his wife and remains her devoted husband.'[39]

In 1860 trade was excellent, employment high, wages better, farmers fairly happy. The Italians were struggling for constitutional liberty—we sympathized but nothing else. Income tax rose to tenpence in the pound. High duties were imposed on sugar and tea but those on French wines and brandy came down as France wished to buy duty-free coal and iron from us. The Prince caught a cold which turned into influenza. The Queen who, during the Crimean war, had promised to visit Canada, as Canada had raised and equipped an infantry regiment, found herself unable to go, and sent eighteen-year-old Albert Edward, Prince of Wales, in her stead. He went to Halifax, Toronto, Niagara, Kingston, laid the corner-stone of the Houses of Parliament in Ottawa, opened the new railway bridge across the St Lawrence at Montreal and was a wild success.

President James Buchanan (1791–1868),* not to be outdone, invited the Prince to Washington. He went, privately, as Baron Renfrew, saw New York, Boston, the tiny city of Chicago, Cincinnati and St Louis. In Washington this great-grandson of George III stood bareheaded before the tomb of George Washington, which made everyone happy. In New York he received an unprecedented ovation.

The Earl of Aberdeen, who had hated the Crimean war, died, and the last contest with bare fists in England was fought. The Food and Drugs Act was at last passed and, to the alarm of some, degrees in science were established at London University. But all in all 1860 was a good and beneficial year for England— prosperous, unentangled, stable and progressive.

'The stability of England', writes a visitor not without reason, 'is the security of the modern world. . . . The English stand for liberty. The conservative, money-making, lord-loving English are yet liberty loving; and so freedom is safe, for they have more personal force than any other people. The nation always resists immoral action of the government. . . . They wish neither to be commanded nor to obey but to be kings in their own house.'[40]

* He was succeeded by Abraham Lincoln, who was elected in November 1860, and took office in 1861.

CHAPTER TWO

Buildings

In accession year a childless eccentric, about whom little is known, began building a vast house on his estate near Liverpool. At the same time the Sixth Duke of Devonshire was in the process of making an important architectural addition to his gardens at Chatsworth, Derbyshire. Charles Scarisbrick's new mansion and the Duke's Great Conservatory illustrate the extremes of early Victorian architecture, while the names of the architect of the first and the designer of the second are, possibly, better known to us today than they were to their contemporaries. Augustus Welby Northmore Pugin built Scarisbrick Hall* and was responsible for much of the decoration of Westminster Palace. Joseph Paxton (1801–65) designed the Duke's Conservatory and the Crystal Palace.† The first created by looking to the past, the second to the future. To the Victorians the distant past was a glory, the future—implicit in the present—was splendid.

Scarisbrick Hall cannot be seen at a glance. The eye cannot apprehend and gather an overall impression in a single look as it can with the classical and neoclassical buildings of the eighteenth and early nineteenth centuries. There are no quiet horizontal lines, no regularity of windows, no gentle curves of cupola or colonnaded wings, no movement in the sense in which Robert Adam (1728–92) defines it, 'the rise and fall, the advance and recess, with other diversity of form in the different parts of the building'.[1] There is no central feature or block to hold the

* Now St Katherine's College, Liverpool.
† Destroyed by fire, 1936.

The Crystal Palace, 1851

whole together and from which the wings flow. It is a magnificent house but does not seem all of a piece. It is asymmetrical, and the irregularities of its outline tend to make it look like the cut-out background of a stage set. Here the eye leaps suicidally from the tall-pointed spire which snuffs the tower of the east wing, on to a conglomeration of pitched roofs with ornamented ridge tiles, and then bounces to the crenellated parapet of the central portion below which is the incised inscription, 'I have raised up the ruins, and builded it as in days of old'.

Absurd as it may sound, this phrase enunciates, as does the house, the underlying concept of the Gothic or Romantic revival in English architecture. The revival did not begin with Scarisbrick, it had begun in a dilettante way in the previous century and had become more serious in the early years of the nineteenth century. Nor did Scarisbrick serve as a model on any scale for meaningless repetition. Since Gothic permits variety and requires

46

imagination, by 1850 Gothic revival architecture in its many aspects had ousted the neoclassical and had become the dominant theme of architecture throughout the country. Most of our major cities are still full of it although, in our reckless way, we are busy tearing down many fine specimens, just as the Victorians, bored by the cool restraint and proportion of Georgian architecture, destroyed many Georgian buildings.

Scarisbrick Hall is the complete antithesis of Georgian domestic architecture. It is said to be one of the 'finest buildings of the Gothic revival in all England'.[2] One may or may not agree, but Scarisbrick is probably the best example extant of how the decoration and carving of ecclesiastical architecture can be used in a domestic building. It was an attempt, both in construction and detail, to return to the real thing but 'the result is that while the western wing remains a simplicity of Gothic, and the central portion is a magnificence of Gothic, the eastern wing and tower are pure fantasy; if the western wing is the bud, the centre is the flower and the eastern portion displays the floridity of decadence'.[3]

Pugin, in his writings, his drawings, his surviving building, was making a most serious and profound effort to return to the first principles of medieval building. As a convert to Roman Catholicism he believed passionately that Gothic was true Christian architecture—'pointed Christian' he called it. In his early days he felt that Protestantism had been wholly responsible for the degeneration of architecture and expressed this in the first edition of his book *Contrasts*, published at his own expense in 1836. In the second edition of 1841 he modified this view and placed the blame chiefly on the Renaissance.

Renaissance architecture, he had come to believe, was simply a revival of paganism. To him every church 'from St Peter's at Rome downwards', was a striking example 'of the departure from pure Christian ideas and Architecture'. Worse, 'this mania for paganism is developed in all classes of buildings erected since the fifteenth century—in palaces, in mansions, in private houses, in public erections, in monuments for the dead; it even extended to furniture and domestic ornaments for the table. . . . The most celebrated palaces of Europe are the veriest heathen buildings imaginable; in Versailles, the Tuileries, Louvre, St Cloud, Fontainebleau, Brussels, Munich, Buckingham Palace, in vain we look for one Christian emblem or ornament. The decoration of garden, terrace, entrance hall, vestibule, gallery or chamber, ceiling, pannel, wall, window, or pediment, is invariably designed from heathen mythology. Gods and goddesses, demons and nymphs, tritons and cupids repeated *ad nauseam*, all represented in most complimentary attitudes, with reference to the modern pagan for whom the sycophant artists designed the luxurious residence. In new Buckingham Palace, whose marble gate cost an amount which would have erected a splendid church, there is not even a regular chapel provided for the divine office; so that both in appearance and arrangement it is utterly unsuited for a Christian residence.'[4]

Indeed, had Pugin but known it, Buckingham Palace when first mooted as a residence for the young Queen was not fit for pagan, heathen or pig. The report on it by a special sanitary commission was so appalling that the government dared not publish it. But the less said about the architectural vicissitudes of Buckingham Palace, the better.

Pugin did not take up Gothic as a fashionable taste. He was, in a sense, born into it. His father, Charles Auguste, a Frenchman, was one of the best draughtsmen and designers in the office of John Nash. The elder Pugin was deeply interested in Gothic and wrote books about it assisted by his son who had spent some time in Europe making drawings of Gothic churches. Even earlier, at the age of fifteen, the younger Pugin had been employed by Sir Jeffry Wyatville (1766–1840) to design Gothic furniture for Windsor Castle. At nineteen, he produced a set for the opera *Kenilworth*, rich in medieval detail. He then went into business for himself and supplied builders and architects with carved Gothic and medieval ornaments. This was a lamentable failure and he was rescued from a debtors' prison by an aunt. After that he was employed by architects as an expert in designing Gothic

Scarisbrick Hall

detail and served them much as his father had served John Nash. Charles Barry first used him for this purpose in 1833 for the King Edward VI Grammar School, Birmingham, but Scarisbrick Hall was Pugin's first big private commission.

His patron, Charles Scarisbrick, came of a very rich, old Roman Catholic family. Although the Catholic Emancipation Act, reluctantly signed by George IV in 1829, had removed most of the disabilities on Roman Catholics, including the ending of all restrictions on the ownership of land, Roman Catholics were still regarded with mistrust and suspicion and a Roman Catholic architect had to find his patrons within a small circle of rich Roman Catholics. Pugin found his in Charles Scarisbrick, who was certainly rich but did not move in the Roman Catholic circle. In fact Scarisbrick had spent much time on the Continent, where he made a fine collection of paintings. When in 1833 he inherited the estate near Ormskirk, he might as well have remained in Europe for all that anyone saw of him. 'There seems to be an obscurity about the early part of his life,' Hawthorne writes, 'according to some reports he kept a gambling house in Paris before succeeding to the estate. Neither is it a settled point whether or no he has ever been married; some authorities utterly ignoring the point; others affirming that he now has legitimate children, who are now being educated in Paris. He is a Catholic but is bringing up his children, they say, in the Protestant faith. He is a very eccentric and nervous man, and spends all his time at his secluded Hall, which stands in the midst of mosses and marshes; and sees nobody, not even his own Steward. He might be an interesting person to become acquainted with; but after all, his character, as I have just sketched [it] turns out to be one of the commonplaces of novels and romances.'[5]

Earlier, Sir Walter Scott (1771–1832) had produced his immensely popular *Waverley*, and the medieval had been given an extra fillip by this. His house, Abbotsford, a medieval castle complete with gas lighting, and his subsequent novels, romantic, colourful and exciting, also gave further impetus to building in the medieval style.

Gothic as known to the mid and late eighteenth century and the early nineteenth was not a style of architecture. Nothing was known of its structure or meaning. It had no nomenclature* and was used almost entirely for decorative effect. Gothic motifs were

---

* Thomas Rickman (1776–1841), architect, writer and ecclesiastical archaeologist, published (1817) possibly the most widely read book on Gothic architecture. In it he defined the phases or periods as Early English, English Decorated and Perpendicular, terms we use today although they overlap.

applied to an existing building to gothicize it, either because it amused the owner to do so or because one could disguise a sadly plain Georgian house in this way. Gothic of no known lineage was also favoured for garden houses. Yet what began in such a dilettante fashion was to become a serious form of architecture. Strawberry Hill and Fonthill Abbey, neither of which are serious buildings, are the direct forebears of the intensely genuine and informed Scarisbrick Hall. Eighteenth-century Gothic was largely a matter of pointed windows and painted glass, of added battlements, pinnacles and bogus buttresses. To Horace Walpole (1717–97), who wrote our first Gothic novel *The Castle of Otranto*, gothicizing was almost a lifelong diversion. In 1747 he had bought himself a plain, square Georgian house at Twickenham and decided to gothicize it.

Scarisbrick Hall, however, is anything but commonplace. Built in Longbridge stone which is very hard and not easily worked, it is a splendid example of how to deal with a recalcitrant material. The west wing or 'bud' was the real starting point as it was the only bit of the old Hall, built in 1595 and considerably added to later, which could be saved. Pugin saved it and touched it up. It is late Elizabethan, has a pitched roof with gable ends and small pinnacled turrets set at the four corners. A three-sided two-storeyed beautifully carved and parapeted bay window rises up the front to the level of the wallplates. The walls are also battlemented, although battlements below a pitched roof are purely ornamental. Chimneys of twisted brick rise above the roof line.

Set at right angles to the west wing is Pugin's central portion —the 'flower'. The battlemented pitched roof has a central pinnacled lantern. Bay windows in front match those of the west wing and there is also a great wide perpendicular and traceried window in the second storey. This is set above a heavy, protruding, buttressed porch enriched with fine carving. Over the massive front door there is another text, 'Ye will show kindness to my father's house'. As the owner was a recluse and lived in solitary gloom, this admonitory text seems unnecessary. Yet the Hall certainly stood where the family house had once stood. It had sprung from a ruin and was a serious attempt to build 'as in days of old'.

This writing on the wall is also carried into the house (Pugin designed its rich interior as well) and around the top of the enormous Banqueting Hall which, like the great halls of medieval and Tudor houses, soared to the roof, was yet another admonition, 'It is vain for you to rise up early, to sit up late and to eat the bread of sorrow, for so He giveth His beloved sleep'. This seems a trifle inapposite, not to say confusing, for a room in which, so far as we know, few banquets can have been held during the lifetime of the owner.

Another state room, for state rooms were an essential to all medieval or Tudor manor houses as royalty might drop in at any moment and commandeer the house for a few days, weeks or months, was the Oak Room, thick with carvings showing the Deluge, the Day of Judgement, Gathering Manna, David and Goliath, the Valley of Dry Bones, Golgotha, Moses receiving the ten commandments, David harping away like a Welshman, a Pope leaving St Peter's, the Holy Ghost, the Eucharist. Where the carvings came from we do not know; it is thought that Charles Scarisbrick bought them in Brussels. Certainly there was neither pagan decoration nor mythology to be found here.

Then there was the Tudor Room—more recently and more aptly known as the King's Room. Lavish with dark wood carving and bright colours—for the Victorians loved both—above is a blue ceiling studded with golden stars, while paintings of the kings and queens, canopied and framed, form a frieze just below. Henry VII and his Queen, Henry VIII and his Queens, the unfortunate boy Edward VI, unhappy Mary Tudor, great Elizabeth I and, curiously for a so-called Tudor room, Mary Queen of Scots, the weak and double-dealing Darnley, James VI and I, Prince Rupert of Bavaria and his mother, the sad 'Winter Queen'. The Scarisbricks had a passion for the Stuarts and had believed firmly in their right to the throne. All this is certainly very idiosyncratic and may express more the character of Charles Scarisbrick than that of Pugin, but its idiosyncrasies are genuine and based on belief, not on taste or fashion. Right here is where the Victorian Gothic revival differs from its eighteenth-century forerunner.

It is, of course, impossible even to attempt to trace all the influences which led to the Gothic revival in architecture. That it was an end product of the Romantic movement of the late eighteenth and early nineteenth centuries, in a sense a revolt against the classical, the traditional, the academic, the 'Augustan', is common knowledge. If the thoughts and works of writers can help make a revolution, poets, too, are revolutionary to a greater or lesser degree, and early in the eighteenth century they began, tentatively, to break away from the formal classical patterns, ideas and content of a good deal of mid to late seventeenth-century poetry. Poets are often prophets who sense and express what is coming before it arrives, and literary influences are never to be ignored.

Alexander Pope (1688–1744) for example, was most certainly a classicist who polished and perfected the heroic couplet. Although he still uses the couplet formally he can give us lines such as :

> In these deep solitudes and awful cells,
> Where heav'nly-pensive contemplation dwells. . . .
> In these lone walls (their days eternal bound)
> These moss-grown domes with spiry turrets crown'd,
> Where awful arches make a noon-day night,
> And the dim windows shed a solemn light. . . .
> The darksome pines that o'er yon' rocks reclin'd
> Wave high, and murmur to the hollow wind. . . .
> But o'er the twilight groves, and dusky caves,
> Long-sounding aisles, and intermingled graves,
> Black Melancholy sits, and round her throws
> A death-like silence, and a dread repose. . . .
> Deepens the murmur of the falling floods,
> And breathes a browner horror on the woods.[6]

This was published as early as 1717 and it is not in Pope's usual vein. Here one observes that the qualifying adjectives

c

speak of darkness, solemnity, doom. All the paraphernalia of frustrated love and horror are there; so are moss-grown domes, and Gothic spiry turrets, foreboding pines and groves, silence, dread repose, graves and the personification of Melancholy. Gradually these became the attributes of a new kind of poetry much favoured by the graveyard school, a school addicted to night, ruined ivy-covered towers seen fitfully by moonlight and all the trappings of decay, dark groves, owls and thoughts of death among the tombs; 'Welcome, kindred glooms!/Congenial horrors, hail!'[7] cries James Thomson (1700–48), while the Rev. Edward Young (1683–1765) in his *Night Thoughts*, revels in gloom, doom, mortality, Heaven and Hell, 'The knell, the shroud, the mattock, and the grave./The deep, damp vault, the darkness and the worm'[8] await us all, he points out, rather gleefully, one feels. Thus melancholy, morbidity and Gothic horror were creeping into literature.

To gothicize Strawberry Hill, Horace Walpole had the advice and assistance of several like-minded friends and, later, that of the adaptable, unreliable and ill-mannered architect James Wyatt (1746–1813). Walpole added battlements to his roof, a few quatrefoil windows set high, some pointed ones with wooden frames, a handful of crocketed finials, a few twisted chimneys and a round crenellated tower with square windows to the typically plain Georgian façade. As his enthusiasm for Gothic increased, inside he let his 'powers of fancy' freely expatiate through the not quite 'boundless realms of invention'.[9] Internally, the house is a mélange of Gothic styles copied from old folio-engravings and drawings of the interior decorations of extant cathedrals and churches, used in a resourceful and fanciful way. There is a monastic hall and a great staircase—an *Otranto* touch here. Recesses are fan-vaulted. The superstructure of tombs, which should hold marble effigies of long-dead bishops or crusading knights, are used as chimney pieces. Recessed bookshelves in the library are elaborated with pointed arch and decorated Gothic tracery and look rather like vast holy-water stoups. Pillars with crocketed finials separate the shelves, adorn the fireplace, and reach almost to a flat ceiling embellished with what is apparently an adaptation of Early English diaper work. Around the circumference, painted knights in armour ride their caparisoned horses, full tilt. Much of the relief work is done in plaster, which could hardly be less medieval, the proportions are distorted and wrong. Yet, somehow, it comes off as a charming and often elegant essay in using Gothic purely as a decorative and fanciful motif. All this provided Walpole—a man of taste and elegance—with a romanticized ambience of the past. Nevertheless, it is a real forerunner of Victorian Gothic, a rococo interpretation it is true, which has nothing to do with the Middle Ages as such. Strawberry Hill, which took twenty-eight years to complete, was so successful that visitors came in hordes to see it, and it is perhaps our first stately home which was open to the public on certain days. Undoubtedly it spread the taste for Gothic.

Of an entirely different type and on a different scale was Fonthill Abbey, built by Wyatt for William Beckford (1759–1844). Beckford, fabulously rich, much travelled, eccentric and incurably romantic, also wrote a novel, *Vathek* (first published in English in 1784). This, an Arabian Nights fantasy, bears no relation to the house which is indeed a fantasy, but a Gothic one. Its beginning lay in a garden feature, a bogus ruin of a convent built by Wyatt in 1790. The convent had a few habitable rooms as a retreat for its owner but five or six years later Beckford decided he really wanted a Gothic abbey as a house. For this Wyatt was also the architect. Wyatt, a brilliant man trained in classical architecture, was by now considered to be a master of the Gothic style. He had built various Gothic houses, Lee Priory in Sussex for one. Here the Gothic features were more fully detailed than at Strawberry Hill. Battlements, small octagonal turrets at each end of the front, an octagonal tower and a spire, a chapel at the back, an oriel window and a two-storey porch. The house had that irregularity of front and roof-line, that asymmetrical look which more than anything distinguishes, externally, Gothic from Georgian. Wyatt had also restored—some say destroyed—Lincoln, Durham and Salisbury Cathedrals under the direction of antiquaries who could now, with relative accuracy, date a building or a part of it as far back as the thirteenth century, but who had no idea of how a structure had been built or, sometimes even why. Neither had Wyatt, but he certainly grasped the effects.

Fonthill, completed in 1807, was an effect—and a theatrical one. Ill-built though it was, it staggered the Wiltshire country-folk—and others—with its great octagonal tower, rivalling Salisbury Cathedral in piercing the sky. It was a roughly cruciform, irregular building, probably about 312 by 250 feet, and at the crossing rose the vast, gimcrack octagonal tower (it fell down within twenty-five years), which soared above a mass of irregular roofs, turrets and smaller spires. Here were cloisters, cortiles, halls and other buildings, all decorated with rich Gothic detail. There were sets-off, buttresses and flying buttresses in profusion, none of which strengthened a building which had bad foundations. Wyatt, reasonably, wanted to give the impression that the Abbey had been built over a long period of time, hence the Early English of the Western Hall and the buttressing turrets of the lower part of the great tower progress to Perpendicular in other parts of the building. The entrance gate was a fair copy of St Augustine's Abbey, Canterbury; some of the windows were reproductions of the Royal Monastery at Batalha, Portugal, where Beckford had been entertained and much impressed by the great church, the cluster of Abbey buildings, the pinnacles and fretted spires.

Inside, Fonthill was equally fantastic. Torches flared from cold grey walls—all very new. The Great Hall, 78 feet high, embellished with armorial bearings, had, at the far end, a flight of steps climbing through a high Gothic arch to a salon below the tower. There were dining-rooms, galleries, other salons, a huge organ, and possibly a chapter room, for Beckford dressed his servants as monks and in his chapel, rumour ran, he indulged in Black Magic or even the Black Mass. It was a vast and probably ridiculous building, but it was impressive at a distance and it did show, possibly for the first time, that Gothic was not just a matter of taste, applied decoration, fancy or a garden folly enormously magnified. Fonthill was a genuine and romantic attempt to re-create groupings of towers and buildings, cloisters and halls which had been the true nature of medieval abbey buildings. Wyatt understood planning and massing. Walpole did not. Neither understood structure nor saw medieval building as expressing a way of life (and craftsmanship) long passed. Nor did Beckford. He ruined himself in building Fonthill, retired to Bath, built himself an Italianate tower and remainded there, reclusively, until his death.

For all this, Wyatt could be called a real link between the uninformed Gothic of the eighteenth century and the real Gothic revival which came later. Nevertheless, the sham Gothic proliferated to such an extent that by 1808 Humphry Repton (1752–1818) says this about it : 'Since the rage for Gothic has lately prevailed, the sudden erection of spruce Gothic villas threatens to vitiate the pure style of those venerable remains of ancient English grandeur, which are more often badly imitated in new buildings, than preserved or restored in the old.'[10] Repton worked for the upper classes, then the leaders of fashion and taste, and these spruce Gothic villas were often built for those who had become rich enough to ape the upper classes. 'Palaces, halls, villas, walled parks all over England', says an American visitor not quite accurately, 'rival the splendour of royal seats'.[11] The aristocracy, particularly those with castles, were not to be left out of bringing their castles up to date, or, rather, backdating them by adding medieval bits. Medieval in those days included Norman. So Arundel, Belvoir, Eastnor and others sprouted sham Norman keeps, towers and turrets, thus demonstrating visually the lineage of the family (which is perfectly admissible); but some of the keeps and towers had Georgian sash windows in their upper storeys. These did not invalidate the ancestry of the owner but were a give away as to the date of the addition. The work at Windsor Castle begun by George IV and James Wyatt and finished by Wyatt's nephew Sir Jeffry Wyatville was, when completed in 1830, an enormous and deserved success. All this was large-scale work, neither spruce nor Gothic.

As to those spruce Gothic villas, the word villa had come a long way from its original Italian meaning. It was no longer a country seat, or even a large country house. It had become a superior middle-class dwelling, large or small, set within grounds of not necessarily great acreage, and was to be found chiefly in developing suburban areas. On the brow of a hill, overlooking Birkenhead and Tranmere, which gave a fine view of Liverpool and the river, Hawthorne observed that, 'all round about were new and neat residences springing up, with fine names—Eldon Terrace, Rose Cottage, Belvoir Villas, etc. etc.—with little patches of ornamental garden or lawn in front . . . shopkeepers and other respectabilities of that level are better lodged here than in America; and what I did not expect, the houses are a good deal newer than in our new country'.[12] This was written after mid-century, when villas had grown even smaller and were more the size of houses on our modern housing estates. Earlier villas often were large and set in ample grounds, and as far as Gothic architecture was concerned all this amounted to was an eighteenth-century squarish house with the more obvious and picturesque parts of Gothic added—battlements, pointed arches, perhaps a bartizan projecting from the angle of parapet or tower, and of course a tower itself, and if the tower were asymmetrically placed so much the better. It was not medieval but it had the look of an ancestral home (if not examined too closely) and very satisfying it was to its owner. This kind of Gothic had a certain snob appeal about it. It was all very eclectic, unreal and scenic—a part of the 'picturesque' element of the Romantic movement. The Victorians, Sir John Summerson says, had 'an intense desire to have a style of their own while remaining convinced that style is a matter of ornament'.[13]

Although in the end the 'battle of styles' was to be fought out between the Classical and the Gothic, in the first forty years of the century there were endless variations on, as well as deviations from, these two themes. Architecture reflected many influences, many tastes. Italianate was a favourite (the English have had a long love affair with Italy), but Indian, Moorish and, most unusually, Turkish, were all used—after a fashion. Hope End, Herefordshire,* built by Elizabeth Barrett Browning's father and completed probably by about 1815, was Turkish, that is to say it had domes, minarets and wide windows with very flattened ogee heads which occupied the first two storeys of the garden front and the third storey of the entrance front—but there were square and rectangular windows too. Ornamentation was not particularly Turkish though there were crescents dotted about. This not so Turkish delight must have looked a trifle odd set in the wooded Malvern Hills. But such deviations, apart from the Italianate, were eccentricities. They, in their diverse ways, are also a statement of the Romantic movement—or perhaps Romanticism is the better word.

The year Hope End was completed saw the defeat of Napoleon at Waterloo and the end of more than twenty years' war with France. During those twenty years much had happened; old beliefs were being challenged, old ways of doing things, of behaving, of thinking were being questioned, and the England which emerged in 1815 was a very different England from that of 1790. We were faced by the totally new problems created by the Industrial Revolution. We were sick of the Age of Reason. We had been swept overboard—as far as it is possible for us to be swept overboard—by the great wave of Romanticism which was common to all European countries, 'that complex phenomenon which flourished in the first half of the nineteenth century' and which 'after about 1850 . . . came to be replaced by a host of other movements, less universal and less profound'.[14] Nevertheless, we were the leading nation in the world, the most powerful, and there was a great upsurge of national pride in our victory.

Another thing had happened too, there had been an unprecedented growth in population, a growth which continued with such rapidity that it gave rise to alarm. Tiny towns and villages, particularly in the industrial north and midlands, had developed out of all recognition; London, Liverpool, Manchester, Sheffield, Birmingham, Bristol, sprawled into the surrounding countryside

* Demolished 1873.

and ate it up together with nearby villages. There were far more factory chimneys than there were church spires. This was very worrying indeed. It worried the good, solid, respectable well-to-do middle classes as well as members of the aristocracy. Thousands, perhaps millions, had no place in which to worship—had never heard the word of God; never set foot in a church and boasted of it. Even the Church of England, which had slept peacefully throughout the greater part of the previous century, was shaken. Leaving aside the controversies within the Anglican communion—the squabbles among the 'high and dry' (a rather unkind name for the old-fashioned high church party), the Latitudinarians (considered doctrinally unorthodox) and the newer Evangelicals (total depravity of unregenerate human nature, justification by faith, and the free offer of the Gospels to all)—the church, although it disagreed on forms of worship, certainly agreed that people should worship, preferably within the Established Church. The Methodists were gaining converts, the Dissenters were building their horrid chapels. The Church of England was doing neither.

It was a dreadful and shocking state of affairs from a religious, moral and material point of view. A godless, atheistic people could spell revolution, and many sound English men and women felt that that was what had happened in France. There were many liberals in England, not to say radicals; did not this smack of Jacobinism? Where would it all end—kneeling at the communion table or the guillotine?

The eighteenth century had not been, to any extent, a church-building century. Parish churches had sufficed for a small population and many had stood for centuries. Henry VIII had been foolish enough, or brave enough, to dissolve the monasteries, but he was not so silly as to destroy the churches. He was head of the English Catholic church, and all over his kingdom were medieval churches and cathedrals now freed from the papal yoke, in which his people could hear the word of God in the English tongue. So the medieval Gothic had persisted in our churches and magnificent cathedrals. It was English. Even old Dr Fuller had said so when he saw the chapel of King Henry VII. 'Indeed,' he wrote, 'let the Italians deride our English and condemn them for Gothic buildings; this they must admire, and may here take notes of architecture (if their pride would permit them) to perfect theirs accordingly.'[15]

This was all very gratifying and it is perhaps not unimportant to note that the Rev. Dr Fuller's *English Worthies** had been reprinted in 1811, and that a newly edited edition came out in 1840. It was witty and learned, full of antiquarian interest, of the splendours of the past, the deeds—good and bad—of the illustrious long-dead. It was anecdotal, it spoke of rich and poor, it told of people who knew and did not know God. No one doubted his sincerity when he claimed that he wrote, 'to gain some glory to God'.[16] National pride plus glory to God; unusual and, perhaps, contradictory but expressive of Victorian feeling. Feeling was what mattered, not cold reason. To be deeply moved was important. The wild beauties, and the terrors of Nature, God's handiwork. The beauty, the solemnity of great cathedrals, of churches with high pointed arches to carry the eye upward; man's inspired handiwork to proclaim the glory of God. Religion now required a feeling of the 'numinous', one of awe—and fear; or of enthusiasm (a dirty word in the eighteenth century) and, on the practical side, good works. But what of those who had no churches?

Many devoted Christians were engaged in good works. Many societies had been founded to spread Christian knowledge. In 1818 the Church Building Society was incorporated and gained enormous support, particularly from the safe, powerful, large, prosperous and church-going middle classes. Even the government could no longer ignore the need for churches, any more than it could ignore the powerful Church Building Society, to say nothing of the revolutionary spirit abroad in the land. People smashing machines, burning hayricks, nagging for parliamentary reform . . . religion might be a safeguard. So a Bill was passed allocating a million pounds to be spent, under the watchful eye

* First published in 1662.

of the Church Commissioners, on building new churches. Two hundred and fourteen churches were erected as a result of the Church Building Act (1818), and of these 'a hundred and seventy-four were in a style then described as Gothic, and which it is perhaps impossible to classify in any other manner. Most of them had pointed arches, and the pointed arch is, at this period, the only workable distinction between Gothic and the other styles.'[17] Between 1818 and 1833, Kenneth Clark estimates, at least £6 million went into church building.

The number of so-called Gothic churches of this period suggests that the Commissioners loved, appreciated and understood Gothic. Some of them may have done so for by now antiquarians, archaeologists and architects were really at work at it, and a good many books were written on the subject. But the fact was that the need for more churches was imperative and both time and money were the governing factors. Stone was expensive (even good artificial stone was costly and had a habit of cracking). To produce enough stone and to build quickly in stone was out of the question. Bricks could be produced in quantity and quickly. Cast iron could be used to support galleries. There was no need for elaborate richness of ornament—this was high church and smacked of popery. Simple, reverent décor, which looked venerable and which could be mass-produced by machinery was what was needed. A portable font and Britannia metal church plate were also economies. With this kind of Gothic a church could be made to hold a large congregation at no great expense; further, 'if there were a vault or crypt, it should be designed to hold coal or the parish fire engine'.[18] These 'Commissioners'' churches were built chiefly in the industrial north, Yorkshire, Lancashire and in the London suburbs.

Henry Crabb Robinson (1775–1867) out for a walk one day, strayed by mischance into a suburb. 'I found myself at Chelsea,' he writes, 'saw the new Gothic church, and was pleased with the spire, though the barn-like nave and the slender and feeble flying butresses confirmed expectation that modern Gothic would be a failure. Poverty and economy is fatal in its effects on a style of architecture which is nothing if it be not rich.'[19] Richness was to come later with William Butterfield (1814–1900) and the High-Church-Gothic-Revivalists.

Some of the Commissioners' churches fell rapidly into disrepair; some even fell down, not surprisingly, as their average cost ran out between £4,000 and £7,000. Classical churches were also built, and Sir Robert Smirke (1781–1867), the leading Greek Revival architect of the day, designed a number of Commissioners' churches in Greek revival style. Yet Smirke, who gave us the British Museum (1823–47) with its stupendous colonnade, had begun as a medievalist and among his first domestic buildings were Lowther Castle (1808–10), built for the Earl of Lonsdale, and Eastnor Castle, Herefordshire (1815), built for Earl Somers. Neither displays any great knowledge of Gothic forms but they are very dramatic, one might call them 'Waverley novel' architecture. At this time too the Inwoods designed the church of St Pancras, London (1819–22), a fine example of Greek revival and largely based on the Erectheum in Athens (it cost £70,000). All Saints, Camden Town, is another Inwood church but, with few exceptions, classical churches were for the most part uninspired and uninspiring. It was the Gothic which became the symbol; the medieval, the crusading symbol of Christianity. The cross (though not the crucifix) as St Augustine had once put it, was 'the devil's mousetrap'. The Victorians were very ready to set this kind of mousetrap, even though they could not keep rats out of the sewers. Despite the political and social upheavals which followed the great victory of Waterloo, 'England remained a deeply religious country and was probably becoming more religious every day'.[20] Or at least the middle class was.

But then came a problem, so much more was now known about Gothic, about medieval architecture, how could this be adapted to modern building? The 'spruce Gothic villas' went on being spruce, but there was more to the medieval than that. The later medieval merchants had built houses—just as the feudal lords had built castles. There is still a beautiful medieval merchant's house at Glastonbury, also the George Inn and Greville House,

Chipping Campden, and the stone-built Elizabethan manor house, Great Bidlake, Devon, and there are other examples throughout the country which have lived on, just as the parish churches have, but they were not really very useful models for Victorian suburban architecture, town houses, or even great new houses built on old or newly acquired estates. A medieval manor house was really out of the question. Such manors had been little more than an enlarged yeoman's house : more rooms, of course, a bit of ornament such as an heraldic beast or two here and there; simple gables and a hood-mould, or dripstone, above the front door, and mullioned windows, all sadly lacking in richness, variety and splendour. As for the classical, England was already full of it and there was disagreement about its suitability for public buildings although many were still being built in this style. There was for example the beautifully proportioned Corinthian Fitzwilliam Museum, Cambridge (begun 1837) by George Basevi (1794–1845), first cousin to Benjamin Disraeli. Basevi had also designed the classical terraces of Belgrave Square, *circa* 1825, Pelham Crescent, Kensington (1820–40), fashionable and excellent town residences; how tragic his early death, a fall from a scaffolding when examining the Bell Tower of Ely Cathedral. Classical squares were being built all over London. Thomas Cubitt (1788–1855) had built Belgrave Square to Basevi's design and in squares and terraces the classical still prevailed.

Thomas Cubitt was a remarkable man, so were his brothers and sons. The son of a Norfolk carpenter, and beginning as a ship's carpenter himself, he became a master carpenter in London and worked with James Burton (1761–1837) who was in a great measure responsible for planning Russell Square, Bloomsbury Square and Bruton Street. Cubitt from the 1820s carried on with Burton's work, but he was a man of great vision, enterprise, imagination and energy, and he founded the first building firm in our sense of the word. That is, he and his brother William employed their own bricklayers, carpenters, joiners, masons, plumbers and labourers on a permanent wage basis.

Apart from the private work he did for others, Cubitt was also a large-scale speculative builder and a good deal better than many of his successors. He did no subcontracting, his standards were high; he built solidly, well and beautifully. His houses lasted. They still do. Cubitt was particularly interested in drainage and in sewage arrangements and for his building estates he provided first-class amenities, lighting, good roads, proper drainage of land. He had begun in the suburbs of North London, Highbury Park and Stoke Newington (he had already won the contract for the London Institution, Moorfields, in Waterloo year, which enabled him to set up his own business). He then built terraced houses in Tavistock and Euston Squares and also in Woburn Place. These were in Greek classical style and stuccoed. He redesigned Buckingham House, which had been pulled about a great deal and it became Buckingham Palace; later he became builder to the Queen.* It was during work on Buckingham Palace he realized the potentialities of the swampy area nearby and leased it from Lord Grosvenor. This derelict land he turned into squares and streets suitable as a new aristocratic quarter of London. It was, and still is, called Belgravia, though at one time it was nicknamed 'Cubittopolis'. Belgrave Square is its heart and is little altered externally today. The façades are classical with evenly-spaced windows, columns, pilasters, pediments, urns and balustrades. Its classical blocks of houses rise on each side, but they vary.

Cubitt and his brother, Lewis, an architect, also designed and built Lowndes Square, but it is Italianate. Cubitt and his men are also largely responsible for Eaton Square (which is a rectangle). The north and central terraces are classical but the third is definitely Italianate. Chester Square is largely the work of another builder, Joseph Candy (1795–1875) who also built what is now South Eaton Place. The most fashionable square was Belgrave, but the adjoining streets and squares were just as carefully planned and laid out and drew to them many rich and solid families. All through traffic was banned, public houses were per-

* Cubitt refused to call himself an architect or land surveyor. He was proud of being a builder and also refused a title.

Terrace House in the Italianate style

mitted only in the mews, and shops were relegated to the out-skirts of Charles Street and Pont Street. Later Cubitt went into Pimlico and the suburb of Clapham Park.

It is quite impossible to name or describe all the new streets, squares, architects and builders working in ever-expanding London at this time (or anywhere else for that matter), and who developed new or extended existing areas. Hyde Park Gardens came into being 1836–38; the Bayswater district was extended, Gloucester Square grew between 1837 and 1850, and West-bourne Terrace with its fine houses belongs to 1845. There were many others, most at this period classical or Italianate. But Gothic was creeping into squares and streets too. One of the earliest examples is Lonsdale Square, Islington, built in 1838 by

66

Richard Cromwell Carpenter (1812–55) who also designed a number of churches.

There are only two entrance streets to rectangular Lonsdale Square, north and south. Thus the east and west sides are longer than the ends of the rectangle so that houses in the long blocks have wider bays. Recesses separate the bays and form the entrance to each house. The doors themselves are further recessed, so entrances are effectively narrow and enclosed. They are Tudor-arched and over the arches of some there are straight drip-stones with plain spandrils; other entrances are decorated with diaper ornament of Decorated Gothic type. Doors are also Tudor arched with four straight upright, rebated panels set in an equally plain heavy bottom rail. Panels are defined by vertical moulding. Two storeys rise above the entrance floor, each with a rectangular single mullioned window, to a plain parapet which continues around the sides of each bay and is carried a bit beyond the front cornice. The bays rise four storeys, first, second and third have rectangular windows; large bays have four mullioned windows, smaller ones, three. The bays rise to a plain gable which springs not from the roof line but from the horizontal parapet. The gable has a single, rectangular window, which makes a fourth, or attic, floor, and the ornamented point rises well above the roof ridge. Chimneys are square, high, with round chimney-pots which define the dividing walls of the houses and are set between recessed entrance front and bay. Areas are rectangular, curbed with spear-topped iron railings set in the curb. By now with the Commissioners' spires rising all over the place, the skyline of the metropolis must have looked rather like the small bespired London which had existed before the Great Fire. And had one cared to investigate the narrow, stinking alleyways and streets of the old parts of many a great town or city, there, in the filthy slums were gabled houses with jettied top storeys, all rotting away, tumbling down and packed with the poor, the miserable, the criminal. Such dwellings were every bit as authentic as the centuries-old parish churches; they too had survived, but they were as neglected and uncared for as their wretched inhabitants.

While Gothic revival architecture was slowly creeping into London and other urban centres, classical still predominated and new classical public buildings to meet new needs were built. The Royal Institution,* Manchester (1824–35) by Charles Barry; St George's Hall, Liverpool, (1839–54) by the architect Harvey Lonsdale Elmes (1813–47) who died young. The National Gallery, London (1832–8) on the site of what had once been the Royal Mews, was intended to be the dominating feature of the newly constructed Trafalgar Square.† Built by William Wilkins (1778–1839), who had initiated the Greek revival in England, it is surprisingly ineffective. The façade is too long, or looks too long because it lacks interest despite the giant pedimented portico, behind which is a ridiculous little cupola. Few now wanted a country house which looked like a public building and there were those who thought Greek revival unsuitable for public buildings too. Westminster Hall on the other hand was in the true, ancient and noble English style. So too were the beautiful old colleges of Oxford and Cambridge, built centuries ago.

But colleges, like public buildings, were hardly relevant to great country house architecture. What, then, was there left for the country house; the great new house which must symbolize the glory of the past and the splendid, equally glorious and rich present? If medieval and Gothic could be stretched just a little, if it could be thought to end not with Henry VIII and the Anglican Reformation—which had taken years to accomplish anyway—then there was indeed a domestic architecture which in the late Gothic (and Renaissance) tongue spoke of national pride, of greatness and thus satisfied the Romantic myth. The Elizabethans and Jacobeans had built magnificent prodigy houses; a great age, great men, great actions, great houses, a perfect parallel or, perhaps, a typically English compromise. 'If rich Elizabethans built for show, which they did, so did the Jacobeans,' and 'if a house was often boastful and vulgar . . . there is no mistaking its virility, animation and enthusiasm.'[21] There

* Now the City Art Gallery.
† Not so-called until 1830.

is no mistaking the energy, the vitality and enthusiasm of the Victorians either—great energy and vulgarity often go hand in hand. So many a great Victorian country house was built in the Elizabethan manner but outdid and surpassed in size, magnificence—and convenience—the real thing. Harlaxton Manor, Grantham, Lincolnshire, is one of these and bears a certain resemblance to Burghley House, Northants (1557–87).

Harlaxton was begun in 1831. Its architect, Anthony Salvin (1799–1881), a pupil of John Nash, was already considered an expert on restoration and improvement of castles; he worked on Warwick Castle, Windsor, Rockingham and the Tower of London, but his real love was domestic architecture. In 1828 he had already used a sober Tudor style for Mainhead, in Devon, and between 1864 and 1875 he produced the very 'Jacobethan' Thorsby, Nottinghamshire, but the earlier Harlaxton is in the most elaborate almost over-exuberant late Elizabethan style. Built in stone on the favourite Elizabethan E-plan, it is authentic in detail and manner. The enormous impressive central entrance has a two-storeyed oriel window above the ironwork door which, as at Burghley, is flanked by towers topped by ribbed and slightly elongated pepper-pot domes. Rising behind and above the entrance is a great square clock tower; below the clock in stone relief is the date, 1837. From the square tower, an octagonal cupola with a horizontally-ribbed dome springs. Each end of the entrance front is extruded, and rises to finialed Dutch gables (Burghley is not gabled), and at each end of these extrusions towers with ribbed domes overtop the gables. The extruded ends have bay windows with strapwork parapets. A perfect Elizabethan touch are the small obelisks which stand at the corners of the parapet, like little sentinels. String courses are well defined but not entablatured as at Burghley. The whole roof line is lively, animated by turrets and well-set square chimneys. It is mere carping to feel that the domes would have been nearer the real thing had they been vertically ribbed—horizontal ribbing suggesting the fourteenth century—for the house is one of great complexity and richness. It achieves what the Elizabethans and Victorians wanted, a Prodigy house, great and exciting enough 'to stun the eye with splendour'.[22] If it has a fault, it is that Harlaxton looks a little too perfect. Time, if permitted, will remedy that.

An entirely different house, Highclere Castle, Hampshire, was remodelled or reconstructed between 1842 and 1844 by Charles Barry,* probably the most versatile of leading early Victorian architects, for the Earl of Caernarvon. This is not an E-plan house, but belongs to the High Renaissance period. In 1837, when Elizabethan Harlaxton was building and Pugin just beginning Gothic Scarisbrick Hall, Barry built the Reform Club, more reminiscent of *Cinquecento* than anything else; prior to that he had built in a variety of styles, 'inventive' Gothic, Greek revival and *Quattrocento*. Highclere is a departure. It is rectangular with four strong square towers slightly extruded from each corner of the three-storeyed house. Another vast square tower rises centrally, high above the roof line. This great tower has at its four corners small towers which repeat, in little, those at the corners of the house. Fenestration is regular; long rectangular cross windows, for the most part, set above entablatured string courses. The parapet is sectionalized with rectangular crossed and crested panels set above the vertical lines made by the window jambs. Between, are uncrested panels which use the Elizabethan 'cipher and square' motif (much seen all over the house); small, free-standing obelisks mark the divisions. The great central tower is richly ornamented, possibly too much so, as if enrichment could never be overdone. This makes for a certian busyness, whereas the rest of the house shows restraint. In a way Highclere suggests a backward look at Wollaton Hall, Nottinghamshire (1580–8) combined with Hardwick (1590–7), both probably by Robert Smythson, but it also suggests the new Palace of Westminster where Barry and Pugin's work met.

There is another kind of grand country house which after the

* Barry also designed Bridgewater House, Cleveland Square; worked at Cliveden and Harewood House; laid out part of Trafalgar Square; and constructed the embanked terrace in front of the National Gallery. His London clubs and public buildings are numerous. He was knighted in 1852.

1840s became very popular. The best known today was designed by a very gifted amateur—I use the word in its true sense—an intelligent, sensitive, musical man who played and composed very well, drew and painted, had a high sense of duty, a great concern for social welfare and was married to 'a fiery little devil'[23] as James Buchanan when Minister to the Court of St James (1853–6) once privately referred to the Queen.

Prince Albert and the Queen wanted a private home of their own. Palaces are all very well for court ceremony but not very private. With a growing family and so little time for a life of their own, the Queen and Prince Albert looked for a quiet retreat. The Queen had visited the Isle of Wight as a girl in 1831 and 1833 and liked it. She consulted Sir Robert Peel and Osborne seemed ideal. It was not too far away to get to London quickly by rail, yet it was separated from the mainland. So the estate, about 1,000 acres, was bought from Lady Isabella Blachford and, as the existing house was too small it was torn down and the present Osborne House built. The Prince designed it Italian palazzo fashion because that particular indented bit of coastline reminded him of the Bay of Naples. Thomas Cubitt prepared the working drawings and carried out the building, and on June 23rd 1845 the Queen and Prince Albert laid the foundation stone. So quick, so efficient was Cubitt they were able to take up residence in the main block or Pavilion Wing in September the next year. Cubitt did not skimp for the sake of speed, nothing could be—or look—more solid than Osborne. As he was interested in new building techniques, and Osborne was to be fireproof, he made an intense study of cast iron and used cast iron beams throughout.

Osborne has a slightly too heavy look, but its tall campaniles —one, the Flag Tower, rises 107 feet, the other, the Clock Tower, 90 feet—are very Italian against an English sky, and the first floor loggia is also Italian in manner. The windows, unusually enough for the period, are big and wide, particularly those overlooking the Italian Garden, and the Terrace Garden which slopes to the Solent. They let in as much sunlight as possible, which is not characteristic of Victorian houses, but then royalty need not worry about fading carpets. The drawing-room, with a big curved bow window, has on its west the vast ornate billiard-room—the Prince was very fond of billiards—and the small hideous Horn Room. The billiard-room is really part of the drawing-room, set at a wide angle to it but out of sight and screened by large imitation marble columns with Roman-Corinthian capitals. On the east side is the dining-room with another big three-sided window. The first floor holds the private apartments of the Queen and the Prince, and the royal nurseries occupied the top floor. A further extension on the east side consisted of the household apartments.

Thus the house is built around three sides of a courtyard and the rooms connected by a grand covered corridor. On the east side, at first floor level, the corridor becomes the loggia, open-sided and with the end stopped by a Seralina which is rather similar to a Venetian window, but unglazed. A further and much later extension of the west wing, and occupying what was once a lawn on which, in Osborne's early days, a large marquee was put up for receptions too large for the drawing-room, is the fantastic Durbar room, but this was not built until long after the Prince Consort's death.

The Queen—and perhaps Prince Albert too—was never happier than at her beloved Osborne, and her affairs were so well managed that she could 'provide for the whole expense . . . out of her own income without difficulty . . . by the time it is finished it will have cost 200,000 l'.[24]

Harlaxton, Scarisbrick, Highclere and Osborne, four great private houses all begun and virtually completed within a fifteen-year span. All different yet very expressive of early Victorian architecture—the first three, as well as the Commissioners' churches are a prelude to the High Gothic revival of the later part of the century. Italianate Osborne differs in style but it too is a part of Romanticism.

If the feeling, thinking and needs of an age can be expressed in architecture, buildings of each age depend on available materials, old and new; on technological discoveries; on new inventions. Where the Elizabethans and Jacobeans, save for the very rich, had to use local materials because they lacked transport facilities—hence the half-timbered houses of Cheshire, the brick of Sussex, the stone of the Cotswolds—the canal-building boom of the eighteenth century meant that not only the very rich but the moderately rich could build in other than local materials if they wished. The coming of the railway in the nineteenth century, which could carry heavy loads much more rapidly, speeded up building enormously, so did new machines. Romanticism and the Industrial Revolution seem strange partners but admirably illustrate the Englishness of the English.

We needed so many new houses, buildings, railway arches, tunnels, so many more bricks, so much more mortar all over the country. Bricks were not new, the Romans had taught us how to make them—the first prefabricated building material in history—but after we ceased to be a Roman province, we forgot how, and in the late fourteenth century began importing bricks from Flanders. Soon we built up our own industry. But until almost mid-nineteenth century bricks were made from clay dug out in the autumn, left in piles to weather in the winter, and in spring spread, tempered by water and trodden on by countless hired feet until it was soft enough to be thrown into moulds. In the early Victorian period the pug-mill was invented ('pug' means to temper) and these upright mills kneaded clay and water into a soft, plastic condition, forced it out through a hole in the side or bottom for men to hand-fill the moulds. This speeded up the process considerably. A few years later a horizontal pug-mill was used which pushed the tempered clay through a rectangular opening into a correctly designed die. This long, soft column was cut by a wire apparatus very much in the way a grocer still cuts cheese. This made for greater speed and increased production. These were known as wire-cut bricks. About thirty per cent of bricks used today are still wire-cut.

With the ever-increasing demand for bricks the soft surface clays, used for centuries, began to run out; harder, drier clays of earlier geological eras had to be used, particularly in the great brick-making areas of the north and midlands. These hard clays had to be broken up before the pug-mill could operate, so heavy cast iron rollers were mounted above the mill, which ground and fed the clay into the mill through a hopper. Increased production of bricks meant open air drying was too slow, so hot-floor drying was evolved. A large shed with an iron floor which could be heated from below was constructed; the shed protected the 'green' bricks from the weather, yet allowed for the evaporation of moisture. After drying, the bricks were ready for firing in the newly-built great kilns. Bricks, a very old building material, due to the development of new processes, first became mass produced in the early Victorian era.

Bricks need mortar and this too was improved by the addition of Portland cement,* a cement first perfected and so named by Joseph Aspidin in 1822. He called it Portland because he believed it looked like, and was as hard as, Portland stone, also it could be moulded into slabs and blocks. As nearly one-third of all brickwork consists of mortar, this improvement was timely as it made mortar more waterproof.

Then there was iron, by no means new, but now being used in new ways and helped by new processes. In 1825 our production of iron was just above half a million tons per annum; by 1851 it reached three million tons. As strong permanent material it was needed for railways, bridges, machines, pillars to support factory floors, and for iron beams. Wrought iron, both for utilitarian and ornamental purposes has a long history. Beautiful old hand-wrought iron can usually be distinguished from the newer by the fact that wherever curved pieces are used at a tangent to each other the join is concealed by a firm, small band or collar and is never welded. The village blacksmith had certainly done more than shoe horses; he was often a craftsman like the village mason or carpenter. Cast iron had also been used for several centuries, but now so many new houses needed railings,

* We still use the name but modern Portland cement differs from Aspidin's formula and there are at least five different types now used.

balconies, grates, cookers, gas pipes, brackets and so-called Gothic decoration for roof ridges and so on, that cast iron, looking as much like wrought iron as possible, was much in demand.

Structurally, iron was little used in building until nearly mid-nineteenth century, when architects began to realize that iron had aesthetic possibilities as structural material. J. B. Bunning's Coal Exchange,* London (1846–9) was the first building in England whose aesthetic character was entirely dominated by iron. Here structurally and decoratively iron was used with amazingly beautiful effect, although Bunning did enclose his building with a stone skin. As Sir Giles Gilbert Scott† (1811–78) wrote in 1858, 'It is self evident . . . that . . . modern metallic construction opens out a perfectly new field for architectural development'.[25] This was written after the Great Exhibition of 1851, and the building, designed by Joseph Paxton made of iron and glass, was the first prefabricated building ever. Pugin, who arranged the Medieval Court, thought it a monstrosity. John Ruskin called it a 'cucumber frame', but today we can see that its influence on twentieth century architecture has been enormous.

The influence of the writings of John Ruskin (1819–1900) upon architecture was also great. Author, artist and social reformer, his *Stones of Venice* (1851–3) no less than his earlier *The Seven Lamps of Architecture*, encouraged the real Gothic revival, and his underlying arguments in favour of Gothic are very similar to those of Pugin.

Pugin saw Gothic as the true Christian architecture, and the Middle Ages as truly Christian. The loving craftsmanship, the wonderful, rich, hand-carved detail in stone and wood (now so easily and inaccurately churned out by machines) all spoke to him of a society whose values had been ultimately overlaid and debased by Renaissance and Reformation. To Pugin, the zealous

* To our great discredit and against serious opposition, we were stupid enough to destroy this historic building in 1962.
† He built the massive Gothic St Pancras Hotel which hid the vast iron and glass station designed by W. H. Barlow. Giles Gilbert Scott is not to be confused with his sons George Gilbert (1839–97) and John Oldred (1842–1913) nor with our modern Sir Giles Gilbert (1880–1960).

A. W. N. Pugin's house at Ramsgate

Roman Catholic convert, the Middle Ages was the only time in history when men worked for, and were inspired by, the glory of God. He believed that architecture created by such men must accordingly be, the only true Christian style. The intervening centuries revealed nothing but a falling away; apostasy permeated everything. So one should start again, return to and recreate the Christian past—and only a good man, a moral man, could create good work—a point of view which found ready acceptance among many Victorians. Sham eighteenth- and early nineteenth-century Gothic, like spruce villas and the economically built Commisioners' churches, were anathema to Pugin. Such work was not authentic in inspiration or material. No medieval architect would use plaster to fudge up stonework, or iron pillars to support galleries. This was shoddy, shabby, bogus and hypocritical.

The ecclesiastical movement,* much as we deplore certain aspects of it, was also concerned with medieval architecture and capital 'M' morality. Morality, so called, was in the air. Ruskin held that 'All practical laws are the exponents of moral ones', and that the only 'mode of averting the danger of an utter dissolution of all that is systematic . . . in our practice, or of ancient authority in our judgement, is to cease, for a little while . . . and endeavour to determine, as the guides of every effort, some constant general and irrefragable laws of right'.[26]

Architecture, he believed, is the first of all the arts and is now in a sad way; man's lower nature had triumphed over his higher. Architecture should be true and honest. It is not. He numbers its deceits :

'1st. The suggestion of a mode of structure or support, other than the true one; as in pendants of late Gothic roofs.

'2nd. The painting of surfaces to represent some other material than that of which they actually consist (as the marbling of wood), or the deceptive representation of sculptured ornament upon them.

'3rd. The use of cast or machine-made ornament of any kind.'[27]

To the average Victorian with a love of over-ornamentation this would have sounded perfectly irrational. The average Victorian did not read Ruskin.

Deceits of structure are also numerous, and detailed. Among other things, Ruskin is dead against iron framework. 'Abstractedly there appears no reason why iron should not be used as well as wood,' he says, 'and the time is probably near when a new system of architectural laws will be developed,

---

* This sprang from a union of the Oxford Tractarians (the Apostolic wing of the C. of E.) and the Camden Society, Cambridge, founded 1839. In 1841 this society began publishing a journal, *The Ecclesiologist*, which gave much valuable information on medieval churches, measurements, building, etc. Ecclesiologists held that fourteenth century or middle period Gothic to be the only right style. Rather more bossily they laid down rules for church ritual and also believed that only good men should build good churches!

adapted entirely to metallic construction. But I believe that the tendency of all present sympathy and association is to limit the idea of architecture to non-metallic work. . . . Its [architecture's] first existence and its earliest laws must . . . depend upon the use of materials accessible in quantity, and on the surface of the earth; that is to say, clay, wood, or stone.'[28] He forgot there were now very many more people on the small surface of English earth than ever before and was soon disabused of the notion that 'all present sympathy' was 'to limit the idea of architecture to non-metallic work'.

As for houses, they were to be sacred edifices. 'There must always be a certain limitation to views of this kind in the power, as well as in the hearts, of men,' he admits, 'still I cannot but think it an evil sign of a people when their houses are built to last for one generation only. There is a sanctity in a good man's house which cannot be renewed in every tenement that rises on its ruins : and I believe that good men would generally feel like this . . . I say that if men lived like men indeed, their houses would be temples—temples . . . in which it would make us holy to be permitted to live. . . . I look upon those pitiful concretions of lime and clay which spring up, in mildewed forwardness, out of the kneaded fields about our capital—upon those thin, tottering, foundationless shells of splintered wood and imitated stone—upon those gloomy rows of formalized minuteness, alike without difference and without fellowship . . . with a painful foreboding that the roots of our national greatness must be deeply cankered . . . those comfortless and unhonoured dwellings are the signs of a great and spreading spirit of popular discontent. . . . When men do not love their hearths, nor reverence their thresholds it is a sign that they have dishonoured both, and that they have never acknowledged the true universality of . . . Christian worship. . . . Our God is a household God, as well as a heavenly one.'[29]

Victorians agreed about the household God (papa became his vice-regent) but a foreign visitor questions himself on this point. 'On Sunday', he says, 'there were prayers read by Mr A. [Peter Ainsworth] in the oak dining-room, all the servants coming in, and everybody kneeling down. I should like to know how much true religious feeling is indicated by this regular observance of religious rites in English families . . . if an American is an infidel he knows it, but an Englishman is often so without suspecting it—being kept from that knowledge by family prayers.'[30]

Oak dining-room, servants, family prayers—rich, middle-class. 'Gloomy rows of formalized minuteness'—lower, not-so-rich middle-class (family prayers there also). But thousands of people all over the country for whom all those churches were being built lived in houses, hovels, tenements which mocked the new churches. New houses were being built for them too, but there were so many more of them now that house building could not keep pace with the increasing population—besides, it had been slow to start.

In cities and towns the poor crowded into the once good houses of the older quarters long since vacated by their owners who, as these urban centres grew, moved outward into the ever-widening perimeters. In Liverpool, 'with all its commerce, wealth and grandeur, a full fifth of the population, more than 45,000 human beings, live in narrow, dark, damp, badly-ventilated cellar dwellings of which there are 7,862 in the city. Beside the cellar dwellings there are 2,700 courts, small spaces built up on all four sides having but one entrance, a narrow covered passage-way, the whole very dirty.'[31] This is Engels who might be accused by some of exaggeration or prejudice, but anyone who cares to read Hawthorne's *English Note Books*, and Hawthorne was a fair-minded man, cannot but believe Engels right.

In Bristol a survey of living conditions of 2,800 families showed that forty-six per cent lived in one room only. Birmingham was as bad, if not worse. 'In the older quarters there are many bad districts, filthy and neglected, full of stagnant pools and heaps of refuse.'[32] There were two thousand such courts in which the greater number of working people lived. In some courts, and this did not apply to Birmingham alone, pigs were kept.

The 'classic soil' about that 'central city', Manchester, where English manufacturing achieved its masterwork and which had

been, a bare half century before thinly populated open countryside of hills and lowlands was 'now sown with towns and villages
and is the most densely populated strip of country in England'.[33]
These once-small towns and villages such as Bolton, Preston,
Bury, Rochdale, Heywood, Middleton, Oldham, Stalybridge,
Stockport, Ashton, now held from thirty to ninety thousand inhabitants each, most of whom were factory hands. Their streets
and alleyways were narrow, small, crooked and filthy. Courts
were filled with ageing refuse and where new red-brick houses
had been built they were black with smoke. Outside the towns
lived the manufacturers, in villas surrounded by gardens.

Villas on the hill outside Stalybridge were particularly fine,
as were their gardens. Engels calls them 'superb' and adds that
they were usually built 'in the Elizabethan style; which is to
Gothic precisely what the Anglican church is to the Roman
Catholic church'. A remark which would have pleased Pugin
for its religious connotations, and Ruskin because he disliked
the Elizabethan or Tudor style. But down near the river Tame,
where the river lay in a narrow, crooked ravine, conditions were
vastly different, particularly in the valley bottom where decrepit
houses had ground floors airless, damp and filthy, half buried in
the hillside. Closer to the river flooding was as common as over-
crowding.

Conditions in that prosperous 'central city', Manchester, seem
even worse than in the satellite towns. Manchester had proud new
public buildings in its business district and proud, new great
houses on its outskirts, but the quarters where the working people
lived were a maze of narrow, stinking alleys and courts; of old
half or totally ruined buildings where the ground floor was, more
often than not, bare earth, where broken windows in ill-fitting
frames were patched with paper or stuffed with rags, where rotting doors swung drunkenly on worn hinges. Streets and courts
were close packed with people as well as with piles of rubbish,
garbage and offal. The courts leading down to the river Irk
were, possibly, the worst. One had a privy at the end of a
covered passage so filthy that the court dwellers could reach it

80

only by wading through pools of stagnant urine and excrement. Beside the river in this quarter stood tanneries, bone-mills, gas-works which spilled their waste into the water; this collected in a thick, slimy mass behind the weirs so that even on the bridge forty or fifty feet above the river the stench was unendurable. Most poor quarters of all towns were without sanitation, sewers or drainage of any kind; water, when supplied, came from a communal standpipe. The shortage of housing meant that many lived in old cattle sheds. Epidemics carried them off in thousands. They died young.

Often in a single house several families—and families were large—lived in two rooms. They all slept in one room together and used the other as kitchen, dining- and sitting-room. Twelve to sixteen people could live in a rat-infested underground cellar. Many families who lived in one room only, took in a lodger to 'help out' with the rent. Common cheap lodging houses in every city took in twenty or thirty people who slept on the floor six to a dozen in a single room; men, women, children, thieves, beggars, prostitutes, huddled together. These, understandably, were hot-beds of vice, but then it was generally believed of the poor that they were an evil, vicious lot anyway.

Samuel Bamford (1788–1872), and others like him, did not subscribe to this general view. 'The great mass of the poor and unfortunate are not, in my opinion', he says, and he speaks from experience, 'so vicious as by the "well-to-do" multitude of the world they are supposed to be; and judging from what I have seen of them, from my childhood to the present time, which has not been a little, I should say they are more entitled to pity than condemnation'.[84]

Yet new houses for factory hands certainly were being built everywhere, row upon row. Those which fronted a street were best and commanded the highest rent; they had back doors and a small court which opened into an alley built up at both ends with a single, covered, narrow passage leading into it. Another row of houses faced directly on to this alley—which was little better than an open sewer—and these were the cheapest, darkest, smallest and foulest houses. Their rear wall was the party wall for the next row which faced a street running parallel to the first street, thus these second street houses had frontage but no back court and were let for more money than the alley houses. This back-to-back building saved space, but whereas the first and third rows, both facing an open street, were better ventilated, the squalor and filth of the row facing the alley rivalled that of the courts and alleys of old parts of towns.

This system of building was common and was usually in the hands of contractors who did not own the land. Houses were of brick and walls were thin because the bricks were often laid narrowside down to save materials. Such thin walls could scarcely support roofs, and houses soon cracked. As the contractors did not own the land on which these 'estates' were built, they found it unprofitable to keep houses in repair as the land, due to the leasehold system, would revert to the landowner, complete with any buildings, when the lease expired. Often within forty years these new houses had become so dilapidated they were barely fit to live in; the more prosperous occupants had died or moved away. The poor stayed and were joined by the even poorer.

London was just as bad. Dickens does not exaggerate when he describes 'Tom-all-Alone's'* in *Bleak House* or those who lived by the waterfront and in forgotten pockets of the city in *Our Mutual Friend*. One has only to read Henry Mayhew's *London Labour and the London Poor* or look at the engravings of Gustave Doré to realize this. Nor does Mrs Gaskell overpaint her picture in *North and South*. Samuel Bampton and Robert Owen, no less than Engels, assure us of the truth about how people lived. For the majority in England the bitter words of a song written *circa* 1848 must have seemed painfully true :

> We're low—we're low—mere rabble, we know
> But, at our plastic power,
> The mould at the lordling's feet will grow
> Into palace and church and tower.

* The original 'Tom-all-Alone's' was in Chatham; it was destroyed in 1820 to make way for a prison.

Then prostrate fall—in the rich man's hall,
And cringe at the rich man's door;
We're not too low to build the wall,
But too low to tread the floor.[35]

Yet there were those who tried to, and did, build well for the poor and for people who worked for them. Sir Titus Salt was one. Good housing was designed by many who were deeply concerned with human welfare and Prince Albert was among these; he designed flats for the poor at Kennington, provided with *bathrooms* (my italics), a virtually unheard-of refinement. Surely the poor were dirty because they preferred dirt!

Osborne House, and the flats at Kennington. The Commissioners' churches to hold as many as possible, and the common lodging houses which did the same thing. Ruskin's household God and the rotten courts of the cities. Scarisbrick Hall near Liverpool, where 45,000 human beings lived in cellars. Belgravia and back-to-back houses. The 'battle of the styles', and the battle for existence. More people, more money, more houses. New men, new materials, new techniques—and new problems. The early Victorians could not solve them, though many of them tried.

Good
Conc.

CHAPTER THREE

Interiors

When Archdeacon Grantly and his father-in-law, the Rev. Mr
Harding, paid their first respects to the newly consecrated Bishop
of Barchester, they were shown into the 'well-known room' where
the old Bishop, Dr Grantly's father, had used to sit. The furniture which had been bought 'at a valuation' was the same and
in its accustomed place, yet to both men the room looked very
different. It is true the occupants were not the same, this they
had certainly expected, but that the old room, which was
virtually unchanged, should look, should seem, so very un-
familiar, was indeed a sad business. Why should a room, 'as well
known to each of them as their own bedrooms',[1] be so meta-
morphosed?

The answer appeared to lie in two things. To the Archdeacon
it was the sight of a new sofa which had been introduced into
the room, 'a horrid chintz affair, most unprelatical, and almost
irreligious'. To Mr Harding the change seemed expressed in the
new curtains. Gone were the reddish brown ones which over the
years had faded from their original rich ruby colour; in their
place were those of a 'gaudy buff-coloured trumpery moreen'
which, although the gentle Mr Harding did not know this, the
Bishop's wife deemed good enough for the palace in the provincial city of Barchester.

But the Archdeacon certainly had very pronounced tastes in
furniture. There was that incident when he and his protégé, the
Rev. Francis Arabin, a fellow of Lazarus and sometime Professor
of Poetry, were looking over the parsonage of St Ewold's, before

84

Arabin moved in. The Archdeacon paced off the dining-room, discovered it to be but sixteen feet by fifteen, or nearly square, and decided the room simply would not do. It was much too small and when Mr Harding in his mild tentative way said it would do very well for a round dining-table, the Archdeacon's wrath descended upon his sanctified head.

Dr Grantly could not abide round dining-tables; they were either of oak, which seems inoffensive enough or, and we feel that here is what bothers him, were of such new construction it would take centuries to give them the proper patina of hand polishing. The only decent dining-table was the long, extending table, dark with age and richly polished. Further, the Archdeacon, ignoring King Arthur, associated the round table with what he thought was 'the nasty new-fangled method of leaving a cloth on the table, as though to warn people that they were not to sit too long'. Regrettably, Dr Grantly thought there was also something 'democratic and parvenue in a round table' and fancied that 'dissenters and calico-printers chiefly used them, and perhaps a few literary lions more conspicious for their wit than their gentility'. In fact, to Dr Grantly a round dinner-table was, 'the most abominable article that ever was invented',[2] and he said so heatedly.

This emphatic expression of the Archdeacon's old-fashioned taste in furniture took place in the 1850s. Had he visited the Great International Exhibition of 1851 and seen Class XXVI, which was devoted to furniture, Dr Grantly would undoubtedly have had a fatal seizure. As a contemporary account puts it, 'the contributions to this section' included 'every species of decoration for churches, for palaces and for private dwellings, upholstery and paper hangings, japanned goods and papier-mâché', and then adds, not without reason, that the display gave birth to one legitimate regret, 'amidst all the ornamental works in furniture collected at the Exhibition' there were 'so few specimens of ordinary furniture for general use'.[3]

This sad little sentiment was not shared by the average visitor who went to be stunned by marvels of all sorts. Certainly, among furniture fit for a palace, the gigantic Kenilworth Buffet* must have had the desired effect. This monstrous beautifully made piece, had everything, size, elaboration and practically no square inch left untouched. Further, it told a story, or part of a story. Carved on it were scenes from the life of Queen Elizabeth, as erroneously narrated by the late Sir Walter Scott in his novel *Kenilworth*. To the Victorians, where every picture had to tell a story, a buffet with a literary equivalent must have seemed the pinnacle of art and utility combined.

To create the right atmosphere and just to make sure everyone understood what century was under review, carved statuettes of Elizabethan immortals such as Shakespeare, Raleigh, Sidney and Drake are prominent. Another panel troubles to show the Queen meeting the unfortunate Amye Robsart in a grotto, of all places, and historically this is pure fudge, albeit of the best variety. However, the chief purpose of this gigantic buffet was achieved in the great central back panel, carved from a solid piece of oak taken from a tree felled near Kenilworth, and no expense nor detail has been spared. Here Robert Dudley, Earl of Leicester, gorgeously arrayed, bareheaded and on foot, leads his magnificently dressed sovereign, mounted on her charger, toward the castle. The usual conglomeration of attendant ladies, knights, warriors, statesmen and pages are there, some mounted, some on foot. An admiring and awestricken crowd of local citizenry watches from the background. Side shelves are supported by the Bear and Ragged Staff, and other carved figures, and are crested with cartouche, coronet and baroque scroll work. Missing are those houses accidentally set on fire when the dragon, a part of the fireworks' display, exploded in the wrong place. It is perhaps just as well, for the buffet is so carved, so ornamented elsewhere with what the Victorians so mistakenly believed to be Elizabethan decoration, there scarce seems a plain bit of wood to rest the weary eye upon.

The buffet was designed by Messrs Cooke & Sons of Warwick and, as *The Art-Journal Illustrated Catalogue of the Industries*

* Still to be seen in Warwick Castle.

of All Nations puts it, rather wearily, 'Any attempt to describe this elaborately-carved piece of workmanship would, in our limited space, be out of the question. All we can do is explain that the designs are chiefly suggested by Scott's *Kenilworth*.'

If the Victorians of the fifties judged the beauty of a piece of furniture by the cubic foot and by the amount of ornament which could be carved, applied on to or inlaid into every square inch, then the sideboard exhibited by Messrs Jackson & Grahame in what the makers were pleased to call the Renaissance or Elizabethan style, runs the Kenilworth buffet a close second. It, too, was gigantic and this kind of sideboard, scaled down, was a prerequisite for the Victorian dining-room of any pretentions at all. Conversely, the sideboard in the dining-room of Osborne House is positively chaste. Large, and made of solid mahogany, the board is supported at each end by gigantic paws which curve upward and turn into winged sphinx-like creatures. The back has two square crested panels at each end and the middle panel between is curved, scrolled and crested with a small crown. Above hangs a very large portrait (after Winterhalter) of the Queen, Prince Albert and five of the royal children.

Speaking generally, sideboards, an innovation in the previous century, had at first been beautifully proportioned and plain topped, the top supported by pedestal cupboads ornamented, perhaps, with inlaid work or by cross banding. At either end of the board there was often a reeded urn with an acorn finial, charming to look at and useful too, since frequently the urn was lined so that it could hold hot water; the water was often used for washing up the flat silver, *in situ*, so to speak. Later knife boxes came in and a gallery was added at the back and, bit by bit, or so one imagines, the plain top became rather cluttered. Possibly this first suggested that sideboards should be given additional surfaces so that more objects could have a place on them. Whatever the cause, by the 1850s sideboards were literally climbing up the walls. Tall backs had been added, sometimes of looking glass heavily framed, sometimes of wood heavily carved and pedimented while all sorts, sizes and shapes of shelves scrambled up

Sideboard and standing lamps, *circa* 1850

at the sides. These shelves were also carved and supported by brackets in the form of heavy leaves, or by pilasters, figures or by carved 'beam ends' more proper to a roof than a sideboard. Yet such shelves rarely held anything as useful as a knife box. They were there as ornaments on which to put more ornaments.

Below this solid superstructure was the surface of the sideboard, often supported by large recessed cupboards with elaborately carved doors. The point of recessing the cupboards seems to have been that it allowed the designer to produce a pair of projecting plinths at either side of each cupboard on which stood pilasters, columns or caryatids (in the form of over-fat cupids) which helped to support the top central board. This, in turn, had been shaped with projections merely to give cupids or columns something to support! The space between the cupboards and just below the central surface board, with its heavily gadrooned or egg-and-dart edge, could hardly be left unscathed, so a kind of apron piece, heavily ornamented, appeared here. This still left ample room below for an elaborate wine cooler, often enriched with vast bunches of grapes and a scramble of vine and acanthus leaves with perhaps a bacchante or two, head only or suitably draped, as further ornament. The cooler often sat on its own special rug placed over an already heavily carpeted floor. Had this space remained clear, such a sideboard would have resembled more than anything else a rich Elizabethan fireplace, where the chimney piece (or back of the sideboard) became the most important piece of decoration, and 'yet another glorious opportunity for ornamentation'.[4] As it is, one finds oneself rather astonished that the wine cooler was not made to resemble logs placed across andirons enriched with brass or carved flames.

The Victorians were, in many ways, good and bad, like the Elizabethans, but they came three hundred years later and could have been a bit wiser. With their passion for the medieval, the Renaissance, the Elizabethan, the Gothic and what they called Louis XIV (it was really Louis XV and loved for its curvilinear design and scrolls) they really had little excuse for not understanding the basic principles of good design and proportion as both had been features of eighteenth-century furniture. Even what is now called Primary Victorian (which includes much of Regency in its many different styles, Greek, Egyptian and even, briefly, Norman) is often very beautiful though much of it is large and heavy, such as the monopodium table—and even a monopodium table looks right when set in a bow-window where curve embraces curve. Whereas a magnificent great sofa with a heavy and beautifully carved mahogany frame looked and was vast, it was also more often than not an unhappy medley of styles. Large claw-and-ball feet often protruded from great scaled legs with rococo shell knees, while wings supported ponderous arms. Vastness was doubtless necessary, for if in Regency times women went in for the vertical and so-called Grecian silhouette which went well with the more restrained, delicate and well-pro-

portioned furniture, by 1840, from the waist down, women looked
like enormous bells. By 1850 the hooped skirt had been replaced
by the crinoline with its horizontal whalebone bands over which
were worn innumerable petticoats so that the bell would not look
dented. By the late 1850s the cage-crinoline arrived with its cross
bars; this lessened the number of petticoats, but it gave skirts
a positively balloon-like look. Just how women managed to
manoeuvre themselves about rooms already overcrowded with
furniture and ornaments, defies the modern imagination. It would
be too much to suggest that women's dress accounted entirely
for the shape of Victorian chairs and sofas, yet it certainly played
its part.

But not all Victorian chairs were vast and they varied in design.
The Gothic, which had been light-hearted and amusing in late
Georgian times, and the bogus Elizabethan and Jacobean seem
to have been the chief, if heavy, inspiration of much Victorian
furniture, and the Gothic had become very solemn indeed. As for
the Elizabethan–Jacobean, it became inextricably muddled. In
fact, both styles were so distantly related to their originals they
were hardly upon speaking terms. The prie-dieu chair, however,
was new and a great favourite. Usually made in mahogany with
tapestry upholstery, it was low in the twirled leg, high in the
back and had a heavy projecting padded top rail. It was used
doubtless by papa for family prayers. Then there was the double,
or tête-à-tête chair, heavily carved and upholstered. Here a lady
and gentleman could sit and flirt, though a safe distance was kept
between them, as these two chairs were joined at a wide angle
by a large triangular piece between the seats. Although hardly a
chair, another piece to sit upon was the ottoman. Some of these
were square with a central back, others were round and divided
into three huge cake-like slices, with a palm rest on top of the
central back. Heavily upholstered and buttoned, sometimes in
velvet, often in good slippery horsehair they were made even
more uncomfortable by tasteful cushions of Berlin work with
bead embroidery which added a touch of novelty to a room.
The papier-mâché chair reached its peak of glory in these days,

Tête-à-tête chair, gladiatorial table and lamp, *circa* 1850

inlaid with mother of pearl and cane-seated, scrolled and gilded, small or large, it was a light-hearted chair and is, today, much sought after. But the balloon-back chair, born in the 1830s, remained the most popular chair until the 1860s.

Some time during the 1850s the bentwood chair really became fashionable, although Michael Thornet, of Vienna, had first made bentwood furniture as early as 1830. It was easy and cheap to produce since the wood could be bent quickly by steam; furthermore it was light and plain. It could be painted in any colour, but for the Victorians black was a favourite. Darkness was all. Rosewood, easily faked, and mahogany were favoured woods and there was nothing like French polish to give a high shine.

Here, one remembers the ungainly Miss Podsnap, brought up in a gloomy house in a shady angle of Portman Square. Having no friends of her own age, she was 'restricted to companionship with not very congenial persons and massive furniture chiefly of walnut and rosewood' and 'giant looking glasses of sombre cast', to say nothing of ceremonial dining plate of 'hideous solidity'. In fact everything was made to look as heavy as it could and to take up as much room as possible'.[5] Miss Podsnap is a caricature but the description of the furniture is not.

Looking-glasses were popular and ponderous; they enlarged and reflected the sobriety as well as the clutter of a room. Certainly they were not meant to reflect light and add brightness to an interior for to these Victorians sunlight was abhorrent, nay, dangerous to beauty. It faded furniture and drew the colour out of the dark, busily-patterned wallpaper, which now stretched from brown painted wainscot to picture rail and was encrusted with oil paintings, water-colours, engravings, silhouettes, daguerreotypes, samplers and hand-embroidered reproductions of famous paintings. It also made pallid the rugs and carpets, and the Berlin-work cushions. Its effect on a woman's complexion was disastrous, it darkened the skin, etched wrinkles and caused freckles. Despite fog, lowering skies and the increasing and menacing pall of smoke belched by the chimneys of thousands of new factories and new houses, the sun did shine. This unwelcome intruder in drawing-room, parlour or dining-room could be defeated by blinds, Nottingham lace curtains and heavy plush, velvet or rep side-curtains in dark colours. Such curtains, brass-ringed, were hung on great poles. On bright days they were often kept drawn in the best rooms and loveliness, inanimate and animate, was happily preserved.

If one existed in unacknowledged poverty and quiet gentility, as did Miss Deborah and Miss Matilda Jenkyns and countless others, one did not possess rich, heavy curtains or blinds and a new carpet for the drawing-room was a luxury to be preserved at all costs and for life. 'Oh the busy work Miss Matty and I had in chasing the sunbeams, as they fell in the afternoon, right down upon the carpet through the blindless window!' says her friend, Mary Smith. 'We spread newspapers over the places and sat down to our book or our work; and lo! in a quarter of an hour the sun had moved, and was blazing away on a fresh spot; and down we went again on our knees to alter the position of the newspapers.'[6]

It seems almost axiomatic that new money has a lamentable facility for driving out good taste, and probably at no other time in our history were there quite so many newly rich people. It was hardly their fault design degenerated. They had not the background to appreciate a quiet elegance of form and ornamentation so their taste was, like that of a child's, unselective. As they had made money quickly they, very humanly, wished to show what their money could buy. But the fault did not lie entirely here. Speaking very generally they belonged to an age when making money was relatively easy if you knew how. Many knew. To be poor, it was believed, was largely the fault of the idle, drunken, irreligious poor themselves, and they had it on Authority, anyway, that the poor would be always with them. Certainly they contributed to charities and Bible societies. They built innumerable churches and sent countless missionaries scurrying into darkest Africa to convert and clothe the nakedness of the heathen native. This was a moral and very respectable thing to do but this 'growth of a morally earnest and largely uneducated rich class coincided with the development of mechanized industry', while 'the mechanical production of furniture . . . was from its early days dedicated to cheap, slick imitations of handmade models'.[7] The word 'cheap' need not necessarily refer to price, it can also mean 'offensive'. By mid-century the muddle of styles had reached its height and furniture was as costly as it was dark and elaborate. What seems evident is that an almost total adherence to what were believed to be historical styles, improved by self-congratulatory wealth of ornamentation, is indicative of poverty of invention.

Again, this taste may have been a reaction to the lightness of much Regency furniture belonging, as it did, to what was considered to be a highly immoral past, mercifully ended with the accession of the Queen. But bad design was not entirely due to the nouveaux riches. When one thinks of the Kenilworth Buffet and other pieces, 'as supplied to the nobility and gentry', the morally earnest and largely uneducated cannot be made to shoulder all the responsibility. Yet the nobility, generally, had inherited enough good eighteenth century furniture to counter-balance, if incongruously, the new.

Nevertheless, a few thought design had deteriorated and to overcome this Henry Cole (1808–82) a member of the Society of Arts—of which Prince Albert had become president in 1843—under the pseudonym of Felix Summerly, founded, in 1848, Summerly's Art-Manufactures. Well-known artists were persuaded to supply manufacturers with designs and the products were then marketed under the name of Felix Summerly as the brand of good taste. It was a splendid idea but a totally wrong one since Summerly and his friend thought Art was something which could be added to a manufacture, thus Art meant merely ornament designed by a well-known artist. The result was a fearful elaboration and no improvement in basic design, as painters and sculptors, no matter how good, are not qualified to design furniture without a good deal of technical knowledge of how furniture is made.

With the alarming increase in population the mechanical production of furniture was a necessity, although it brought death to one of the oldest and best of English crafts, working in wood. The day of the loving craftsman who had worked as his father and forefather had done; the day of the village joiners, carpenters and cabinet makers who, in the previous century, had studied the great pattern books of the period and produced from them, as well as from their own store of knowledge, major and minor hand-carved pieces of great quality, was over. Demand was by now so great that only machines could satisfy it by churning out furniture at a great pace; so furniture manufacturers became rich. Investing one's capital in a furniture factory brought a handsome return, but not always.

In the early 1840s the future poet laureate, Alfred Tennyson (1809–92), was induced by a glib promoter to sell his small estate in Lincolnshire and invest all his money in a *Patent Decorative Carving Company*. This speculative venture collapsed with the utmost rapidity and the poet was left completely penniless. Subject as he was to melancholia, this cast him into such a state of despondency that his life was despaired of. Complete rest and isolation under the care of a hydropathic doctor at Cheltenham brought him round and his friends persuaded Sir Robert Peel that he was worthy of a pension. The pension, granted in 1845, was a munificent £200 per annum. The following year Tennyson was at work on *The Princess*. When published, it was Thomas Carlyle and Edward Fitzgerald who then despaired. They gave up hope of him as a poet. But Tennyson's description of Sir Walter Vivian's ancestral home is doubtless accurate, for 'on the tables every clime and age/Jumbled together' lay an indiscriminate collection of

> Claymore and snowshoe, toys in lava, fans
> Of sandal, amber, ancient rosaries,
> Laborious orient ivory sphere in sphere,
> The cursed Malayan crease, and battle clubs . . .

Small wonder the poem is subtitled *A Medley*.

Although new-built houses now far outstripped ancestral houses there was nothing quite like a medley and muddle inside to show off success. The more a room could be overcrowded, the more beaded, fringed and upholstered, the more stuffed birds, reptiles, small animals, wax fruit or flowers under glass domes, the more ornamental china and glass knick-knacks, paperweights, albums of water colours and drawings, the more boxes of all shapes and sizes, mats and coverings for tables, chairs, desks and chimney pieces, the better it served its purpose. Its wearisome purpose was to show that the possessor had arrived; but if money made him respected and respectable it also made him a snob. 'Among the respectable classes', Thackeray says, 'the greatest profusion of snobs is to be found'.[8] And he stoutly held that John Burke's *Peerage and Baronetage*, first published in 1826, had become 'the Englishman's second Bible', and suggests that children were brought up to respect it equally with the Bible.

One of the chief signs of respectability in these times was the pianoforte, grand, upright or cottage. Often a house was doubly respectable in that it had two, a grand in the drawing-room, an upright or possibly a cottage piano in the parlour. Playing the piano was now a very necessary part of a young lady's education, so woefully lacking in other respects, and if she could sing too she was indeed fortunate. If Victorian novelists are right, few young ladies lacked this accomplishment, and the sight of pale, pink-tipped fingers running up and down the keyboard, added to the angelic purity of the young female voice, was calculated to pierce the manly bosom and drive the stricken one to such confusion he would forget to turn the pages for the fair performer as she sat upon the four-legged, tapestry-covered music stool, at the keyboard of an upright which bore a strong resemblance to a solid bookcase, save that the strings were often concealed behind pink silk.

The Queen played the piano, as did Prince Albert, although the organ was his favourite instrument. The large grand piano by Evard in the drawing-room at Osborne has its case decorated with oval porcelain plaques painted with a variety of saints. Double music stools stand by the keyboard, for the royal pair loved to play duets. In the Queen's sitting-room which, for the period, is only moderately crowded with bric-à-brac, is her 'baby' grand piano (not like our modern ones). It is square with a heavy base and large barley-twirled legs; the whole instrument is dazzlingly inlaid with ivory. But both pianos are restrained in decoration; whereas really expensive and grand grand pianos were carved, had ormulu mounts and were often also inlaid with brass.

Poor Mary Russell Mitford may have owed her single state to the fact that she was totally unmusical. She seems to have taken this deficiency with humour. Her tone-deaf father, however, was absolutely determined that his daughter should become an accomplished musician. From the age of five, she says, 'he stuck me up at the piano and, although teacher after teacher had discovered that I had neither ear, nor taste, nor application, he continued fully bent upon my learning'.[9]

Miss Mitford does not describe the countless pianos or the music stools upon which she sat while undergoing what must have been a painful process for her unfortunate teachers but, around 1850, the four-legged square or round stool was replaced by a new invention, the adjustable stool. This had only three legs heavily carved and attached to a central cylinder into which a stout spindle was screwed, enabling the seat to be twirled up or down. The round padded seat was circumnavigated by a deep heavy fringe which concealed the mechanism. Plainer stools often had a simple curved back, but on really grand ones the back, resembling a hollowed-out inverted pear, was deeply curved and padded. The small end of the pear joined the stool and the space between pear bulge and seat was filled in with supports—outward curving scrolled wood. As a lady sat bolt upright at the keyboard —tight-lacing saw to that—the deep curve of back and side supports took care of the crinoline.

In the tall houses in cities and towns and the equally tall but narrow semi-detached suburban villas the drawing-room was reserved for special occasions. Everyday living required a parlour. Both dining-room and drawing-room were filled with large furniture—a carved pedestal table, sideboard, perhaps an Omnium (a what-not on wheels) and several easy chairs in the dining-room. In the drawing-room a big horsehair or velvet upholstered sofa with its brightly-embroidered cushions ornamented with beadwork, a grand or very tall upright piano, a cabinet with brass stringing to display china, rich velvet curtains, the loo table, other tables and elaborate and plain chairs. But the parlour was, generally, the intimate family room—all cosiness, comfort and clutter. Emerson says of the Englishman : 'If he is in the middle condition, he spares no expense on his house . . . within it is wainscotted, carved, curtained, hung with pictures and filled with good furniture. 'Tis a passion which survives all others to deck and improve.'[10]

'Decking', by mid-century, particularly in the parlour, reached heights at which even Emerson might have been dismayed. The parlour required less massive furniture and this meant even more of it could be put into this room, enlivened and brightened by pretty individual touches, which displayed the needlework, bead and shellwork and the indoor gardening skills of the women of the household.

A large, solid round pedestal table, its surface protected by a circular lace or crocheted mat and dotted with boxes, ornaments, a potted plant or two and, as its main decorative object, wax or shell flowers under glass, was the central feature. One table was certainly not enough, so across a window that old-fashioned gate-legged table—a regrettable legacy, perhaps, from a great-aunt—could be placed, its plainness disguised by an all-enveloping chenille cloth, a patent Axminster cover, or a straight hand-embroidered, fringed runner placed crosswise to bisect the table. The pendant flaps showed off the runner to perfection. Here was just the place for the ubiquitous aspidistra plunged into a large pumpkin-shaped outer pot of painted china or pottery. This obscured the window even further. Naturally, this table was put to good use as a medium for displaying vases, boxes and knick-knacks of all kinds and shapes—a crochet box ornamented with a metal bas-relief of scrolls which would have been denounced by Vitruvius; a bronze cup and cover, ribbed and swagged, its cover surmounted by a pot-bellied cupid or Puck seated on a snail; a long-necked glass vase, gilt at top and bottom and with a floral design in vitrified colours painted on its bulging body.

More useful was a plentiful supply of small tables, some of them of papier-mâché which had reached the height of popularity. There was sure to be something or several things—chairs, boxes, tables—of papier-mâché in parlour, drawing-room or bedroom. In the parlour a round black tea-table, with its top inlaid with mother-of-pearl in a floral design, rested on a pedestal with a spindle and knopped baluster stem, and a flattened-dome base. This in turn stood on three raised protruding feet which had their tips rolled back in a volute. Sometimes the base consisted of three short, intensely cabriole legs; but stem, base and legs were also painted with little flowers and splotched with gold. A hollow work-table of the same substance was also a necessary piece. Shaped like a large up-ended trumpet, its interior concealed the necessary appurtenances for sewing and needlework. The hinged lid was also painted and inlaid—Windsor Castle was a favourite subject. The painted trumpet was set in a triangular base, but a plain straight-sided equilateral triangle would never do, so the sides curved inward and the exterior angles were rounded, the roundness repeated again in bun feet. There might also be an inlaid games table with a tip-up top. But fortunate indeed were the possessors of a papier-mâché piece known as a cabinet, which was a games' table and writing desk combined. Shortly after 1850 the craze for papier-mâché, which had begun in the previous century (and in England we made 'papier-mâché of the highest quality')[11] died out.

In the room there was also a plain and useful writing table, which could be used for sketching. And, with the number of children being turned out—women, allowing for the slowness of nature were, as always, almost as productive as machines—there had to be many chairs of varying designs, sizes, and degrees of comfort; from papa's antimacassared easy chair to cane-seated upright chairs.

In many parlours there was a square piano standing in one of the embrasures created by fireplace and chimney breast. The piano with its flat top could be used to display small ornaments, but at one side there was usually a very necessary oil or candle lamp with painted porcelain or brass base to light the music. The round-globe gas chandelier, which hung from a now plainer white ceiling, gave but a flickering, dangerous and inefficient light, for by now gas was laid on in cities and towns and had become a common form of lighting in principal rooms. That the iron pipes rusted and clogged, and burners rapidly silted up, was no deterrent, but it meant candles and oil lamps were still very necessary. The central light, plus a goose-necked gas wall bracket or two, in a room was not sufficient to dispel the gloom of a winter evening, so candles were still much used and they had been greatly improved. The discovery and introduction of a hardener, stearic acid, and the impregnation of wicks with boric acid, which eliminated guttering—both had been discovered in the 1820s—was a great advance and the invention in the early 1830s of the plaited cotton wick which was snuffless, all meant that candles no longer smoked because of imperfect combustion, nor did they constantly have to have the snuff cut. Even more useful, they no longer poured torrents of wax. By 1847 the cheapest candles cost only 6d a pound, and better-quality spermaceti ones sold at 1s 11d. By 1855, paraffin wax, produced by the distillation of coal and oil shales, was being used and when, in 1859, the discovery of enormous oil fields in America caused the price of candles to drop considerably even the poor could afford to use a candle from time to time instead of a rush dip. Candles were no longer hand-dipped or rolled because in 1834 Joseph Morgan had invented the first machine for the continuous wicking and ejection of candles. It operated by movable pistons, and candles could be turned out with speed although it still took twenty minutes for them to cool and dry.

These snuffless, less smoky, and all but dripless candles influenced candlestick design in a most intemperate way. Since tallow or wax no longer overflowed, large grease pans were reduced to an ornamental frill, and as wax or tallow no longer cascaded down the sides of vase-shaped candelabra and girandoles, they were no longer difficult to clean, which meant they could be as ornamented as possible. The plain candlestick turned itself into a candle lamp with baluster base often of painted china or ornate brass. The baluster fitted into a base which often looked like a hat with leaves and flowers on the upper side of the brim. The candle itself was artfully disguised by a bell-shaped dome of opaque, painted glass, the top opening concealed by a stand-up frill or a small hollow pot-shaped object. The vase-shaped candelabrum was, naturally, more elegantly ornamented. Set on an ormolu, brass or Muntz* metal base, the whole vase could be patterned with the applied metal twisting out from its handles. From the top sprouted a metal jungle of leaves and flowers in convoluted shapes and from these daffodil or lily-shaped candle holders shot up in tiers. More superior and expensive candelabra often had a figure or figures such as Daphne clutching a Herculean Apollo who holds aloft floral branches in which

* Invented by G. F. Muntz in 1832 it is sixty per cent copper and forty per cent zinc.

the candle-holders are set, or a rather fat Prometheus reaching up to take the fire not from Zeus but from the candles above. Birds and beasts were also much seen, they generally clustered at the base of the candelabrum with a jungle of leaves emerging from a central trunk. What could be done with a metal girandole was a wonder and a delight. It could stand on crocket feet from which heavy leaves, unknown to any botanist, climbed to an equally crocketed leafy summit where a single flower-shaped holder soared in triumph above. On downward-curving side leaves, ornaments often shaped like the number six, sat on the central spine of each heavy leaf, and surprisingly blossomed into a flower to hold the candle—daffodils with a short trumpet and small perianth, bolt upright Canterbury bells, small thick-petalled tulips, all were used. Art-manufacture which sought to combine beauty with utility could hardly go further.

Yet it did, for this contorted ornamentation could also be seen, though to a lesser extent, in fender and fire furnishings. Steel, bronze, brass and iron, either alone or in combination, snaked its way around the hearth; also popular were deep rectangular fenders where highly ornamented Vitruvian scroll work lodged between a base and a crenellated top, happily combined the pseudo-Gothic with the pseudo-classical. Fire tongs matched. The operative bits, often reeded or fluted, could be fitted into handles of brass, bronze or polished steel. A pair of tongs with a metal handle with a finial—made like a trefoil window with ornamental cusps—above the hinge, was another Gothic touch. The long shovel and poker also had fitted, contrasting metal handles, twirled, knobbed or shaped like a small, round, petalled fleur-de-lis or fleuron. A black painted oval coal box with a meat-cover lid, had ornamented handles and feet. Grand ones for use in the drawing-room were of japanned iron and shaped like lidded urns or a Christening font—they were called coal-vases. The grate itself, usually of the hob type in cast iron, had plain or ornamented bars. To this could be attached a perforated iron shelf, useful to keep the muffins warm and there might even be a small, sliding, iron shelf at one side for a hot-water jug.

The low, flattened-arch fire opening, now surrounded by marble or cast iron, was topped by a mantelshelf of stone, marble, iron or painted wood. From this a straight or draped dark green, red or purple-fringed plush pelmet could be hung. The shelf bore all manner of objects; a straddle-legged clock wearing above its face something rather like a miniature fontange; vases, candlesticks, china or brass ornaments and even a small picture or two. Finer and more exclusive ornaments were kept for the drawing-room. Things like bronze figures or statuary porcelain; the last, first made, it was said, by Mr Copeland in 1847, just like Parian marble but not so expensive. It was made by other manufacturers too and one could get almost anything one pleased in this splendid new Parian ware—heroines from Scott's novels, the Duke of Wellington, the Queen, Prince Albert, gods and goddesses of classical antiquity and groups of happy children at play with animals—all too fragile for the parlour. The same could be said of the beautiful Coalport vases in elaborate rococo style or the 'illuminated glass' with a design of fruit, flowers, snakes and flags incised on the underside and filled in with silver, or the Derby plaque beautifully painted with a Venetian scene. These, even if they had not been delicate and costly, were not appropriate for the parlour. Nor was the drawing-room clock writhing with carvings of floral and naturalistic design, which sat on the mantelpiece below a chimney breast, on which a portrait, reputedly by Sir Thomas Lawrence, hung.

On the chimney breast in the parlour was a large looking-glass to double these decorations; or a good-sized engraving of the Monarch of the Glen, Sir Walter Scott with his dogs, a scene from The Battle of Waterloo or the more recent Fall of Sebastopol. In some homes this place of honour was occupied by the Queen, the Prince Consort and various Royal offspring—such a splendid example of virtuous home life. A tall adjustable fire screen with bandy legs was as useful as it was ornamental. The screen, usually of hand-worked petit point in an undulating frame, gave great scope for talent. Floral designs and pastoral scenes were favourite themes, but after 1851 the Crystal Palace, enclosed in a garland, became enormously popular. In front of the writhing fender, a long tapestry-covered fire stool was as handy to trip over as to put one's feet on. The wooden floor, covered by a large patterned carpet, had a dark brown painted surround which matched wainscotting, doors and window frames. Above the door was an excellent place to hang a picture to cover that unsightly bare space between the top rail of the door, with its four sunk panels, and the high picture rail.

If the parlour were one of the back rooms on the ground floor, as it often was, it opened into a narrow passage which widened into the square or oblong front hall. Here the staircase rose to the first floor double drawing-room and then on up to the bed-room floors. But from the front hall to drawing-room floor, as the staircase was meant to impress visitors, the balustrade was of ornamental cast iron with a mahogany or dark painted wooden handrail. Balusters were no longer upright or 'S' curved bars, so common in Regency times, they were scrolled and twisted into floral or so-called Gothic shapes. Typical of the Gothic in-fluence was a balustrade with three or four vertical, plain bars broken at regular intervals by flat ornamental ones. These flat ones were more or less heart-shaped scrolls at top and bottom and were joined together by a miniature rose window, minus the glass. Or they might be oblong open panels containing a diamond shape, the diamond with a round central whorl and the inter-stices and spandrels entwined with scrolls. Stairs were narrow and carpeted; the carpet held in place by brass or iron rods set in the right angle made by the brown painted treads and risers.

Victorian cast iron was by no means confined to balustrades, bal-cony or garden railings (the last vanished during World War II), or to charming garden furniture. For weight, solidity, ornamenta-tion, durability and near immobility nothing could compare with cast iron. Further, it was relatively cheap. How Victorian ser-vants ever managed to dust, and polish, a Victorian room is one thing, how they coped with a six or seven foot long cast iron hall table, or pseudo-Jacobean dining chairs, is another. Sprained backs, dislocated shoulders and ruptures must have been some of the occupational hazards of the servants of the day. Still, servants were cheap. In London, where there were at least ten thousand female servants always looking for a place, 'from £6 10s to £10 with allowances for tea, sugar and beer'[12] was an adequate yearly wage for a maid of all work. An upper housemaid was paid £12 to £20 a year, with allowances, though a lady's maid was paid only £12 to £15, but she had perks in the way of cast-off clothing. A cook, without allowances, could earn from £14 to £20 a year, and a footman £15 to £20. The average middle-class household did not usually have a valet, footman or butler, but a cook, housemaid and a maid of all work were absolutely essential. They worked from dawn to dusk (and later), had very little time off and slept in sub-arctic attics. When the family entertained on a large scale, a footman, butler and waitress could be hired.

To return to cast iron. A combined hat and umbrella stand, towering a good seven feet against a windowless wall, set sometimes with a heavy looking-glass, could burgeon with all manner of ornaments and came in a wide variety of shapes and sizes. Then there was the umbrella stand, uncomplicated by hat or coat rack. These displayed the utmost ingenuity. A sexless Eros or Cupid holding what purported to be an inverted bow in his arms, right-angled from his winged body, stands on curly shells which catch the drips (cupids of metal or ormulu, used as applied decoration to furniture and vases, were a chronic part of ornamentation). Another admirable umbrella stand is a very satisfied and complacent heron standing on a shell-decorated plinth, holding in his beak an astonished-looking large, coiled snake. An unusual stand was made like a young girl wearing only her underclothing and the uncovered frame of her crinoline; the frame held the umbrellas. It sounds a trifle incongruous and is a bit difficult to reconcile with the Victorian idea of respectability. Certainly those given to the rampant Podsnappery of the time could never have permitted such an object to stand in a hall for, as Mr Podsnap pointed out to a singularly unfortunate foreign visitor, 'there is in the Englishman a combination of qualities, a modesty, an independence, a responsibility, a repose, combined with an absence of everything calculated to call a blush into the cheek of a young person, which one would seek in vain among the Nations of the Earth'.[13] An unblushing iron maiden revealing very nearly ALL to the world was certainly in flat contradiction to the rules of behaviour proper to a young girl in whom a delicate blush and a downcast eye was a sign of modesty. A girl who didn't blush was either unwomanly or, worse, hardened to impropriety and lacking decorum.

Cast iron door stops were in great demand and would not flush the cheek of the most modest. Very popular were those shaped like a dog lying, front paws crossed on a floral plinth, or a merry child with outstretched skirt. Both were delightful and 'homey'. There are half bells, leafed and reeded; and heavy double scrolls sitting lumpily on a ribbed fan-shaped plinth. Hunks of fern or bracken grew from speckled knobs to spray out against a door, while small floral wreaths in oblong leafy bases were commonplace. Manufacturers of cast iron furniture, umbrella stands, door stops and even boot scrapers often patented their designs. Many pieces bear the initials of the manufacturer, together with a diamond-shaped date mark on the back.

Below the hall stairs, a plain boxed-in staircase led to the kitchen and lowest regions. The subterranean, subfusc middle-class kitchen had certainly improved over the years. The open fireplace with its variety of spits, hanging hooks and portable ovens had long since given place to the coal-burning, cast iron kitchen range. But now there were great innovations in the range. On one side, flush with the grate, was a lidded boiler with a tap for drawing off hot water. On the other side the oven, or ovens. The grate had a detachable perforated iron plate on which an iron tea kettle stood and steamed. Rather grander versions of this type had an enclosed fire with an iron door and the the whole iron top had detachable lids with a plate rack above which must have been highly inconvenient. The iron mantelshelf held plates, candlesticks, ornaments and a large salt shaker or salt box. Salt still had to be kept as dry as possible and only heat could do this. In these kitchens the stone sink, with wooden cupboards below and wooden surround and draining board, was now fitted with a cold water tap. Although water was still supplied only for a few hours a day or on several days a week, this tap was a decided improvement on the old method where water had to be fetched from a cistern standing in the below-pavement-level court. Drinking water could now be drawn and the sediment allowed to settle before the water—more or less clear—was poured into jugs.

The floor, stone-flagged, was uncarpeted and what wall space was not covered by an enormous brown-painted dresser—all shelves, cup hooks, drawers and cupboards—was usually painted green. A variety of pots, pans, lids, small mops and jugs stood upon and also hung from open, scrubbed wooden shelves set in the recess made by the chimney breast. A fat wooden towel-rail held a roller towel above the sink, an iron gas chandelier hung heavily above the large, scrubbed kitchen table. A cheap chair or two was permitted—allowing for cook's bad legs—and the whole room, despite the stone floor, was probably the warmest in the house.

This simple range had certain disadvantages. As the oven tended to roast unevenly, sometimes a thick iron bar was run through it and stuck out into the coals, thus conveying heat to the furthest side. Or heat could be carried into oven or boiler by a complicated arrangement of dampers and flues. The 1840s saw the development of the close-range; this was more stove than grate or open fire as the barred grate could be closed off by an iron door and the front of the chimney opening sealed off. Unfortunately, no matter how little cooking was done, the fire could not be damped down unless the cook were skilful and brave enough to remove a few of the front bars, the doors of the smoke chamber and to cope with an intricate series of dampers. If she couldn't manage this then the fire 'could burn like a blast furnace, and was known to melt its bars'.[14]

For those who liked meat spit-roasted, a smoke jack with a spit was used. The spit hung from a central box placed above the opening of the grate; this was rotated by a fan set inside the chimney which revolved with the smoke and hot air. Also in the 1840s, Brown's Patent Cooking Apparatus was invented. Here a flue-heated boiler was set on one hob farthest away from the fire; an addition was the Automatic Toasting Jack. This, a Dutch oven affair, enclosed on three sides, had a vertical spit, and when placed in front of the open fire-grate, a tube below ran into the air inlet allowing a current of air to turn the fan, which rotated the spit. It must have been an awkward addition sticking out in front of the fire.

Other popular jacks were the Bottle Jack which looked, as its name implies, like a gigantic bottle on legs. It was open on one side and had a hook and spring to turn the vertically suspended meat. The Improved Spring Jack was a desperate-looking affair with chains and wheels to operate the horizontally spitted meat inside the squarish container. It required to be manually operated by a turning handle on top and this probably provided roasted hands as well as meat. A useful contrivance, highly recommended by one of the authorities of the day, Mrs Eliza Acton, was the Conjuror, a large round roasting pan with a lid which fitted snugly into another deeper pan which contained air inlets. Into the top tin went steaks and butter, into the bottom, lighted paper. The Conjuror, it was claimed, cooked in from eight to ten minutes at practically no cost at all.

For larger kitchens there was the Sylvester Apparatus. A huge intricate cooker with the bottom of the side oven open to the fire. This was alleged to be a great improvement, the hot air being supposed to ensure roasting meat instead of baking it. One wonders if a smoke-begrimed joint might not have been the unhappy result of this. Even more involved was Harrison's Apparatus, used for any number of different and difficult methods of cooking. It was a solid, two-tiered monster which, at will and at risk, could be converted into a close, semi-close stove, or an open grate. The boiler at one side still had to be hand filled, but it had a steam escape pipe reputed to stop steam filling the kitchen and running down walls, cupboards and crockery and other cold surfaces in rivulets. The Apparatus had innumerable ovens and plate warmers of varying degrees of efficiency or inefficiency. The whole thing looked like an iron wall with eight different-sized doors and a small open fire in the middle.

Very large private houses could, by now, have a giant range or 'kitchener' which filled both fireplace and recesses. Narrow hobs on each side gave a much larger open fire-grate. Behind was a larger boiler which still had to be hand filled, a feat of strength which could hardly be accomplished while the fire was burning. A pipe ran from the boiler which had a tap protruding from the surround, so hot water could be drawn off. Above, on the chimney breast was a smoke jack, and in one of the recesses stood a two-storey baking oven heated by a separate close-fire. Next to this stood a waist-high, very large hot plate with closet below for heating dishes. This was topped with iron to keep kettles hot after they had been boiled or filled from kettles already boiled on detachable trivets over the open fire. The hot plate was heated by water from the back boiler. Occupying the other recess was yet another waist-high hot plate, also with a plate-warming closet and detachable grills and grids on top. Such huge creations of cast iron, on which mountains of black lead were used, were trimmed with highly polished steel or brass. Keeping them, as well as all the fireplaces in the house, clean and polished, took hours every day. The Americans, then as now, were much better with stoves and arrangement of kitchen. Their stoves were free-standing and kitchens had better working surfaces. But Americans were more given to frying than to grilling and broiling. So although their stoves were better than ours and created quite a stir at the Great Exhibition, Americans were also noted for their indigestion.

Kitchen boilers had to be large; they supplied water for washing up, scrubbing floors and for washing the face too, that is, if the mistress of the house and her daughters had taken to the habit of washing before going to bed. This practice was firmly advocated by Mrs Beeton. 'There is', she says authoritatively, 'no greater preservative of beauty than washing the face every night in hot water.'[15] So last thing at night, after the exhausting duties of the day, up at least three narrow flights of stairs, the housemaid toiled with cans of hot water, careful not to spill a drop en route. These were set beside the bedroom washing stands, now no longer the graceful tripod of the early Regency but rectangular objects which resembled more nearly than anything else a midget partners' desk gone slightly demented. Usually marble-topped or, occasionally, mahogany, they had one or two large holes cut in the top in which large round pottery basins were sunk with matching ewers for cold water standing inside the basin—both with painted floral designs. At the back, as a splash board, there was often a low bow-shaped looking-glass set in a scrolled and crested mahogany frame. There was nothing quite so useful as a looking-glass for showing up splashes, or a sluttish housemaid who didn't clean it every day. Below, on each side, were cupboards or drawers with a space left between for the all-important slop bucket. Slop bucket, basins and ewers were designed and sold en suite and many were made by famous potters.

Washing the face each night as an aid to beauty was one thing, but the thought of washing the whole body in a tub was another, and it was now gaining ground. Women were even encouraged to have a bath in warm water—soap did not figure largely in bathing until the 1880s—but for an Englishman to have anything other than a cold bath was a sad sign of degeneracy or, worse, effeminacy. Muscular Christianity demanded cold-water washing of face and hands every morning. At the great public schools, boys washed at a stand pipe set out of doors, even on the darkest, wettest days of winter.

Baths, steam and wet pack, had long been considered as medicinal, and taking the waters, internally and externally, at spas such as Bath, Brighton, Scarborough, Buxton and Cheltenham had been the thing for the rich (and adventurers) to do every season. Seaside watering-places had become fashionable too. Bathing in sea water—the colder the better—was good for the health. This was still believed, but gradually the idea crept in that one could bathe at home both for health and for pleasure. The health-giving properties of the cold bath were emphasized by many physicians, although the eminent doctor, Marshall Hall, was dead against plunging infants over their heads in cold water.

During the first half of the century, as running water was rarely piped farther than the kitchen sink, it was usual for the up-to-date family to descend to the back kitchen for a Saturday night bath. This was taken in a tin lounge bath or round tub which had to be filled with cold water, plus a hot can or two, from the kitchen. After the operation was over the bath had to be emptied by hand, cleaned, dried and stood up-ended against a wall.

It was the Great International Exhibition which popularized the bath and removed it from the kitchen premises. The variety of tubs exhibited—grand French ones were particularly ornate—was as bewildering as it was astonishing and only a few of the more ordinary English ones can be mentioned here. The hip bath had become a thing of beauty; made of sheet iron or zinc (sometimes of copper) it had the outside painted or japanned in brown and the inside marbled. With its high, curved, sloping back and large, deep, oval basin, it had a great advantage in that it could be stood on a large bath-sheet in front of the open bedroom fire and filled with water lugged up in buckets from the kitchen. It, too, had to be hand-emptied. The Sitz bath, square or oval, and provided with a little seat, was also most useful—particularly for gentlemen. To use this, it was not necessary to remove the clothing other than the nether garments and the coat, then tuck the shirt up underneath the waistcoat, button it firmly and sit with a blanket or knitted woollen 'throw' around the shoulders. The bent knees, it would seem, could remain cold. How a gentleman, unless he had a valet, extricated and dried himself without getting his shirt cuffs wet, one does not know. There were lounge baths with mahogany railings, slipper and steam baths, also the portable metal hip bath for travelling. This, a large, drum-shaped affair, had handles, a lid, straps, a padlock and, possibly, detachable wooden legs. It was taken along with the rest of the cumbersome luggage by the English when travelling on the continent—so full of filthy foreigners. Much later, the portable gutta-percha travelling bath was introduced and this lightened luggage considerably.

Yet, even as early as the 1840s some of the larger houses of the rich had a cold water supply laid on, piped and pumped upstairs into a lounge bath or a large oval tub. This, often set in a recess of a huge bedroom, had a cold water tap but no overflow or escape drain, so it had to be hand-emptied. Doubtless effete people cheated and had a few cans of boiling water brought up to temper the cold. A large cold bath in a large cold bedroom must have intimidated all but the most hardy and could not really be regarded as a pleasure, no matter how health-giving. Fairly soon, however, effeminacy did creep in for, in time, tin baths were made and set inside a metal case or jacket around which water, heated by a small furnace, flowed. This circulating hot water, in turn, warmed the cold water within the bath proper. A separate room for the bath was a great advantage— even though bath and stove were portable—a small bedroom could be converted into a bathroom merely by replacing bed with bath. The rest of the room, furniture, curtains and patterned wallpaper which, alas, was horridly affected by steam and splashing, remained the same. One of the chief difficulties of this type of tub was that it still had to be filled and emptied by hand. Further, the stove burned coal or charcoal and had a tendency to fill the room with fumes as well as smoke. Also, it took a good half hour before the bath became reasonably warm. Nevertheless, the modern bathroom began here. Yet at Osborne the Queen had no separate bathroom. Her bath, short and very deep, occupies what looks like a vast wardrobe in her dressing-room and is not visible when the doors are closed. Presumably they remained open when the Queen bathed otherwise she would have smothered—and in darkness, too. There was only one bathroom in Windsor Castle when Prince Albert married the Queen.

Then there was the shower bath. A hip or round bath with a round tank held aloft on three or four iron bars, one of which was a pipe. Water was driven up pipe to tank by means of a bucket and hand pump, not very unlike the stirrup pumps of the last war. The water then came through the perforated bottom of the tank upon the bather who, not surprisingly, suffered some shock at this sudden rain of icy water descending upon his unprotected head and naked body. But it was all very healthy and some baths even had shower curtains which hung damply from the sides of the tank.

Nevertheless, no matter how great the sudden shock of cold water, it caused an American visitor to note in 1847 : 'A Frenchman may possibly be clean; an Englishman is conscientiously clean.'[16] There is no definition of conscientious here, a matter of conscience, a belief that bodily cleanliness was next to godliness, or mere scrupulousness? But the French were an ungodly lot, everyone knew that. And the Lord strengthened the island race and approved of cold showers. The heavens themselves perpetually proclaimed this.

As for the even more necessary water closet the w.c., as we know it, did not come into use until the 1880s. But as the late eighteenth century turned into the nineteenth the very rich often had a closet of sorts tucked away somewhere in their country houses—a chummy two- or four-holder—but in smaller London houses the privy, convenience, boghouse or necessary place, as it was variously called, was at the back of the house or at the end of the long, narrow garden near the stables. Under the house ran a brick drain attached to the public sewer. If there were no sewer it ran into a cesspool. In some w.c.s, a thin and notoriously ineffectual trickle of water swirled into the primitive pan when the water was pumped from the water-works at the usual infrequent intervals. So night soil men did a thriving business and were in chronic demand to clear out cesspits and clogged drains.

It was in the mid 1770s when Alexander Cumming, F.R.S. (1733–1814), mathematician and mechanic, first patented *A Water Closet upon a New Construction*. This was very simple. Water was supplied by an overhead cistern but the real secret of the invention was that Cumming had the soil pipe bent and recurved a foot to eighteen inches below the pan. This double bend, shaped like an S set sideways, was kept filled with water.

It was called the stink trap as it, supposedly, sealed off the smell from the soil pipe and drain. The valve at the bottom of the basin closed it off and was connected with a flush—a pull-up handle—which opened the sliding valve to let the water and its contents fall into the trap. A few inches of water was brought into the basin very low down by a separate pipe, and there it remained to evaporate or be flushed away when the handle was jerked up. Unfortunately, the sliding valve was not efficient, particularly if the handle were not jerked hard enough and the curved and recurved stink trap became horridly congested. Nevertheless, this double bend pipe is still basic to all western w.c.s.

Then came Joseph Bramah (1748–1814), cabinet-maker, inventor of the famous Bramah lock, a fountain pen and a hydraulic press. He had installed many a 'water closet upon a new construction', had seen the disadvantages and worked out a better one—a two-valve closet which he patented in 1778. This was a great improvement, the contents were emptied and the water—cold, hot or medicated—was let in at the same time. Bramah's valves were hinged and did not stick as the sliding valve had done. These closets became very popular and the firm went on making w.c.s until the late 1880s.

How uncomfortable the early, mustard-coloured, stoneware seatless pan must have been and what a relief to have a wooden seat. Possibly that is one reason for the popularity of the earth closet. This was invented in 1860 by a parson, the Rev. Henry Moule (1801–80), one-time vicar of Fordington, inventor and gardener, who took a great interest in sanitary science, a subject upon which he wrote, doubtless with more real fervour than his sermons. The earth closet was simplicity itself. A large ample rectangular wooden seat stood high on four legs; below the hole in the seat a large shallow bucket was attached. Behind this, as a back, was a triangular-shaped hopper, up-ended and held in place by wooden sides. This could be filled with dry earth or ashes and the contents of the hopper were let into the pan, layer upon layer, by a pull-up handle. When full, another bucket was

113

placed under the earth pan. The user was assured that the contents quickly became quite sterile and were most useful for gardening. Further, there were special little stoves to be had which dried out the earth before it was put into the hopper. London Medical Officers of Health were greatly in favour of the Rev. Dr Moule's Earth Closet. Grand closets of this type could be completely enclosed by wood with cabinet doors to conceal pan and hopper, but the simpler type could be installed in tenements where there was no water. Such bad sanitation was a frequent cause of typhoid and other diseases, but no one knew that.

Then there was the invaluable chamber pot. Doubtless the very rich still had silver ones, which were common in the seventeenth and eighteenth centuries. In fact, among the civic plate at York there is still the silver chamber pot for th : use of the Lord Mayor. Some of these silver pots had another handle added by the Victorians. They could then be used as flower bowls, for the Victorians dearly loved a display of silver, and who would see a silver pot were it hidden under a bed or in a bedside commode cupboard?

Simple unornamented pottery pots were for the humble. The glazed pottery pots decorated with floral designs were for the well-to-do. Noblemen had armorial bearings on theirs as they did on their dinner services. Elaborate pots often had flowers painted inside and pottery flowers in relief on the outside. These were kept under a bed and hidden by a long valance, or in the bedside table-cabinet. Banished were the coarse and immoral chamber pots of the late eighteenth and early nineteenth centuries with a fully modelled frog squatting on the bottom, or Napoleon's head, modelled or transfer printed, looking up expectantly. With this last one, the vulgarians of fifty years before could show the Emperor exactly what they thought about him. To the respectable mid-Victorians such 'joke' pots were very unfunny and showed a despicable want of delicacy. The ruder functions of nature existed, since the Lord had made man that way, but they were not a subject to be spoken of, much less joked about.

Victorian bedrooms were numerous; the larger the house the greater the number of bedrooms. In town or country mansions, newly built or old, there was usually a central block with wings at each side. One wing with kitchen, pantries, laundry, storerooms, servants' hall, housekeeper's room and servants' bedrooms, the other for the children and their retainers, with necessary night and day nurseries, schoolrooms, governess's room, rooms for the upper nurserymaid (later called 'nanny'), the under nurserymaids, and the children's bedrooms. Master and mistress had their own bedrooms, dressing-rooms and rooms for their personal servants in the main block. But in houses of the middling and lower middling sort, and with these we are chiefly concerned, such as the four or five storeys high detached or semi-detached houses in suburban Brompton, or the villas with grounds at Blackheath, or those of the new terraces in Bayswater, there were two or three bedroom floors above the drawing-room. The first bedroom floor for master and mistress and, possibly, elder children, the attic floor for servants with the children's floor sandwiched between.

No matter which floor it occupied, the master bedroom was the largest and often had a dressing-room attached. In houses built in the previous century which had escaped being torn down to allow three or four narrow-fronted houses to be built on the same site, the dressing-room remained, but the powdering-room was swept clear of wigstands, boxes, tables, chairs, puffers and powder bags—all the paraphernalia associated with a frivolous and immoral age—and turned into a w.c., a bathroom or, even, a small bedroom.

The most important feature of the master bedroom was the commodious, connubial double bed. No longer was this bedroom used as a morning reception room where the lady of the house received visitors, male or female, in bed, as she had done from the time of Queen Elizabeth until well on in the eighteenth century; the double bed of the 1840s and 1850s had to be beautifully but strictly utilitarian. Here husband and wife slept and begot quantities of children. Misbegotten ones were conceived elsewhere, in houses of assignation or accommodation of varying expensiveness; more cheaply in the stews and lodging houses around Covent Garden and St Giles. If a man kept a mistress and was both rich and cautious he set her up in her own house in Richmond or in a neat villa in the newly developing St John's Wood, where the high-walled garden plus the unpretentious and secluded carriage drive concealed his secret. If he had the 'publish and be damned' kind of personality, which was rare, he kept her where he pleased. Illicit love had become furtive for men. For women of any standing or pretentions, it spelled complete ostracism. If an unhappily married woman with an unfaithful or brutal husband even saw another man at frequent intervals, no matter how innocent the friendship, she compromised herself, as Caroline Norton had done with Lord Melbourne in 1836 and with Sidney Herbert ten years later. If she took a lover it was best to escape to the wicked continent with him; if she returned to England as Marguerite, Lady Blessington, did, no lady called upon her. Lady Blessington was not called upon at Gore House, Kensington, although she entertained and amused other women's husbands by her wit, conversation and good food. Lesser female violaters of the marriage bed were generally given no quarter. They were as dead to spouse and family alike.

This seems a trifle harsh. A marriage settlement usually meant the bridegroom received the bride's money—and kept it—which made nonsense of that bit of the marriage service 'with all my worldly goods I thee endow'. Often it was the other way round. The dowry was the husband's. The wife was his personal property, part of his goods and chattels. Too often the nuptial bed turned out to be a sacrificial altar.

Indeed, the mid-Victorian double bedstead often looked like a misshapen altar with its half-tester as a skimped baldacchino. Half-testers were back in favour after a lapse of some four hundred years. This ungainly kind of bed often had two tall, square posts at its head which rose seven to eight feet above floor level. About three-quarters of the way up, huge projecting scrolls were attached. Posts and scrolls supported the half-tester. The tester

Half-tester bed with side and back curtains, 1840–50

had plain sides with heavy moulding at the top and lighter moulding at the bottom, rather like a cornice. Ornamentation was reserved for the front panel which was joined to the two sides by the square entablatures of non-existent pillars. From the bottom of these a brace of 'S' shaped crockets or other ornament depended, each with a pendant drop often resembling an outsize acorn. This all-important front panel was curved like a wavy bow, the wave greatly emphasized by double moulding. In the space left between the high curve of the wave and the straight bottom moulding rail of the tester, there might be a cartouche from which leaves curled and diminished toward the capitals. A dark silk curtain fell from the back of the tester, and silk curtains were drawn at night to protect the sleepers' heads from draughts, to which gentlemen must have been extremely susceptible as they also wore nightcaps. By day the curtains were looped back and held in place by heavily-tasselled cords, or the ends were folded across the pillows. A padded headboard repeated the bow shape of the tester and was set within a mahogany frame relentlessly scrolled at each end where it joined the headposts. A twisted knot, shell, or leaf, adorned the highest point of the curve. Sometimes the head was of solid wood ornamentally carved and ran straight up to the half tester.

The heavy and shorter footboard was also curved at the top and was held with unshakeable solidity between two square columnar footposts set on plinths with a stepped base and capital to match the tester. As a central embellishment of each plinth a patera or bellflowers were used. The posts were entablatured like the tester, but here crockets stood upright and wore the giant acorn as a finial. The central motif of the footboard was often a heavy round or oval of applied strap-work embracing a cartouche to match that of the tester. The cartouche was perfectly plain, though one feels it should have had the words *Hic jacet* carved upon it. More heavy curlicued scrolls ran from each footpost for about eighteen inches or so and were joined onto the deep side panels with their triple or quadruple mouldings at top and bottom, these helping to keep the mattresses in place. The whole bedstead was a riotous mélange of styles; the half-tester, a hangover from late medieval times; strap-work, **Elizabethan**; curves, scrolls and curlicues, heavy-handed baroque; paterae, eighteenth century neoclassical; bellflower, decorated **Gothic**. There is a definite ecclesiastical flavour about such beds.

Fortunately there were other much lighter and prettier bedsteads. A single iron-framed half-tester of lesser height was often made with attractive papier-mâché head and foot boards. The tester was a half circle with valance, back curtain and straight hanging side curtains of silk or velvet. Another deep valance, which touched the floor, concealed the iron frame and the bed was covered by a counterpane to match. Other bedsteads, single or double, were iron-framed and head and foot pieces of the same height were of brass. They were usually rectangular, made of thin brass rods, round or square. Foot and head posts had a knop and finial on top, with the top rail fitted into the knop. Inside the rectangle made by the posts and the top and bottom rails of the iron frame, brass squares or rectangles were set, often held in place by thin leafy ornaments to disguise their joints. A floor length valance and counterpane completed this simple and charming bedstead. These were the forerunners of the heavy brass bedsteads of late Victorian and Edwardian times. The old and rather ugly tent bed of the previous century now took on a new, more graceful shape. It was no longer the cheap bed it had been and was now renamed a canopy bed. It had four posts with head and foot of light iron or brass, the top rails were curved, and below open-work designs in slim iron rods filled in the space between the posts. Four curved iron rods soared from the four posts and converged to an open iron or brass frilled ring which looked very much like the neck frill worn by men in the days of Edward VI. Around this the silk curtains were gathered and fell on all four sides. They could be drawn by day exposing counterpane and floor-length valance.

Bed-making in those days was no easy task. The great half tester double bedstead could not be made up single-handed. But people who had such great beds could also afford to employ upper and under housemaids to cope with them. Nevertheless, to make a bed was certainly considered an art. 'In bed-making', servants are told, 'the fancy of the occupant should be consulted; some like beds sloping from the top towards the feet, swelling slightly in the middle; others, perfectly flat; a good housemaid will accommodate each bed* to the taste of the sleeper, taking care to shake, beat, and turn it well in the process. Some persons prefer sleeping on the mattress, in which case a feather bed is usually beneath, resting on a second mattress, and a straw palliasse at the bottom. In this case, the mattresses should change places daily; the feather bed placed on the mattress, shaken, beaten, taken up and opened several times, so as thoroughly to separate the feathers; if too large to be thus handled, the maid should shake and beat one end first, and then the other, smoothing it afterwards equally all over into the required shape, and place the mattress gently over it. Any feathers which escape in this process a tidy servant will pat back through the seam of the tick; she will also be careful to sew up any stitch that gives way the moment it is discovered. The bedclothes are laid on, beginning with an under blanket and sheet, which are tucked under the mattress at the bottom. The bolster is then beaten and shaken, and put on, the top of the sheet rolled round it, and the sheet tucked in all round. The pillows and other bedclothes follow, and the counterpane over all, which should fall in graceful folds, and at equal distance from the ground all round. The curtains are drawn to the head and folded neatly across the bed, and the whole finished in a smooth and graceful manner.'[17]

As a bed had three mattreses and there were probably half a dozen or more beds to be made, each according to the 'fancy of the occupant', bed-making sounds as if it might be a whole day's work for the housemaid or housemaids. But this was only one of her daily chores and let us hope there was more than one housemaid. Even before she began on the bedrooms she had to dust and polish the furniture in the breakfast parlour, prepare the

* We no longer distinguish between the words 'bed', which here refers to mattresses, and 'bedstead', the frame upholding the bed.

table, then attend to all the downstairs fireplaces and that meant polishing the grates as well. Then she went up to her mistress's dressing-room or bedroom, lit the fire there and put hot-water cans next to the washstand. If no lady's maid were kept, she put her mistress's clothes on a horse to air in front of the fire—failing a horse the backs of the chairs would do. Then she called her mistress.

While the family breakfasted she saw to the bedrooms, pulled up the blinds, drew the curtains, stripped the bed and placed the bedclothes over the horse or chairs to air. Slops were emptied into pails and all vessels containing slops—a rather euphemistic word—were rinsed with scalding water to which, if necessary, a little turpentine was added. Hand-basins were rinsed in cold water and dried. Ewers were emptied, washed and refilled with cold water. Water jugs were also emptied, well rinsed and wiped dry; this was most important since, during the night, what sediment was left in the water settled at the bottom of the jug. The pails were then carted down to the kitchen, emptied, washed, scalded and dried. This scalding, a very necessary precaution, must have been ignored by many an overworked housemaid. After this she began the business of bedmaking. Before doing so she had to remove all velvet chairs or any other objects which might become dusty, into another room. Then came the bed and after that was done she was free to do the rest of the room, thoroughly.

This was no job for the faint-hearted or the easily wearied; the bedroom was just as cluttered with furniture as every other room. There were small chairs and a table or two, one perhaps of papier-mâché, to be dusted. There was the washstand to be cleaned, soap dishes washed and mirror-back polished. Then there was the Victorian wardrobe which, from about 1830 onwards, had developed from the smaller Regency press type, with bottom drawers, into the hanging wardrobe—a massive piece of great solidity—standing between seven and eight feet high and proportionately deeper than its forebears. Often it had three doors to close off the hanging cupboard and the deep single drawer below, two narrow side doors with recessed panels and a central door set with a long plate-glass mirror, which meant that the cheval glass of the eighteenth century was out; it made a brief comeback in gentlemen's dressing-rooms in late Victorian and Edwardian times. Crowning the wardrobe a heavy cornice—the favourite was ogee or reverse ogee moulding—frowned down upon the rest of the room as if, in a forbidding, *pater familias* fashion, it particularly disapproved of the feminine, inlaid and carved mahogany dressing table with its toilet mirror and stand draped in ephemeral muslin, which fell in a rounded widow's peak above the centre of the looking-glass and was held there in a most unwidowly fashion by a large flat pink silk ribbon bow. This draped mirror stood upon a cabinet, with inlaid doors and gadrooned or reeded bun feet. Around the top was a ruffled valance and the cabinet itself was sweetly pretty; it, too, was draped with frilled muslin which allowed only the mutin (often carved) and part of the shutting stiles with their keyholes to remain visible. On the flat top stood the silver candlesticks, the ornate silver-backed brushes, the tortoiseshell combs with their silver handles, the scent bottles and other articles of dressing silver, as well as a ring stand and, possibly, a *cabaret de toilette* of china, all these had to be removed daily, dusted and replaced. The night-table cabinet-commode had to be cleaned and polished and the clean, necessary article returned, the door closed and polished, the candle and water jug removed from the top, which also needed dusting and polishing.

Then there was the iron grate to be dealt with. If the fire were burning it was not black leaded until later, but the brass fender and fire-irons had to be well rubbed and polished with dry chamois leather. The rest of the fireplace was usually of marble. Pilasters with rosetted plinths to match the bed upheld the mantelshelf with its beaded, nailhead or guilloche moulding— sometimes the three were combined as a further fantastic en-richment. The fireplace opening was low, curved and also finished with a moulding, often crested with a floral ornament. Marble needed to have dirty marks removed and there was nothing better for this than a home-made paste of two parts soda, one each of pumice stone and chalk, carefully sifted, rubbed well into the marble, washed off with soap and water, then dried and polished.

The mantelshelf was a welter of china ornaments which needed dusting, and if there were gasoliers at each side of the shelf with hanging flower-petalled china shades the openings had to be cleared of rust and the shades dusted. The large looking-glass, with its bogus baroque or rococo frame, of mahogany or gilt pine had also to be dusted. Should the wallpaper—large floral pat-terned—have dirty patches, such patches could be removed with the soft inside of a fresh loaf of bread rolled into a ball and used as an eraser, the dirty crumbs fell on the polished floor or painted surround or even on the large floral-patterned and baroque-scrolled carpet. The hearthrug—and a Berlin wool-work hearth rug was fashionable—had already been removed and shaken. The framed pictures, landscapes and even photographs, which adorned the walls, were dusted, then all the dust, crumbs, feathers and bits of wool, were swept toward the fireplace to be gathered up on the hearth. After this the velvet-upholstered chairs, which had been removed to the passage, were brought back and this bedroom was finished. There were at least five others to be dealt with, but they were less elaborate.

The simplest and barest rooms of all were those of the ser-vants on the attic floor. The housemaid's bedroom, which she shared with another maid, was furnished with an old double or two single beds, a chest of drawers, a small hanging looking-glass—not to see her face in, but to enable her to adjust her cap —the old Regency tripod wash basin and ewer and, possibly, the clothes press, much battered, for her clothes. Failing that a pegged board was screwed to the wall and served to hang her clothes upon. Above this was a shelf to hold a few boxes. Often a cheap curtain tacked to the shelf, or a separate calico curtain on rings, concealed the clothes. The scrubbed floor had a rug, possibly relegated from a child's room, a table for candlesticks and trinkets or ornaments of her own, a cheap chamber-pot, a chair or two and that was that.

In grander houses with a servants' wing, the rooms were better and here there was a servants' hall, and a hierarchy to be preserved among the servants. Housekeepers were, of course, grander and in great houses servants took enormous pride in being in 'good service', but we are not speaking of family retainers who, generation after generation, served the same family and were, in a sense, a part of the family as they had always been.

Yet even the most ill-housed, ill-fed and underpaid servant was far better off than the poor who lived in the teeming tenements of London, Manchester, Liverpool and in the mushrooming industrial towns with their squalid rows of back-to-back houses, or in the tumbledown cottages of farm labourers. Anyone who reads Henry Mayhew's great work on the conditions of the poor in London alone, emerges half-blind with rage and pity—and apt to forget how many good and sincere Victorians spent their lives in trying to help better conditions.

Page after double-column page of Mayhew's book gives innumerable case histories. Although he does not cast his net so wide as Sir Frederic Morton Eden had done at the end of the eighteenth century, as he deals only with London, he is far more detailed. One family of five, he tells us, lived in the front basement kitchen of an old house in which every room was let to a different family. This family of five was very unusual: although all they had to sleep in was one bed, the room was spotlessly clean. To have kept a room spotless when water came from the nearest pump or conduit and had to be carted home in a battered bucket or in buckets hanging from a yoke over the shoulders so that the stone floor could be scoured daily; to live five in a room and yet keep that room clean and neat, to take turns in sleeping two or three in the one bed, must have taken unbelievable determination and endurance. But this family was an exception to the general rule.

Another 'terrible hovel' which he visited had the broken windows stuffed with rags or brown paper to keep out the cold and damp. In this house with a sloping roof and half the tiles missing, he groped his way up a tottering, broken staircase to a room filled with smoke from a defective chimney. The room—where three women lived—was about nine foot square, the paper hung in shreds from the walls, the ceiling was broken and patched, but the occupants didn't lack water as they caught it in jugs placed on the chimney piece. A rag of a carpet made from old mats inadequately covered the rotting floor. It was useful as it prevented things dropping through the floor boards. The rent was ninepence a week—a penny per square foot—and the room was furnished with three broken chairs, backless and nearly seatless, a rickety table and some bits of crockery. On a mattress on the floor lay a girl 'eighteen years old last twelfth-cake day'. She had just been confined but the baby had died, said 'an old woman of sixty'. The other occupant, also a girl, was healthy and a street pedlar. As they were very, very poor the parish allowed them one shilling and two loaves of bread a week, but the neighbours, when they could, helped out with the occasional vegetable, 'but mustn't grumble' the old woman said and added, Mayhew tells us 'as long as they kept out of the "big-house"* she wouldn't complain'.[18]

As the rent was ninepence a week that left them with threepence out of the parish shilling and what few pence or shillings the healthy girl could earn, and earnings must have been scanty. Few streets sales could be made on wet days, so these three lived well below subsistence level. 'Three wet days', Mayhew was told by an ex-clergyman who sold stenographic cards in the streets, 'will bring the greater part of 30 thousand street people to the brink of starvation.'[19] As statistics from the Royal Society showed the average number of wet days in London to be 161 annually, that meant a rough average of two and a quarter wet days a week. Had the weather stuck to this average, weekly, starvation would not have been the commonplace it was, but weeks on end of rain in spring, summer, autumn and winter, brought the most dreadful suffering and since food was more expensive than gin, the really poor took to gin.

In another poverty-stricken household, where starvation was a

* The Union work-house.

member of the family, a girl said she thought Christ must indeed be 'a very kind gentleman because he gave a good many poor people a penny loaf and a bit of fish each'.[20]

In Liverpool, where Hawthorne walked almost every day 'in the darker and dingier streets inhabited by the poorer classes' he notes 'at every two or three steps a gin shop' and the people 'filthy in clothes, and in person ragged, pale, often afflicted with humors, women nursing their babies at dirty bosoms; men haggard, drunken, careworn, hopeless, but with a kind of patience, as if this were the rule of their life. . . . Sometimes a decent woman may be sitting sewing or knitting at the entrance of her poor dwelling, a glance into which shows dismal poverty.'[21] Hawthorne does not detail the poverty of their furniture. He had no need to.

Dickens does not exaggerate when he describes the interiors of the poor. Trollope tells the truth when he describes the home of the perpetual curate of Hogglestock : 'By degrees the carpet had disappeared . . . now nothing but a poor fragment of it remained in front of the fireplace. In the middle of the room there was a table which had once been large; but one flap of it was gone altogether, and the other flap sloped grievously towards the floor, the weakness of old age having fallen into its legs. There were two or three smaller tables about, but they stood propped against the walls, thence obtaining a security which their own strength would not give them . . . there was one armchair in the room, a Windsor-chair, as such used to be called, made soft by an old cushion in the back . . . and there was an old horsehair sofa, now almost denuded of its horsehair, but that, like the tables, required assistance. Then there was half a dozen of other chairs, all of different sorts, and they completed the furniture of the room.'[22]

Mr Crawley, the curate, was a beneficed clergyman of the Church of England and, like many clergyman, was desperately poor. He was also a Greek and Latin scholar. His poverty irritated the worldly Dr Grantly, the more so since his son wished to marry Grace Crawley 'who was as poor as poverty itself'.[23] There was nothing 'unprelatical' about Mr Crawley's sofa, and no dissenter or calico printer would have been seen dead—except of starvation—at Mr Crawley's table.

There were indeed two nations. One, of the great half-tester bed, the other of the mattress in that smoky room. There were ornate chairs, heavy tables, rich carpeting, contrasted with back-less chairs, and old mats; marble fireplaces and mantelpieces, with damaged chimneys and jugs set on the mantelshelf to catch the rain. There is the Kenilworth Buffet, and the rickety table. The gas chandeliers, the elaborate branched candlesticks, and the stump of a candle stuck in a bottle, and the woman sitting in the doorway knitting because there was no light inside. The world where the housemaid prepared the lavish breakfast—and that of the girl who thought of the kind gentleman who gave a penny loaf and a bit of fish to the poor.

CHAPTER FOUR

Food

'Man, it has been said, is a dining animal. Creatures of the inferior races eat and drink; man only dines.' This is a trifle confusing, the simple mind may wonder if the inferior races do not belong to the genus homo—if not sapiens. The next sentence does not clarify matters. 'It has also been said', it reads, 'he is a cooking animal; but some races eat food without cooking it.' Just what that would make a cannibal chief and his ritualistic, tribal dining customs is a question which need not detain us, for we are soon given the marrow of the subject: 'Dining is the privilege of civilization. The rank which people occupy in the grand scale may be measured by their way of taking their meals, as well as by their way of treating women. The nation which knows how to dine has learnt the leading lesson of progress.'[1]

These sentences were written in 1861 by a woman whose name was destined to become a household word, Mrs Beeton. It is difficult when reading Mrs Beeton not to think of her as a formidable, middle-aged, dictatorial and overweight dragon. In fact she was only twenty-five when her articles on household management and cookery, which had appeared as a regular magazine feature for two years, were collected and published in book form. Four years later, at the age of twenty-nine, Mrs Beeton died in childbed.

It was Robert Burton (1577–1640) who, back in the seventeenth century said, 'England is a paradise for women and a hell for horses',[2] so on the treatment of women we were reputedly civilized. But when it came to cookery! To quote Burton again: 'If we study at all it is *erudito luxa* to please the palate, and to

128

satisfy the gut. "A cook of old was a base knave (as Livy complains) but now a great man in request; cookery is become an art, a noble science; cooks are gentlemen." [3] This great man knew little about women, horses or cookery and confesses that he had lived a silent, sedentary, solitary, private life. As for Livy, he is often sarcastic.

Mrs Beeton is not. She is a teacher but she does not make use of the teacher's weapon, sarcasm. What she is trying to drum into the heads of the newly rich is how to dine if they wish to be accepted by society and how to give a dinner—if accepted. She attempts to show how the aspirant must behave in her own home so that she (and he) can move up the intervals of the 'grand scale', not necessarily to the top but well into the middle; the secure, comfortable, safe, smug middle, where the top can be gazed at with envy and admiration—and feverishly emulated—while the bottom can be looked down upon with scorn and contempt. Yet her remark that a nation which knows how to dine has learnt the leading lesson of progress must have shaken many an early Victorian. Were we not far and away the most progressive, most powerful, richest nation in the world? Certainly we were. Few Victorians entertained the smallest doubt of it or of our superiority over all other nations. But here is Mrs Beeton making dining the criterion of civilization and progress. And here she knew what she was about.

We were, and always had been, noted for bad cookery and repulsive table manners. We had driven French and Italian visitors to despair by what we did to food. We cooked, it is true, but we cooked and ate abominably. On the continent we had been known for centuries as a nation of gross feeders. In the late seventeenth century what we did to a bit of boiled beef had M. Henri Misson shuddering, for we 'besieged it with five or six heaps of cabbage, carrots, turnips, or some herbs or roots well salted and swimming in butter'. [4] Some time around the middle of the eighteenth century we began to Frenchify food, to the horror of Mrs Hannah Glasse, and a good many Englishmen who thought it all silly nonsense. No less horrified, but for other reasons, was the young visitor, François de la Rochefoucauld, who bewailed our lack of ragouts and sauces as late as 1784; who found our table manners and after dinner conversation disgusting, and dinner itself the most boring and tiring of all his experiences in England, because it lasted four to five hours, and English guests seemed bent upon little else than stretching their stomachs beyond endurance to please their host. It was not really until that man of many talents, Dr William Kitchiner (1775?–1827), epicure, writer on optics and music, produced his *Apicius Redivivus, or the Cook's Oracle* (1817) that English cookery began to look up. Dr Kitchiner—his book had gone into seven editions by 1827—was the first to produce the kind of cookery book we know today. He gave exact measurements for every recipe followed by clear instructions as to method. It may be said that with Dr Kitchiner's work, those other than the rich (most of whom imported French chefs after the manner of George IV) were initiated into the meaning of good cooking.

Bit by bit in the first half of the century cooking probably improved. A positive cascade of cookery books, articles on cookery and the new science of dietetics poured from the pens of authors fitted and unfitted to deal with the subject. Even so, it seems there was not enough of the right kind of information or, perhaps, what there was made little impression, for as late as 1856, five years before Mrs Beeton, Eliza Acton (1799–1859) writes in her Preface to *Modern Cookery for Private Families*, 'It cannot be denied that an improved system of practical domestic cookery, and a better knowledge of its first principles, are still much needed in this country; where, from ignorance, or from mismanagement in their preparation, the daily waste of excellent provisions almost exceeds belief. This waste is in itself a very serious evil when so large a portion of the community often procures—as they do in England—with painful difficulty, and with heaviest labours, sufficient bread to sustain existence; but the amount of *positive disease* which is caused amongst us by improper food or food rendered unwholesome by a bad mode of cooking it, seems a greater evil still.'

No nonsense about rank and the 'grand scale' here. Eliza
Acton seems intent on feeding and nourishing a family no matter
what its position in the social scale. Indeed, her whole preface
appears to show a good deal more feeling for the 'have-nots' than
does Mrs Beeton. Isabella is concerned with civilizing us at table,
Eliza with our getting value for money no matter how large or
small the income. 'Why,' she asks, 'should not *all* classes participate in the benefit to be derived from nourishment calculated to
sustain healthfully the powers of life? And why should the English, as a people, remain more ignorant than their continental
neighbours of so simple a matter as that of preparing it for
themselves?'[5]

This sounds splendid and practical but when it comes to reading the book one realizes two things. First, the private families
cannot have been low-income families; haunches of mutton, sides
of beef, three white soups—rich, delicate and oyster—are not the
food of the poor. Second, waste does not mean throwing good
food away. It means cooking it so badly its nourishment is reduced.
Eliza Acton may have thought her book would help the poor for
she says, 'in our cottages, as well as in homes of a better order
goes on the "waste" of which I have already spoken', and then
gives the game away with : 'It is not . . . cookery-books that we
need half so much as cooks really trained to a knowledge of their
duties, and suited, by their acquirements, to families of different
grades. At present, those who thoroughly understand this business are so few in number, that they can always command wages
which place their services beyond the reach of *a modest fortune*'
(my italics). Hence her book is a do-it-yourself cookery book.
Always provided one had the money to buy the food.

It is just as well to remember that the first edition of this family
cookery book, so abundant in its recipes, was published in 1845
when its author—also a not very good poet—was forty-six and
old enough to understand what was happening. For 1845 was
the middle year of the 'hungry forties'. Agricultural labourers
earned on an average six to nine shillings a week and the cottager
and his family were more often hungry than not. This was the

Culinary trophy

year of a scanty harvest and an appalling growth of general poverty and want; it was the year when the miniscule fungus, *phytophthora infestans*, ruined the potato crop in Ireland and brought thousands to starvation and the verge of revolution. But the fungus did in one year what good men had been trying to do for a quarter of a century; it brought about the repeal of the Corn Laws. Thereafter, although we had a bad patch economically for two years, the price of bread fell by fourpence and by the 1850s we were waxing rich and fat. We were also, as usual, being poisoned in droves by what we ate.

The sophistication of food was certainly not new, but with population and consumption of food increasing, those who supplied it had become expert, hardened and practised adulterers. Fears of the various poisons and harmful substances used to sophisticate food had been vividly expressed in horrific terms by eighteenth century pamphleteers, but the writers were not analytic chemists and could not substantiate their work with sufficient proof. Early in the nineteenth century, however, Friedrich Christian Accum

(1769–1838), a German-born chemist, appeared on the scene. Accum became 'chemical operator' to the Royal Institution and in addition to other interests had a positive passion for chemically analysing food. Over the years he worked away and in 1820 brought out a book on the adulteration of foodstuffs and became famous or notorious, depending on the reader, overnight. Adulterers had been fulminated against before but, hitherto, no one had been able to back fulmination with thorough chemical analysis. It was the old eighteenth century story, but now it was informed by specific and irrefutable evidence. Alum added to bread; red lead used to colour Gloucester cheese; cream thickened with flour and arrowroot; beautifully coloured confectionery which, since its colour came from salts of copper and lead could sweetly lead to permanent ill-health and even the grave. Dried blackberry leaves added to tea; sand to the sugar loaf; capsicum added to mustard and copperas (another name for vitriol) added to beer, to say nothing of *cocolus indicus* which gave a nice bitter flavour and a real wallop to the diluted brew. It also stupefied, paralysed, caused convulsions, gastro-enteritis and 'over-stimulated the respiratory system and could, not surprisingly, lead to death'.[6]

Accum's book also gave a list of druggists and grocers who had been convicted of selling adulterating materials to brewers. The work which named names became an overnight success and went into four editions in two years.

But the brewers and their suppliers who had been listed were furious, vocal, many and powerful. Whether they engineered Accum's downfall is now difficult to say. Accum, however, did perhaps give his enemies their chance for when he was Librarian to the Royal Institution it was discovered that someone was removing leaves from the books. Suspicion fell upon Accum, and the Royal Institution, more shame to it, applied for a warrant to have his rooms searched. It was alleged that a number of the missing pages had been found there and Accum was charged with theft. Whether he had taken the pages or whether they had been planted is a matter of conjecture, but the magistrate

who tried the case obviously had his doubts for he dismissed it
on the ground that the missing leaves were 'waste paper' and
that Friedrich Christian Accum had not stolen enough of this
waste paper to constitute theft. The Royal Institution, motivated
by what we shall never know, seemed bent on ruining Accum.
Instead of dismissing him, it brought a charge against him of
mutilating books. He was granted bail but, worried, fretted and
harassed, he jumped bail and fled to Germany.

It is difficult to understand why the Royal Institution hounded
a brilliant member. Accum may have created envy because of
his success, or other members may have been got at by powerful
brewing interests. It may be that he did mutilate books, but one
feels that this offence, nasty though it is, was not the real motive
for the persecution. Of course Accum's flight to Germany was
given great publicity and both he and his book were discredited.
Thus druggists, grocers and brewers could go back quite happily
to their old custom of adulterating food, and they had a pleasant
and profitable ten years in which to poison their customers before they were again attacked.

The attacker this time was an author who preferred to remain
anonymous, and the attack was a pamphlet with the blood-
chilling title *Deadly Adulteration and Slow Poisoning Unmasked:
or Disease and Death in Pot and Bottle.* The work was dedicated
to the then Prime Minister, the Duke of Wellington, and the
author begged the Duke's administration to put an end to 'blood
empoysoning and life-destroying adulteration'.[7] Unfortunately
the pamphlet was not a very intelligent re-hash of Accum's book;
equally unfortunately the author had made the mistake of using
irony to make his point. The Victorians did not care for irony
and satire—secure generations do not. Who would believe the
exaggerated claptrap produced by an author who had not the
courage to put his name to his work? Certainly not the seven-
year-old *Lancet*; it thought the writer belonged to the well-mean-
ing and exaggerated class of alarmists who wrote in a tone of
'half-mad honesty'.[8]

It took another twenty years before *The Lancet* finally took up the cause and even then it was not until a book by John Mitchell (published 1848), dealing with the falsification of food and the chemical means which could be used to detect adulterants, really alarmed the public. The book stated flatly and gave facts that the gross adulteration of food stuffs was still usual, widespread and as fatal as it had been in Accum's day.

Thus, with unaccustomed celerity, *The Lancet*, two years after the publication of Mitchell's book, announced the setting up of an Analytical and Sanitary Commission to investigate the adulteration of food. The editor, Thomas Wakley, appointed two analytical chemists, who were also doctors, to investigate. Wakley, as if to make up for lost time (and lost lives) was now determined to get to the root of the matter, but his first article dealing with the adulteration of coffee would probably not have been noticed other than by medical men, had not the press and in particular the magazine *Punch* taken it up. *Punch* called the investigators 'Scientific Detective Police'. As *The Lancet* had already published the names of those taken in adultery, *Punch* described the function of these policemen as one of investigating and exposing the adulteration of food 'practised by a set of scoundrels' who called themselves 'grocers and tradesmen',[9] and put an immense amount of villainous stuff into coffee. After this first blast *Punch* acted as a popular voice for the professional *Lancet* and subsequently published a series of essays called *Sermons on Tradesmen*. The magazine was in dead earnest but got its effect by creating a series of Imps who infected the food trade. The Baker Imp who ground, not his bones, but alum to make his bread and did in the bowels of the consumer. Alum adds weight and whiteness to bread but it causes dyspepsia. A random sample of loaves taken from all over London showed that every single loaf contained alum. The well-known League Bread Company, which advertised its bread as being of the utmost purity and absolutely alum-free was caught out, for analysis showed every loaf produced contained alum. Then there was the wicked Grocer Imp who enriched chocolate with brick dust, the prototype of that grocer who :

... sells us sands of Araby
As sugar for cash down;
He sweeps his shop and sells the dust
The purest salt in town.
He crams with cans of poisoned meat
Poor subjects of the King,
And when they die by thousands
Why, he laughs like anything.[10]

The Milk Imp went in for taking the blue look off his skimmed and watered milk by adding powdered chalk, and the Confectioner Imp, a real artist, painted his iced twelfth night cake with verdigris which made it a brilliant emerald green and was most suitable at Christmas-tide since it could so easily cause another slaughter of the innocents.

The Publican Imp was praised for giving his beer a fine head with green copperas and additional strength with vitriol. But not all brewers were scoundrels. Although the panic about adulterated beer seemed to include everyone, when Messrs Allsop & Sons began to build 'the largest brewery in the world for Pale Ale' (in 1848) and were reputed to add strychnine to give this beer its bitter taste, they publicly denied it in unequivocal terms and stated : 'no deleterious substance was ever employed in the manufacture of their beer'.[11] This was upheld by the Analytical and Sanitary Commission which, in 1850, tested forty samples of Allsop's various brews and found they were made only from malt, hops, pure spring water and nothing else. Thus the Commission was able to protect the honest tradesman and expose the dishonest.

When in 1855 the whole of the findings of the Commission were published in book form even the government was roused by the report and the consequent public alarm. It now introduced the very first Food and Drug Act. It is true that it took five years to do so and the Act when it came into force in 1860 was full of loopholes yet this was an historic achievement and the beginning of our subsequent Food and Drug legislation.

But we still went on being poisoned by food. Meat pies in hot weather and ill-preserved vegetables produced botulism,* while milk was possibly the best little breeder and carrier of germs of them all. The Elizabethans had been no great believers in the virtues of milk. This was just as well as polluted milk in England was, throughout the centuries, as common as polluted water. But in the eighteenth century people began to drink more milk and in the nineteenth century as the population increased so did the demand for milk. A few rich landowners had their own model dairies and understood the need for clean milk. At Windsor, Prince Albert saw to this, but he was a fussy foreigner. Most milk which reached the consumer was badly contaminated by dirty milking, filthy cow byres or by pollution in transport.

Although London could no longer supply milk for her population and much was brought into the city by rail—and in days of no refrigeration it arrived in bad condition—thousands of cows were still grazed in Hyde Park and other green areas and milkmaids still paraded the streets with their yokes and uncovered milk cans. Cowhouses in London were little more than broken-down sheds filled with cows and dung. As late at 1847 a well-known cowshed in Golden Square housed forty cows, two to a seven-foot stall. Ventilation was totally lacking, save for the air which came in through the broken roof. The stale from the animals drained into a tank which was piled high with dung and stood between the turnip and grain bins. The stink was appalling, the filth indescribable. But this was by no means unusual and it was in repulsive hovels like these that milking was done. When one of *The Lancet*'s detectives, Dr Hassall, microscopically examined samples of London milk he found nearly every sample was contaminated by pus or blood.

Butter and cheese must also have been contaminated. Although it was certainly known that 'Dutch butter and cheese have associations of extreme cleanliness; for, so scrupulous are the makers, that *bare hands* are never allowed to come in contact with the materials',[12] we paid small attention. One thing which

* The word was not used until 1887. It is apposite; botulus is Latin for sausage.

Cows grazing at Hyde Park Corner

was not part of the Englishness of the English was the clean handling of food.

Yet somehow we survived to eat and drink ourselves into apoplectic graves; and the times of meals changed. The dinner hour which had been moving on from the beginning of the eighteenth century had, by the beginning of the nineteenth, reached half past four. By accession year it was two or three hours later. Mrs Prinseps and her daughter who lived in Great Cumberland Street, were not at the top of the 'grand scale' though comfortably off and moving in good circles. They breakfasted at nine and had luncheon at one, which was usual, but, as their footman and general factotum tells us, they had 'Dinner at six which is considered very early'.[13] On one not very special day, the 'Old Lady and Miss P', as the diarist calls them, dined on 'two soles fryed with saws, a leg of mutton, a dish of ox, pullets, potatos, brocolo, rice and rhubarb tart, tabiaca pudding, cheese and butter'. Perhaps the 'dish of ox' was ox tongues as the dinner sounds very substantial for a simple meal for two, but by eight o'clock the pair were obviously gnawed by pangs of

138

hunger, 'and were ready for tea with bread and butter and dried toast, never any supper—it's not fashionable'.

Also when alone they had a small 'parlour breakfast' at nine o'clock, consisting of 'hot rolls, dry toast, a loaf of fancy bread and a loaf of common and a slice of butter'. Hot water came up in 'a hurn that had a place in the middle for a red hot iron that keeps the water boiling. . . . With this they make their tea. . . . They have chocolate which is something like coffee but of a greasy and much richer nature.'[14]

This was an unusually simple meal as the English breakfast, especially when there were guests, astonished continental visitors. Tea, coffee, chocolate, cold meats, game, broiled fish, sausages, eggs, kidneys, bacon, toast, muffins, butter, marmalade, fruit in season graced the table and side tables. Breakfast was taken at nine or ten o'clock after an hour or two of exercise, preferably out of doors. The hapless foreign visitor, unless entertained at a country house, doubtless wandered gloomily about the dank shrubbery of his host's surburban villa, and concluded the English right to consider themselves different from all other races.

Dr Jonathan Pereira (1804–53), however, although he believed in a good breakfast, was not in favour of exercise or work before the first meal. He was particularly opposed to students in boarding schools having to do two hours' work before breakfast and thought it particularly bad for those children 'disposed to spasmodic brain disease',[15] whatever that may mean, as well as young people afflicted with epilepsy.

School meals were notoriously appalling even in public schools. After a dozen years on the continent the young Richard Burton (1821–90) who later became the famous or infamous traveller, scholar and writer, was sent to an English school where he was shocked by the brutality of the English schoolboy and sickened by the food. This 'dark little boy with . . . large black eyes . . . extremely proud, sensitive, shy and nervous, of melancholy disposition' had been intended for Eton (where, as at Winchester, food riots were common) but his father had been persuaded by

some 'blundering friend' to send him and his brother Edward to
a school at Richmond run by the Rev. Charles Delafosse, whose
only claim to fame was that he was Chaplain to the Duke of
Cumberland. This worthy was rather liked by the boys as he
drank too much, was sparing of the rod and knew no more about
school-mastering than 'The Grand Cham of Tartary'. Mrs Delafosse, a thin-lipped woman, who had charge of the ménage, was
another matter. The school, Burton later recollected, 'was a kind
of Dotheboys Hall'. The fees were £100 a year whereas £20
would have covered the expenses. Breakfast was at 8 a.m. and
consisted of 'very blue milk and water in chipped broken mugs
of the same colour. The boys were allowed tea from home but it
was a battle to get a single drink of it. The substantials were a
wedge of bread with a glazing of butter. The epicures used to
collect the glazing to the end of the slice to get a final *bonne
bouche*. The dinner at one o'clock* began with stickjaw (pudding) and ended with meat, as at all second-rate schools. The
latter was as badly cooked as possible, black out and blue inside,
gristly and sinewy. The vegetables were potatoes which could
serve for grape-shot, and the hateful carrot. Supper was a repetition of breakfast. . . . Saturday was a day to be feared on account
of the peculiar pie which contained all the waifs and strays of
the week. On Sunday there was an attempt at plum pudding of
a particularly pale and leaden hue as if it had been unjustly
defrauded of its due allowance of plums. And this dull routine
lasted throughout the scholastic year . . . school was a night-
mare. . . . It was like the Blacking Shop of Charles Dickens.'[16]

The diet of this fee-paying school was almost worse than the
food doled out to paupers in the Newport Pagnell Union Work-
house, as detailed by Dr William Brinton in his book, *On Food
and its Digestion* (1861). For the whole week breakfast remained
the same with $1\frac{1}{2}$ pints of gruel for men and women plus seven
ounces of bread for men and five for women. On Sundays, Tues-
days and Thursdays dinner at midday consisted of five ounces
of meat and one pound of vegetables—doubtless cabbage and

* Children and servants dined at one and not in the evening.

carrots. For supper on these three days each inmate received $1\frac{1}{2}$ pints of gruel and the same amount of bread as at breakfast. Mondays and Fridays were meatless; $1\frac{1}{2}$ pints of soup and only two ounces of bread were the mid-day ration but the protein deficiency was scantily made good at supper by one ounce of cheese eaten with the usual few ounces of bread. Wednesdays and Saturdays were altogether lean days. Men received fourteen ounces of rice pudding and women twelve ounces for dinner; they made do with the usual ration of bread and cheese for supper. Even so, these inmates of the dreaded workhouses were often better fed than the poor and the contrast between what the rich ate and what the poor—as opposed to paupers—survived on is one of the darkest shadows on the early Victorian picture.

Nathaniel Hawthorne notes this frequently in his diary. On one occasion after attending an unimpressive civic banquet in Liverpool where, he says, he ate 'turtle soup, salmon, woodcock, oyster patties and I know not what else, I have been to the News Room and found the exchange pavement densely thronged with people of all ages and all manner of dirt and rags. They were waiting for soup tickets and waiting very patiently too— only patience and meekness in their faces.' He then adds that this seemed to indicate, 'an insolence of riches & prosperity which will, one day or another, have a downfall'.[17]

This was not written in the hungry forties but in 1855 when we were rich, prosperous and well-fed; when the economy flourished and our exports amounted to more than four times those of the United States. But we were engaged in the Crimean War—a costly affair.

Hawthorne has something to say on this too. On a return journey from the Lake District where he found the scenery beautiful, the hotels expensive, the food bad and the meat not over-fresh, he stopped at an inn in Lancaster and fell into conversation about the war with another traveller, 'and heard from him— as you may from all his countrymen—an expression of weariness and dissatisfaction with the whole business. These fickle islanders! How differently they talked a year ago! John Bull sees now, that he was never in a worse fix in his life; and yet it would not take much to make him snort as bellicosely as ever.'[18]

It was in this year that Alexis Benoît Soyer (1809–58) went out to Scutari to reorganize the victualling of the hospitals and introduced the 'cooking-wagon' for army use. Soyer, a great cook, and a writer of cookery books, had left Paris in 1830 and entered the service of the Duke of Cumberland. The year of Queen Victoria's accession he became chef at the Reform Club where he was extremely popular and became known as a brilliant man. He devoted a great deal of his life to remodelling army kitchens and improving barrack food and was indefatigable in working for the relief of the poor. Again there is the contrast between the Soyer who concerned himself with feeding the poor and the Soyer who, in 1850, was called upon to produce what was subsequently called 'The Hundred Guinea Dish' at a banquet given by the Lord Mayor of York for Prince Albert 'to propitiate the Great Exhibition of 1851'.[19]

This work of art of the great chef contained only a small portion of the following ingredients: five turtle heads, parts of fins and green fat, which cost £34; twenty-four capons from which the two small noix were used, cost £8 8s 0d; eighteen turkeys, eighteen poulards, sixteen fowl at a total cost of £10 11s 0d but again only the noix were used. Then came ten grouse which cost £2 6s 0d, a trifle more than 4s 6d each; twenty pheasants and forty-five partridges (noix only) at £6 7s 0d plus the noix of one hundred snipe at £5, and three dozen pigeons at 14s. Six plovers, forty woodcocks and three dozen quail, used whole, cost £11 9s 0d. An undisclosed number of ortolans imported from Belgium came to £5, and a cheaper item was six dozen stuffed larks, at only 15s. The 'garnish', made of cocks' combs, truffles, mushrooms, crawfish, American asparagus, olives, croustades, sweetbreads, quenelles de volaille, green mangoes, and an unnamed new sauce, doubtless invented by Soyer, came to £14. The total cost of this single dish was £105 5s 0d. What it would cost today is impossible to estimate.

'The Hundred Guinea Dish' was not responsible for the aston-

Table silver, 1850–60

ishingly propitious outcome of the Great Exhibition, but the Exhibition's three refreshment rooms of different classes did a roaring business. Refreshments, it had been specified, were to be light and moderate. No cooking was allowed and, wisely, no intoxicating beverages. Nothing resembling a common tavern or alehouse should sully the character of this great enterprise. So visitors consumed more than a million bottles of soft drinks* and 1,804,718 buns—half of them Bath buns. Ice cream was an unsuccessful refreshment. The average person simply spluttered when attempting to eat an ice and and complained of toothache. What turned out to be a run-away winner was jelly. Jelly—like ice-cream—had hitherto been the prerogative of those with money who kept a good table. Now, for the first time, jelly appeared in public and within the reach of everyone with a few pence to spend. People took to this new food—much better than and not so hard on the teeth as ice cream—with such relish and delight there was some danger that supplies might run out, or so a contemporary writer says. How much of his story can be believed is difficult to say but he tells us that, 'during the Great Exhibition . . . buffalo hides, and sheep and calf skins advanced cent per cent in price. This was caused by the great demand for jellies in the refreshment rooms. Visitors there consumed jellies who had never tasted jellies before; and as the usual materials were not available, buffalo hides were purchased in tons in Liverpool, for the purpose of making these delicacies. Size and glue were used at first, but the hides were found to be cheapest.' Then he adds, 'No one knows what he eats in English confectionery', and suggests we are little better than the South Sea Islanders who, when they saw the first pair of buckskin breeches, so little understood their purpose that they 'stuffed them with seaweed and had them boiled for dinner'.[20]

There were to be no inferior jellies for the followers of Mrs Beeton, and for upper-class jellies nothing but the best would do.

* Messrs Schweppes had the contract. M. Soyer did not exhibit but he took nearby Gore House—the erstwhile Blessington-d'Orsay home—and set up his own Gastronomic Symposium of All Nations.

How to tell what is best she is at great pains to explain and if it takes time to distinguish between isinglass, which she informs us is the purest and best gelatine imported from Russia, and the inferior sorts which come from North and South America and the East Indies (hence the hides) it is obviously well worth the trouble—or so she says. Only the isinglass, bought inexplicably from 'wholesale dealers', and three small vessels containing boiling water, cold water and vinegar respectively are needed for this test. 'If the isinglass is adulterated with gelatine (that is to say, the commoner sorts of gelatine—for isinglass is classed amongst gelatines, of all which varieties it is the very purest and best)', it would not dissolve in boiling water, become milky and cloudy in cold water, nor swell up and become jelly-like in vinegar. Pure isinglass dissolved in boiling water, became cloudy and white in cold water, and jelly-like in vinegar. One could, however, buy made-up jelly in bottles—rather an expensive commodity—stand the bottle in hot water until its contents were liquid, then pour into the desired mould and garnish 'as taste dictates'.

Even ten years after the passion for jelly created by the Great Exhibition, Mrs Beeton won't give an inch in the matter of purity or of providing cheap jelly. In the first edition of her *Book of Household Management* elaborate and wonderful jellies are recommended for dinner parties, but in the 168 economical and useful 'Bills of Fare' for 'Plain Family Dinners' not a single jelly appears. Bread and butter pudding, college pudding, fruit tartlets, apple dumplings and, a horror, vegetable marrow with white sauce, arrowroot blancmange, sweet macaroni pudding— which must have been less awful then than now as the recipe calls for two tablespoons of brandy—yeast dumplings, rice pudding and, sadly, 'Half-Pay Pudding' made of suet, breadcrumbs, flour, milk, a few currants and raisins and two tablespoons of treacle—'seasonable at any time', are the stodgy, starchy puddings obviously intended to fill the gaps. One can only think that testing isinglass and producing even a simple jelly was too lengthy a process for every day and the use of bottled table jellies too expensive.

Table jellies as we know them in packets were not extensively used before the 1880s and, as a late edition of *Law's Grocer's Manual* tells us, 'they possess many advantages. The expense of glass bottles and breakage, and about two-thirds of the cost of railway carriage, are avoided.' The jelly, it goes on to explain to the uninitiated, 'is usually stiffer or more concentrated than bottled jellies, and admits of the addition of about double its volume of water, or wine and water, when required for use'. Even at this late date, the *Manual* warns the aspiring grocer that there are many *qualities*. 'Indeed,' it says, 'some of the lower-priced jellies forced into the market are little better than coloured *size*, and retailers who respect their trade should take care to purchase from reliable firms only.'

The use of the words 'reliable firms' indicates that selling food had become 'the food industry'. This industry was born in the first half of the century. It was due primarily to that new method of transport, the railway.

Before railways, before we became industrialized, we were a truly rural nation and in a sense lived off the land. Each city, town or village, depended largely on the surrounding agricultural land for its food, and food was sold in open markets. Unless the urban centre were situated on the coast, a navigable river or waterway, it fed itself from its own locality. This meant that all over the country prices varied for they were conditioned by supply and demand, a good harvest in the south, a bad one in the north meant dear bread where the harvest was scanty, cheaper where it was plentiful. But by the 1840s the first great railway boom was under way; already there were 1,700 miles of track and fifty different lines serving the country and this new and quick method of transportation turned the raising, the selling and the buying of food into a new industry. Foodstuffs could now be bought from numbers of sources, stored in warehouses, shipped by rail to all parts of the country and delivered to city markets or wholesalers with great rapidity. Retailers could be more sure of supplies and also of a greater variety of foodstuffs. All this was of enormous advantage in stabilizing food prices, but there were certain disadvantages, for too little was known about the correct ventilation, temperature, or moisture content of warehouses, and if food was not shifted quickly it became damaged and spoiled.

To take merely one example, that most-used commodity, flour. Flour very quickly went rancid in warm weather because in those days even white flour contained wheat germ, and so great losses were incurred by millers and wholesalers. It took years of milling before the germ, so rich in Vitamin B, could be removed, and an even greater amount of experimenting to learn how to get rid of the faint yellowish colour, due to the presence of carotene, and achieve the fine white flour which produced loaves of almost totally un-nutritious bread. Today, bread nourishes us because it is enriched, but this enrichment was not made law until the middle of the present century. The Utopian, 'bread we have of several grains . . . with divers kinds of leavenings . . . some do nourish so as divers do live by them without any other meat, who do live very long',[21] never appeared, but a new leaven did. Yeast began to replace the old-fashioned leavenings or barm in the first half of the nineteenth century.

Probably the most common barm used by those who made bread at home, or by bakers, was the froth skimmed from fermenting malt—and when home-brewed beer was made this was easily obtainable. Then yeast supplied by brewers or grown in potato mash was used—as it worked more quickly. Later, newer and higher fermenting kinds of yeast were bred and these were the parents of our modern bakers' yeast.

Another introduction of the time was self-raising flour—the raiser was chiefly of carbonate and an acid salt which, when wetted, frees carbon dioxide. This flour was introduced sometime in the 1840s but did not meet with wide approval until around 1870. Baking powder was used for raising some kinds of cake and although it could be made at home, it was also now being manufactured and sold in packets. Baking powder was useful for economical cakes as butter, lard and eggs could be used in smaller quantities.

The keeping of butter, lard, eggs, milk and other perishable foodstuffs was now a big problem which the Victorians had to face, particularly in the summer. In the country, those with estates had had separate ice-houses ever since the seventeenth century. Some of these houses were handsomely designed, small architectural masterpieces, others were 'cleverly concealed . . . in the garden mount'.[22] Ice cut from rivers and ponds and packed in straw would last throughout the summer. Now there were more town dwellers, more town houses, more people—and less ice. So importing ice also became an industry. Ice came from the Scandinavian countries and, surprisingly, considering the distance and the slowness of ships, in large quantities from America. 'Wenham Lake ice is now extensively used in England and many cargoes are annually exported from Boston', Timbs tells us, and claims that this ice lasts longer than any other and was also of extreme purity and crystalline brilliance. 'A block of Wenham ice weighing a few pounds,' he assures his readers, 'will last several days, unless it be broken off for table use, or mixing with drinks.' Such ice lasted, if indeed it did, in a new invention, the ice-chest or Patent Ice Safe, as it was called. This was a cumbersome double-walled chest, the hollow between the walls filled with some 'non-conducting substance'. It opened at the top to allow the ice to be placed in a central upright chamber, and also at the front to allow food to be placed all around on zinc shelves. In such a safe fruit and vegetables could be kept for nearly a fortnight and remain 'quite fit for the table', while 'butter may be almost frozen in it in two hours', or so Mr Timbs says enthusiastically. His *Hints for the Table* is delightful reading but how much reliance can we place on his reports of refrigeration? 'The artificial production of ice has, of late, been brought to great perfection', he runs on. 'A *Freezing Powder* is made by which a bottle of wine may be iced, at the cost of little more than a penny! By aid of machinery and the freezing preparation, a large castle has been frozen in metal from moulds, from the purest spring water; it was five feet in length, the same in height and weighed 7 cwt.' One longs to know where, when and how this miniature evanescent crystal palace was produced, what the freezing powder, what the machinery? But on these points Mr Timbs is expressively silent.

Certainly there were refrigerators on view at the Crystal Palace and certainly by 1856, three years before Mr Timbs produced his handbook, James Harrison of Australia had patented an ice-making machine based on an earlier vapour compressor machine invented by Jacob Perkins of London in 1834. But as ether was the substance compressed such machines were hardly suitable for home use and the production of ice castles. Nor was the machine invented by a Frenchman, Edmund Carré, which made use of sulphuric acid. In 1860 Carré did introduce another ice machine, making use of vaporized ammonia, but this is poisonous too, and such machines were large and clumsy and used only for scientific experiment. The problem of how to reduce size and produce an ice-making machine for home use was not solved until sometime between 1910 and 1920; nevertheless, the real beginning was made before 1850.

Tinned and dried foods also made a tentative beginning at this time. Although they are often thought to have originated in the United States, England seems to have been the first country to have preserved food in tins. Strictly this is a misnomer for the containers were of iron tinned on the inside. Bottled food was used by the Navy—the usual method of preservation in quantity—and back in the first decade of the century a Frenchman, Nicholas Appert, had already devised a new process. He used stout glass bottles, filled and closed them, then subjected them to heat in a large *bain marie*. During the Napoleonic Wars, the French Navy used Appert's method with great success. Almost simultaneously, in England, Thomas Saddington was experimenting with a similar method of bottling but he used wide-mouthed jars, filled them with fruit, put on loosely-fitting stoppers, stood them for an hour or so in water heated to a temperature of 160°–170°F, then filled them brimful with boiling water before fitting the stoppers tightly. For this new method of preserving food in quantity, Saddington, in 1807, was awarded a prize of £5 by the Society of Arts.

Although this is very like our modern method of home-bottling, it was not that used by the Victorian housewife. She had to go through a dreadful process with perfectly dry bottles, in which she first burned a match to exhaust the air. She then quickly filled them up with fruit, stopped the bottles with soft corks, put them into a cool oven until the fruit was reduced by a quarter then, literally, hammered home the corks, cut off any protruding tops, and sealed them with melted resin.

Saddington's method was infinitely more simple. Large jars could be used and thus an enormous supply of preserved food could be had for provisioning troops or sailors. But jars, no matter how stout, are frangible. Army wagons and high seas play havoc with bottled foods. Something other than glass was needed. There was iron and there was Bryan Donkin. Donkin (1768–1855), a civil engineer, inventor and partner in the firm of Donkin and Hall began in 1812 to experiment with preserving meat in specially made tin-lined canisters. This turned out so well that his firm sent samples to the Army and Navy authorities and in 1817 the company issued a booklet full of testimonials to the excellence and variety of this new tinned food. The testimonials were genuine and came from such famous people as Lord Wellesley, Sir Joseph Banks and Admiral Cochrane, all of whom had had occasions to use them at sea.

The Naval authorities, more up and coming than usual, actually ordered this tinned food—but only to be used as medical supplies in naval hospitals. By 1831 the authorities decided that His Majesty's ships should carry these foods too, but again, only for use as medical stores.

But the idea that this new method could bring profits, soon drew other manufacturers into the field. Donkin's food had been preserved in canisters which held only two to six pounds of meat. Why not use larger containers? Larger containers holding from nine to fourteen pounds were therefore used by rival firms. The results were disastrous. Food poisoning began to take its toll; manufacturers were accused of putting bad meat and offal into their tins and an outcry was raised. It is perfectly possible that unscrupulous manufacturers, eager for as much profit as possible, did use inferior meat but the real culprit was lack of proper sterilization. It took years of detective work before it was realized that heat sufficient to preserve from two to six pounds of meat would not penetrate to the centre of a canister holding a far larger amount, thus the food in the centre remained unsterile and bacteria flourished. In the end, after much investigation, the Admiralty decided not to contract for tinned foods but to build its own factory, which it did in 1856. This, then, was the beginning of the enormous tinned food industry, although, as such, it did not really start forging ahead until 1866 when we first started importing tinned meat from Australia. By 1870, Cincinnati, Ohio, and Chicago, Illinois, were hot rivals for the tinned meat market in England.

Experiments in the dehydration and evaporation of milk were also taking place at this time, and very unpromising the early experiments were. First attempts at evaporation over an open fire gave a brown, sticky mess well known to all those who have let milk boil away in a saucepan. In 1835 a process for reducing milk and added sugar by steam heat, was invented, and resulted in a honey-like substance which kept fairly well in pots. Whether this 'milk' was ever marketed we do not know. Ten years after Queen Victoria came to the throne, F. S. Grimwade successfully produced a milk evaporated by a steam-jacket process and this was used by Arctic explorers. Then in 1855 he patented a process for making dried milk.

Here the liquid was first evaporated in vacuum pans and ended up looking like dough. Sugar was then added and the mass run through rollers, emerging by the yard in a thin ribbon. This ribbon of milk was dried off and powdered, but the use of powdered milk in any great quantity was not taken up until a good fifty years later. Across the Atlantic, however, Gail Borden had perfected his process for evaporating and condensing milk. This was in 1853 but it took him another three years to get his process patented in the United States and England. So with packaging, tinning, dehydrating and evaporating all beginning in the first half of the century a brand new side of the food industry came into being and with it 'brand names'.

The food industry also included hotels and restaurants. Londoners and visitors to London—native and foreign—often found dining out away from their lodgings and hotels a necessity and there were a number of restaurants and cafés to serve them. Few were good. As the anonymous writer of *London at Table* puts it, where we fell lamentably short at the Great Exhibition 'was in places for visitors to dine, not sumptuously, or gluttonously, or licentiously, but plainly and well'.[23] For those who did not wish to be licentious gluttons, a few respectable places are recommended. The Bedford Hotel, Covent Garden, had good claret, which hardly sounds a recommendation for food or sobriety. The Café de l'Europe in the Haymarket, despite its foreign name, went in for good English dishes; fresh fish, well-dressed joints, excellent steaks, sound sherry and port at a reasonable price. Turtle soup, entrées, venison and vin de Bordeaux came more expensive, but there was a well-ventilated smoking-room for those who indulged in 'the fragrant weed'.

The Blue Post in Cork Street was 'very snug' particularly in winter for a dinner for four in a private parlour on the ground floor—which sounds as if licentiousness just might be creeping in; it also possessed two coffee rooms for those who wanted to dine in a hurry. Good, sound food could be had at Dolly's Chophouse in St Paul's Churchyard and the 'Clear Turtle' provided by the Ship and Turtle in Leadenhall Street rivalled that found at either the Adelphi or Waterloo Hotels. Simpson's in the Strand had a high reputation for its excellent mutton and in the West End were the Clarendon, Fenton's, Ellis's and a few others, but it was never very easy to find a restaurant where a gentleman could take his wife and daughters with propriety (ladies, when alone, went to a confectioner's and men had their clubs). The Albion or the London Tavern seemed suitable for mixed dining or, better still, St James's Hall on the corner of Regent Street and Piccadilly. This café-restaurant had rooms for public and private parties and supplied refreshment, 'whether Breakfasts, Luncheons,

Dinners or Suppers'. The smoking-room was beautifully fitted and contained; 'Periodicals and all Novel Publications emanating from Mudie's Library, with all the Papers of the Day', while 'the department appropriated to Families and Ladies' was 'replete with every convenience and accommodation'.[24]

To return to that criterion of civilization and progress, dining, and its natural concomitant, the dinner party. The size and arrangement of the dining-room, the quality of the plate and china, the quantity and elaborateness of the food and the time at which one dined—seven or half-past in the higher, six in the middle and midday in the lower ranks—all indicated with a fair degree of accuracy just where the party-giver stood in the social and economic scale. It also showed whether the host had progressed with the times.

The old-fashioned host was as suspicious of foreign dishes as he was of foreigners. No French chefs for him. No fallals or dishes *à la Française, Allemande, Italienne* or *Turque* graced or, rather, disgraced his table no matter how dearly his wife longed to be in the fashion. Good broth, roast beef, venison, saddle of mutton, lamb, pork, cod, salmon, fowl, game, followed by a heavy, sweet pudding, tart or apple-pie, the favourite of the late Lord Dudley, were good English fare. Lord Dudley had certainly not been taken in by foreign dishes and 'could not dine comfortably without an apple-*pie*', as he insisted on calling it, contending that the term 'tart' only applied to open pastry.* Even when he was, briefly, Foreign Secretary and attended a grand dinner party given by Prince Esterhazy, 'he was terribly put out on finding his favourite delicacy was wanting, and kept on murmuring pretty audibly in his absent way, "God bless my soul! No apple pie." '[25] Nor could the victor of Waterloo be charged with a preference for foreign or fancy food. Had not his French chef, Felix, left him out of sheer despair?

But the old-fashioned host (whose wife probably still did the carving, as women had done for centuries, unlike the modern

* Canadians and Americans still agree with Lord Dudley, Chaucer and Shakespeare on this point.

hostess) was fighting a losing battle, although in the floods of new cookery books coming off the presses, all full of outlandish dishes and strange ways of service, a few still catered for his tastes. Eliza Acton, for one. Her book contains only a few non-English dishes. Doubtless foreign ones were not calculated to sustain healthfully the powers of life. That curiosity, *The Epicure's Almanac: or Diary of Good Living* published in 1841, is another. This work, which gives a recipe for each day of every month of the year, is singularly free of foreign influences. True, for January 30th it suggests *Boeuf à la Flammande*, a giant dish of ribs of beef larded and braised, to which is added, 'a pottle of fresh mushrooms (forced at this season), two pounds of truffles, two dozen force-meat balls, made with plenty of eggs and half a pint of Madeira'. But, the author warns, 'this being an expensive dish, is only applicable to state occasions' and, he adds jovially, 'or, as the sailors say, "for birthdays or bonfire nights" '.[26]

This particular epicure with his Stewed Cheese, Eve's Pudding, English Curaçao—'equal in flavour to that imported from Malines, or any other place in the universe'—his Nag's Head Cake, English Rumshrub and infallible methods for ripening home-brewed and bottled beer, rather blots his cook book on July 27th when he urges his countrymen to eat frogs, 'the favourite dish of our French neighbours . . . who prefer a fricassé of "Grenouilles" to Rost-bif à la G-damn'. Even Mrs Beeton does not go to this extreme although she gives a good many French recipes and includes a glossary of terms used in French cookery in the first edition of her book.

But the old-fashioned, not to say antiquated, way of dining where several dishes were served together in each course, when guests helped themselves and each other and made a long arm or asked a servant for an out-of-reach dish, when the tablecloth became spattered with gravy and encrusted with food, had died out by the late 1830s, save, perhaps, in rural pockets of darkest England, and a new type of service, which entirely broke with the past, came in. This was *service à la Française* and it had made a tentative beginning shortly after the Napoleonic wars. As the memory of the wars and anti-Gallic feeling diminished, *service à la Française* became the fashion and this, together with the wide acceptance of French cookery, was the chief difference between the old, coarse Georgian fashion and the refined and tasteful Victorian.

The new service meant that dishes were served in succession. There was no less food but there was a greater variety of dishes. Dinner was divided into two main courses and followed a fairly regular pattern. The first course began with soups and fish, with a few little light dishes such as oyster or lobster patties on the side. This preceded the *entrée* which was followed by roasts. Then came lighter game birds and fowls and wonderfully elaborate sweets. Finally all was cleared away for the dessert. It will be noticed that all dishes are given in the plural, that is because they were usually in the plural. The smallest dinner for, say, six people might have but one soup and one fish but two *entrées* are the absolute minimum permitted, even by Mrs Beeton. The fashionable insisted on four *entrées* for six or eight guests; six for a dozen; eight for eighteen and so on, increasing the number with the size of the party. Some guests preferred white to red meat so two roasts were a minimum. And guests were not stuck with just grouse or partridge or pheasant or woodcock—a variety of game birds was there to suit every taste, as well as domestic fowl, for those who preferred it or for those who liked contrast. At grand dinners, thirty or forty dishes were quite usual, and at a dinner given by Queen Victoria somewhere about 1840 there were no fewer than seventy dishes, although the Queen preferred plain food. The first course included 'four soups, four fish, four *hors d'oeuvres*, four *relevés*, sixteen *entrées* . . . three joints on the sideboard including a haunch of venison', while the second course comprised 'six roasts, six *relevés*, two *flancs*, *four contre-flancs* and sixteen *entremets*'.[27]

Hors d'oeuvres, sometimes called *entrées volantes* or 'flying dishes', did not begin a dinner, they were served usually with or after the fish. A *relevé* is just a 'remove' or an intermediate dish to fill a gap between two grander dishes. *Flancs* were side dishes placed on the table or sideboard and they literally flanked or supported main dishes. *Entremets*, which always came in with the second half of the dinner, were also 'between dishes' and the term applied to vegetables as well as sweet dishes. Not all waiters could get their tongues round the names of French dishes. Lady Lyttelton, after dining with the Queen at Windsor, writes to her daughter : 'Yesterday at dinner the English servant who hands round the dishes calling them by French names, offered me what he called "Fricassé de *Valets*". I thought Lord Lilford would have died.'[28]

Obviously it was impossible for guests to serve themselves and each other in old English fashion, so the new French Service also required a good many footmen and waiters to hand round the dishes. At very large parties professional caterers were used for very special dishes and waiters could be hired, but it was not uncommon for guests to bring their own liveried and powdered footmen to make sure they got everything going.

The dinner did not end with the sweet. The table was cleared to make room for the dessert and ices, and the dessert, after the triumph of the sweets, must not be anti-climactic. The table must look fresh and new for the flower decorations (and the nineteenth century saw the introduction of flowers as table decoration) after an hour or so in a hot room doubtless looked tired. Even if they did not, dessert was special and required special plates, silver-plated dessert knives and forks* and an epergne—the more elaborate the better.

The epergne, well known to the eighteenth century as a dispenser of sweets or pickles, was transformed by the Victorians into a magnificent dispenser of fruits and an eye-catching ornament. Epergnes came in a bewildering variety of shapes and sizes and the more contorted, ornamented and involved the better. Certainly 'the management of an epergne, plateau or centrepiece' presented 'an opportunity for the display of taste; as these superb

---

* The silver-plating of dessert utensils and fish knives and forks came in in the nineteenth century as it was felt the acids in fruit and in fish sauces would corrode steel.

ornaments' were usually 'of beautiful forms richly chased', but the epergne owner was warned that 'glass pieces and plate should be alike in brilliant order'.[29]

The epergne with its tree-like branches or arms, often detachable, supported as a crest a curved dish, where a variety of fruits rioted in nests of real or artificial leaves—silver-paper leaves were tasteful. Its branches held at the tips glass dishes filled with individual fruits and often glass baskets swung gently below. Pottery or china pine stands shaped like pineapples held this fruit when in season. Tall-stemmed tazze and ornamented baskets held other fresh fruits, low ornate glass or silver dishes and baskets offered dried fruits and nuts as well as delicately-flavoured sweet biscuits and cakes to accompany the ices which were handed round separately. Coffee in small cups and liqueurs ended the dinner. The ladies, after a short interval, left the dining-room to be followed at a longer interval by the gentlemen. During the evening, tea and coffee were served. Guests were often invited to join the party after dinner and could arrive in succession from nine o'clock until midnight and light refreshments were provided. Dinner guests often had after-dinner invitations and thus during the season two or three parties could be squeezed into one evening. The Society hostess contented herself with giving one, perhaps two dinners a week, the middle-class hostess upset the household once a month.

Lighting for a party was important and many still preferred candles to gas. Where money was no object large numbers of candles were used, but where economy was necessary the hostess never economized on food at a party, no matter what saving the family had to endure in ordinary meals; she saved on candles. One to each guest was the bed-rock minimum and she could work out how long the party would last and buy candles accordingly. Mixed wax and spermaceti, four to the pound, would last ten hours, while a short 'six' burned for only six hours. Those who had gas lighting were still slightly wary of it. It could be erratic, it could splutter, it could and did fail. Although it brought out all the brilliance of silver and glass and the ladies' jewels, it had

Epergne with candlesticks, bottle-stand and ewer

an unfortunate tendency to make the skin look yellow and haggard; it was not kind to wrinkles, and lips looked cold and colourless. No woman wanted to be outsparkled by her jewels or made to look like a death's head at a feast.

Although *service à la Française* was certainly *de rigueur*, it should be noticed in passing that an even newer method of dining had made its appearance, this was *service à la Russe* where all carving and serving was done in the kitchen and dishes brought into the dining-room by servants. This required a good deal more china, cutlery and servants.* Mrs Beeton for this reason does not consider it practical and gives only two *à la Russe* menus in 1861. Within thirty years the picture had once again changed completely and in the 1888 edition the editor says : 'Dinners *à la Russe*, as they used to be called, are now so Anglicized and so common that we find them in the houses of people with very moderate incomes.' Also in this edition the dismal word 'serviette' replaces table-napkin.

An early century change for the better was the introduction of individual finger glasses or finger bowls which were placed on the table with the dessert. In the previous century a basin and ewer had done duty for all guests to have a good wash in, but the Victorians had grown a deal more fastidious and even filled their individual finger glasses with warm water in cold weather. Yet a writer whose pseudonym is Greek for Guide or Escort finds it necessary to give instructions on the correct use of the finger glass : 'Wet a corner of your napkin, and wipe your mouth, then rinse your fingers; do not practise the *filthy* custom of gargling your mouth at table, albeit the usage prevails among the few, who think *because* it is a foreign habit, it cannot be disgusting.'[30] Gargling had been a common English habit not fifty years before and guests had been warned not to use the table cloth as a napkin. By the late 1850s even wetting the mouth with a napkin was bad

---

* In Rome, February 21st 1830, Henry Crabb Robinson notes in his diary that he first 'partook' of dinner *à la Russe* at Prince Gagarin's. 'A servant between each couple' and 'the moment your plate was whisked away . . . another was instantly offered.'

manners, although some gentlemen still followed this custom (said to be French by Isabella Beeton), but the ladies were to set a good example here and wet only the tips of the fingers.

Other hints for those dining out, or giving dinners, appear in books of etiquette of the time which were aimed at helping those at the lower end of the grand scale to climb a bit higher. During the early part of the reign a transition in table manners seems to have been taking place, and it was just as well to be *au fait* with what was being done. One should not eat food with a knife as forks and spoons were provided—the broad round-ended knife so useful for eating peas was definitely out in good society. Nor should one eat largely or toss off a glass of wine in one gulp. Fish should be eaten with a fork only, assisted by a piece of bread, but in first-rate society silver fish-knives were replacing bread. Nothing was so vulgar as to make a clatter with a knife and fork and it was also vulgar for a hostess to festoon herself with jewels or to be more richly dressed than her guests. Ladies now stayed longer at table, while gentlemen no longer became inebriated so quickly. All these were pleasing and sure steps in the progress of refinement.

Having a drink before dinner was an innovation. Known in the north as a whet-cup, in the Frenchified south it was called a *coupe d'avant*—a cock-tail then meant a harlot. The *coupe d'avant* might equally well have been called a *coup de grâce* as it was usually a good-sized glass of brandy or rum. This was said to 'crisp' the stomach before dinner. What with the courses of wines served with dinner—sherry, madeira, champagne, claret, burgundy—and gentlemen lingering over their bottles afterwards, it is not surprising hangovers were a common complaint and remedies just as common. Coffee was excellent for counteracting a stupor due to opium or alcohol, and also excellent for relieving a nervous headache provided that this was not accompanied by 'sanguineous conjestion'[31] which may be a Victorian euphemism for a bloody awful headache attendant upon overindulgence. Another remedy which sounds particularly nauseating, but which was held to be a sure cure, called for two drams

of Rochelle salt, one of an infusion of senna, a teaspoonful of tincture of cardamon taken with a wine glass of Ratafia or Eau de
Cologne.*

Considering that a modest dinner of the middle sort for a dozen
people consisted on an average of twenty-six to thirty dishes, that
breakfasts and luncheons were not small, it is hardly surprising
to find Hawthorne noting, 'there is hardly a less beautiful object
than the elderly John Bull, with his large body, protruding
paunch, short legs and mottled, double-chinned, irregular-
fashion aspect',[32] and caricatures of the day bear this out. What
is surprising is that fashion plates and nearly all paintings show
women as slim, elegant, beautiful and young.

This American who, despite his criticism of England and the
English, really liked us, did not see Victorian women with the
romantic eye of a painter. He saw them as they undoubtedly
were and bravely set down what he saw. Englishwomen, he says,
'are capable of being more atrociously ugly than any other human
beings', and his knowledge was not limited to a mere handful,
for he saw many at private and public dinners. To him they
appeared dowdy and coarse. 'Ladies look like cooks and housemaids,' he says coolly. And as if that were not condemnation
enough, adds, 'As a general rule they are not very desirable in
their youth and, in many instances, become perfectly grotesque
after middle age; so massive and not seemingly with pure fat,
but with solid beef. You think of them as composed of sirloins,
and with broad and thick steaks on their immense rears.' When
seated, 'they look as if nothing could ever move them; and, indeed, they must have a vast amount of physical strength to be
able to move themselves'.[33]

This is a most unappetizing picture, but early photographs bear
out these remarks and so does an article in *The Times*: 'Every
doctor will tell you', it reads, 'that there is more harm done in
the middle and higher classes by over-eating than by over-drink-
ing. . . . "Respectable people" as they are called, very seldom

* Eau de Cologne mixed with wine or spirits was commonly drunk, as it was
then made of pure spirit.

drink too much . . . but they certainly are apt to stupefy themselves with excess and variety of viands.'

Early photography, however, does not concern itself to any large extent with the majority. *The Times* does. 'The case of the working classes, it must be admitted, is different', the article continues. 'They seldom get too much to eat and cannot afford to be very fastidious. Their only sauce, as a general rule, is hunger; and their intoxication is generally owing to the cheap and bad quality of their drink. It is either beer with "stuff" in it, or spirits even more adulterated.'[34]

The simple and brutal fact is, the majority lived at subsistence or below subsistence level. 'In the midst of plethoric plenty, the people perish',[35] Carlyle writes in 1843, while another description should purge the imagination of any nostalgic longing for the good old days. Plenty there was, but only for those who had plenty. Londoners, in 'startling numbers' were pale, lank, narrow-chested, hollow-eyed ghosts, whom one passes at every step' with 'languid, flabby faces, incapable of the slightest energetic expression'.[36]

The underfed are never energetic, and the underfed existed in millions throughout England. The machines had enormous energy and production capacity. The men, women and children who fed and minded them had not.

In Elizabethan times the staple diet of the poor had been bread, beef and ale, but the total population of England had been, then, about two million. Further, we were primarily a rural and agricultural country which exported surplus wheat, but by the beginning of the nineteenth century we were eight million and by the middle of the century the figure was double. It had taken two centuries to reach eight million. It took only fifty years to add another eight or nine. There could be no question of bread, beef and ale now. There was a 'grand scale' for the few and for the many—'a graduated scale . . . in the best cases a temporarily endurable existence for hard work and good wages, good and endurable, that is, from the worker's standpoint; in the worst cases, bitter want, reaching even homelessness and death by starvation'. The average is much nearer the worst case than the best, 'while every working-man, even the best, is . . . constantly exposed to loss of work and food, that is to death by starvation, and many perish in this way'.[37]

Today the condition of those who worked in the 'dark Satanic mills' of the midlands and north are so well known to us that it tends to obscure the fact that there were thousands all over the country who were not mill-hands or miners who suffered equally. The chronic fear of unemployment and the certain knowledge that if the job were lost the alternatives were to starve, beg, steal, go to the dreaded workhouse or commit suicide, meant that the Age of Progress for the minority was the Age of Anxiety for the majority.

To quote Henry Mayhew, 'at the brisk season for each trade there is full employment for all; but . . . in almost all occupations there is in this country a *superfluity of labourers,* and this alone would tend to render the employment of a vast number of the hands of a casual rather than a regular character'. In most trades, he calculates, 'one third of the hands are fully employed, one-third partially, and one-third unemployed throughout the year'.[38]

Even full employment did not mean a living wage for a man and his wife; their children had to work too. The Factory Act, which affected all textile mills other than silk, had limited the working hours of children between the ages of nine and thirteen to not more than nine hours a day and forty-eight hours a week. It also provided that those under the age of eighteen should work only twelve hours a day and a sixty-eight-hour week. By 1844 a six-and-a-half day week had been secured for children of eight to thirteen and a twelve-hour day for women. By 1847 a ten-hour day for women and children had been achieved, but this was too often evaded by a relay system as it was legal to employ women and children between the hours of 5.30 a.m. and 8.30 p.m. Factory Acts of 1850 and 1853 finally limited the hours of all textile workers as factories were allowed to remain open for only twelve hours a day. As a compromise the hours for women and children were lengthened from fifty-eight to sixty hours a week. This meant ten and a half hours on weekdays and seven and a half hours on Saturdays.*

These Acts which affected the textile industry did something to protect children, but since children could no longer be put out to work at six or seven years of age and home industry had been replaced by the factory system, a family often suffered acute want until the eldest child was eight or nine and could take his or her place in a factory as a wage earner.

No such rules applied to children who were not factory workers. Children could be and were employed in all trades and were paid very little. But there were thousands who had to pick up a living as best they could. In London alone, in the late 1840s, there were probably thirty or forty thousand children who came from destitute families or who had no homes at all. The homeless lived and lodged as and where they could. They slept in the nooks and crannies of unsavoury rookeries, in doorways, under railway arches. They crept under tarpaulins which covered barges and wagons or sought shelter in deserted, decaying houses. If they had families these families were so poor that every member had to earn a few pence by any means to keep the whole in collective misery. For example, a child could, like an adult, be a bone-gatherer. If lucky the adult made 8*d* a day but the child earned only 2*d* or 3*d*. Sometimes he was fortunate enough to find crusts of bread; sometimes a kind servant would give him a fresh bone with meat on it and this went to feed the family before the bone was sold. A child could be a crossing-sweeper, a bootblack, a seller of lucifer matches, or a runner of errands. If he were of a particularly destitute family, he could become a cigar-end finder. Cigar-ends could fetch a ha'penny a pound when a child was the finder. Adult finders could get from six to ten pence a pound for dry ends. These were sold to middlemen who used the tobacco in making cheap cigars.

Then there were, more particularly in London, the river-

---

* These regulations applied to textile factories. Extensions of the Factory Acts to include other trades came later in the century.

finders or mudlarks. They were of all ages and waded in mud up to their waists. 'These poor creatures are certainly about the most deplorable in their appearance of any I have met with', Mayhew writes. Ages ranged from mere children to the decrepit old—particularly old women. They lived in filthy hovels on both sides of the Thames from Woolwich to Vauxhall and they were mostly 'dull-witted'. They squelched through the mud, the decaying refuse and ordure of the river banks to gather what the tide brought; bits of coal (sold to the equally poor for a penny a stone), chips of wood, bits of metal, bones, rags, old rope—all of which could be sorted and sold. They earned from $2\frac{1}{2}d$ to $8d$ a day but the average, over a year, came to about $3d$. A good many children between the ages of ten and twelve were mudlarks and almost as many were only six years old. They were, it is true, chiefly the children of the very poor so it is not surprising to find they actually liked to be taken up and sent to prison; at least they were fed there. Prison life, appalling though it was, was far better than their daily lives. Many deliberately and repeatedly committed small crimes to be able to enjoy the relative comforts of prison. The girls, however, at the age of eleven or twelve commonly gave up mudlarking to become 'the lowest type of prostitute'.[39]

What did the very poor eat when they did eat? 'Potato parings, vegetable refuse, and rotten vegetables . . . for want of other food, and everything greedily gathered up which may possibly contain an atom of nourishment.'[40] Deficiency diseases were rife —scurvy, rickets, sore eyes; while scrofula, tuberculosis, chest and lung diseases were commonplace. Children carried fat bellies set between spindly legs and thin, narrow chests—hunger-oedema makes a belly look fat. Some never tasted meat, although they were given spirits and laudanum at an early age—spirits warm the stomach and laudanum soothes a crying child to sleep. Many children died in an opium-induced sleep. The poor managed on what bread, porridge and cheese they could buy. The children managed too on a diet so deficient in protein that they could not grow. They managed, unless they were lucky and died before the age of five, which half of them did. The well-nourished children of middle-class families died too, but the figure was about thirty per cent lower. For the majority, 'Death was as true and common as poverty'.[41]

But even those who had money to spend on food could not buy good food. Wages were usually paid on Saturday evening* so the working man could not get to the market until five or seven o'clock and by that time good food, which he probably could not have afforded anyway, had already been bought up and only inferior stuff left—rancid bacon, tired vegetables, green potatoes, old, tough and stringy meat. Sometimes meat was that of diseased cattle or of animals so ancient they had died a natural death. Often it was tainted. As markets had to shut down by midnight on Saturday, anything which would not keep until Monday was sold late at night for a few pence. Frequently by Sunday morning it was bad, but had to be eaten. Often hucksters would buy, very cheaply, market leftovers and sell them at a profit from barrows and stalls.

Some large employers in mining, textile or new railway areas paid part of the wage in 'truck'. Truck was either food or a voucher given in lieu of money which could be exchanged for food and other commodities at a 'tommy-shop'. Tommy-shops sold bad, inferior goods at high prices and were often run by the employer who could pose as a benefactor since he provided shops in areas where there were no shops at all, and no competitive prices.

Not all employers were monsters of iniquity. Sir Titus Salt (1803–76), an immensely rich woolstapler, was not. In 1851–3 he built new works and a model town for his workpeople on the river Aire—which is how Saltaire came into being. Robert Owen (1771–1858) was another exception, he had created an ideal community and a model village for his workpeople. They were

---

* The custom of paying wages out in beer-shops was prevalent. Unless the employees were very strong-minded, they spent a good proportion of their earnings on the spot. What was left over went for food and the necessities of life.

well housed, well paid, good shops provided good commodities, hours were regulated, streets were kept clean, children educated and he still made a handsome profit at his mill—but that was in Scotland; yet he spent thousands of pounds in trying to get his ideas accepted; he printed and circulated his theories of how labour should be treated, how to gear wages to productivity and he envisaged model village communities all over England. His ideas were held by most to be totally impracticable and, indeed, Owen spent too much and died without personal fortune, supported (unknown to him) by his sons.

But there were degrees of poverty and the cost of living index for a better paid fully employed scavenger (street cleaner) in London reveals a happier state. His income per week from all sources, including a few shillings earned by his wife and son, was £1 8s 4d. His expenses per week were : rent 3s; bread 2s 1d; butter 10d; sugar 8d; tea 10d; coffee 4d; cheese 6d; flour 3d; suet 3d; rice ½d; potatoes 10d; fruit 3d; milk 7d; salt, pepper and mustard 1d; butchers' meat 3s 6d; bacon 1s 2d; raw fish and herring 8d; beer 3s 6d; spirits 1s; tobacco 9d. Baking Sunday's dinner cost 2d; it was probably cooked at a bakehouse which was cheaper than buying fuel, and the family must have been relatively clean and tidy for 6d went on soap, ½d for starch, another ½d on soda and blue and 3d on mangling. Dubbing worked out at ½d. Wear and tear on bedding and crocks came to 3d. Clothing and repairs for the family averaged 2s; boots and shoes 1s 6d and 3½d went for candles. A surprise item is 3d a week spent on his daughter's schooling, while a shilling was allowed for amusement and sundries. As nothing appears to have been allowed for heat, perhaps heat was a sundry. The grand total expenditure was £1 7s 6d and by week's end the family had 10d in hand against a rainy day. The annual income of this family must have been nearly £74, so the cost of the famous 'Hundred Guinea Dish' would have kept them for a year and a half.

If the plight of the lower paid workers in cities and towns was bad, that of the agricultural labourer was in general little, if any, better. The myth of happy country folk, bright-eyed, rosy-cheeked with rollicking fat infants and a puppy playing around the door of a rose-embowered rural cot, while mama shells peas, grandma knits and the elder children in an orchard background feed hens or scratch the contented pig, is one to which many Victorians heartily subscribed and wrote about romantically in novels and bad poems.

Broadly speaking the industrial revolution had its parallel in an agricultural revolution, and it is as well to remember that revolution is a misnomer for neither took place overnight. Indeed the revolution in methods of agriculture preceded the revolution in industry and by the beginning of the nineteenth century, English farming with its improved strains of cattle, of seed, its method of crop rotation, the importance it put on fertilizing, drainage and tillage, its new tools, had become the model for Europe. By 1843 enclosures of common land had been completed. Enclosures brought benefits and miseries. Without them we could not have fed ourselves during the Napoleonic wars, but enclosures dispossessed thousands of their little strips and their grazing rights and the dispossessed sought work in the new industries. Cottages became derelict, many were pulled down, many in bad condition were left to house farm labourers.

Through enclosures and by buying up small properties great landowners, old and new, had increased their estates. They had to spend a good deal of money on doing so and in turning waste into productive acres; naturally they expected a return for their money. But Agriculture is also very sensitive to economic fluctuations, not the least to fluctuations in the price of corn, which bedevilled the economy off and on for years.

Landowners and tenant farmers who had to have a return on invested capital, could achieve this in many instances only by keeping the wages of agricultural labourers as low as possible. In good years things were not too bad, in bad years they were appalling. It is very difficult not to paint too dark a picture because wages certainly varied, so did employment from county to county. An agricultural worker in Dorset might earn six or seven shillings a week, while one in Lancashire earned fifteen.

Wages were higher in Lancashire and the northern counties, probably because there was alternative employment for men in mines and industries. But many agricultural workers had to depend on the parish to make up for the deficiency in wages. Many farmers encouraged this, for if it meant higher rates, it meant they could pay lower wages, and as rates were spread the higher rate was shared.

Living conditions varied too from county to county, but generally speaking labourers had little to eat. They had insufficient bread but made do with potatoes—if the crop did not fail—they had a few vegetables but were usually too poor to keep a pig or cow for there was no free grazing now. Better paid workers could buy a bit of bacon or cheese from time to time, but often a sort of gruel made with flour, hot water and a scrape of butter served as breakfast with bread and cheese only for supper. Sometimes the farm labourer was also paid on the truck system and was charged a higher price than if he had bought his wheat elsewhere. Often an unscrupulous farmer would make his men take butter and cheese which were too inferior to be taken to market. As for meat? By this system he could get rid of his diseased cattle at a profit. Unless the worker broke the harsh game laws by poaching a rabbit or a hare he often had to do without meat for months. Out of his miserable wages he had to pay rent and feed his family. If he kept them warm it was usually because he still had a right to turf and brushwood for fuel.

This sounds as if all landowners and farmers were a brutal uncaring lot. They were not. Many of those who improved land, who built new cowhouses and pigsties also built new and better cottages for their hands and kept rents as low as possible. Thereby they lost money and could economize only by employing fewer hands. A vicious circle which was not to be broken until a century later.

Lord Ashley (1801–85), the tireless worker for the improvement of conditions in industry, when he succeeded his father and became 7th Earl of Shaftesbury found that the conditions of the workers on his own estate were almost unbearable. 'I have passed my life', he writes on October 3rd 1851, 'in rating others for allowing rotten houses and immoral and unhealthy dwellings; and now I've come into an estate rife with abominations! Why, there are things here to make one's flesh creep; and I have not a farthing to set them right.'[42]

Nevertheless, he did what he could. He built schools in three neglected villages, made plans for cottage improvement, started cricket clubs in the park and set up evening classes. But he could not afford to live on the estate himself nor finance improvements, to build cottages, improve land and raise the wages of 'my people' as he called them. So in 1853 he had to do something he hated, sell land and pictures. How else could he manage? A pair of good cottages cost £450 and he charged but a shilling a week rent. That he was not successful was not his fault as he had had to leave affairs to a trusted agent. His agent was a rogue.

To attempt to measure the degrees of plenty and want lying between the overfed and those who companioned hunger is impossible in a single, brief, chapter. One can deal only with extremes, with the haves and have nots, yet one can be fairly sure that the have nots achieved numerical superiority. And if we return to the world, not of the ultra-rich and the French chef but of the middle class and the sliding scale of Mrs Beeton with her definitions, we can only assume that, judging by her standards, at least half the population of England were 'creatures of the inferior races'. They ate and drank when they could afford to. And they ate too little and drank too much.

The forty or fifty course dinner. The food and dishes recommended for those on a modest budget belong to one end of the scale, at the other there is an England to which people were being awakened. An England where, 'within the precincts of wealth, gaiety and fashion, nigh the regal grandeur of St James, close on the palatial splendours of Bayswater, on the confines of the old and new aristocratic quarters, in a district where the cautious refinement of modern design has refrained from creating one single tenement for poverty; which seems, as it were, dedicated to the exclusive enjoyment of the wealth that *there* want, and famine, and disease and vice stalk in all their kindred horrors . . . is indeed a monstrous state of things. Enjoyment . . . brought in close contact with the most unmitigated misery. Wealth . . . laughing—an insolently heedless laugh—at the unknown wounds of want! But let all men remember this—that within the most courtly precincts of the richest city of God's earth, there may be found night after night, winter after winter, women —young in years, old in sin and suffering—outcasts from society —ROTTING FROM FAMINE, FILTH AND DISEASE. Let them remember this, and learn not to theorize but to act. God knows there is much room for action nowadays.'[43]

Such conditions did not prevail in London alone. Nor did they refer to prostitutes only.

CHAPTER FIVE

Medicine

On April 7th 1853 the Queen gave birth to a son, Prince Leopold. This was not an unusual occurrence; Her Majesty, then approaching her thirty-fourth birthday, had already produced seven of her nine children. All previous confinements had been very painful. They had left her exhausted and depressed, while recovery had been very slow. This birth, however, was almost painless, recovery was rapid and the Queen was delighted.

The royal delight was due to a new development in medicine, 'blessed chloroform', the Queen said, which 'soothed and quietened beyond measure'.[1] Dr John Snow had provided this boon at the invitation of the Queen's physician, Sir James Clark* (1788–1870). Immediately afterwards, Sir James wrote to Professor James Young Simpson of Edinburgh, to describe the method of administration and its gratifying result.

But the popular press was far from pleased. It expressed astonishment and horror at the dreadful risk taken with the Queen's life. *The Lancet* was equally disturbed (it was only thirty years old) and its agitated editor wrote that the use of chloroform was never justifiable in cases of childbirth, even in women of lesser rank. The Queen was not perturbed. She was a woman. She knew. Again, at her next confinement in 1857 she had chloroform. After that chloroform became popularly known as 'anaesthesia à la Reine'.

Pain-deadeners until the nineteenth century were virtually

---

* Dr Clark when practising in Rome, befriended Keats and was with him when he died. He became physician to the Duchess of Kent (1834) and in 1837 was appointed physician-in-ordinary to the young Queen and created baronet.

non-existent. Primitive peoples had used some very odd concoctions indeed, for when given in doses large enough to kill
pain, they also killed the patient. Opium was well known in
ancient Greece, hashish in Egypt. The early Romans, by com-
pressing the carotid arteries in the neck, which supply blood to
the brain, certainly produced unconsciousness. Unfortunately, if
the patient survived the operation he might suffer irreparable
brain damage. Then there was mandrake, much favoured, poisonous though it is, by many ancient peoples and in use in Europe
until the mid-seventeenth century. The only safe way to mini-
mize pain and help defeat shock was for surgeons to perfect the
swiftest possible operating techniques. The skill of a surgeon was
thus measured in seconds.

Robert Liston (1794–1847), six foot tall and powerfully built,
could amputate a leg in three minutes flat. An incredibly short
time to anyone watching the operation, but an eternity to the
victim. James Syme (1799–1870), later recognized as the greatest
living authority on surgery, a small man without Liston's Samp-
sonian strength, was far less radical in his methods. If he could
save leg or arm, even if it meant a stiff limb for ever after, he
saved it, believing this better than the mutilation caused by
amputation. It was much wiser, if more difficult, to remove an
infected foot at the ankle than to saw off the leg below the knee,
which was usual practice. Syme removed the foot of Professor
George Wilson (1818–1859); the operation is still known as
'Syme's amputation'. When Wilson recovered he wrote to a
brilliant young friend that the operation was more tedious than
some which caused greater mutilation as it could not be done by a
few swift strokes of knife and rapid use of saw. Then he added
'Of the agony it occasioned, I will say nothing. Suffering so great
as I underwent cannot be expressed in words and . . . fortunately
cannot be recalled. The particular pangs are now forgotten, but
the black whirlwind of emotion, the horror of great darkness, the
sense of desertion by God and man, bordering close on despair,
which swept through my mind and overwhelmed my heart, I
can never forget however gladly I would do so.'[2]

Since, as he rightly points out, pain also makes the senses 'preternaturally acute', it is hardly surprising that most people were so frightened of operations, that they neglected a condition which required one until it was too late.

Professor Wilson's brilliant young friend was James Young Simpson (1811–70). Simpson, born on the seventh day of the seventh month, 1811, was the seventh son of a baker. As every Scot knew, an authentic seventh son is born with remarkable gifts and potentialities. So the whole Simpson family made great sacrifices to send clever James, at fourteen, to Edinburgh University. Here he studied under the great Liston and at one time nearly decided he could not go on. This was when he saw a woman undergo the excruciating agony of a mastectomy. To his credit, he made the brave decision to continue, and, if possible, to try to find something to relieve the pain of operations. Mandrake had only just been officially removed from the Pharmacopaeia and, although a patient could be loaded with opium or alcohol, both had disadvantages. Generally speaking, doctors had to depend on ropes or strong-arm assistants to hold the patient down.

Yet even at this time there was something which could have been used as an anaesthetic. In 1800 Humphry Davy (1778–1829) had published a work on nitrous oxide (laughing gas) in which he suggested it might be of some use in surgery as it seemed to kill pain. Small attention was given to this idea save by an almost unknown general practitioner, Henry Hill Hickman, of Ludlow. Fascinated by the thought, he spent a long time experimenting with nitrous oxide on animals. In 1824 he published a paper with the excessively dull and lengthy title, *Letters on Suspended Animation containing Experiments showing that it may be Safely Employed during Operations on Animals, with a View of Ascertaining its Probable Utility in Surgical Operations on the Human Subject*. But who was going to pay any attention to the work done by an insignificant provincial doctor? Certainly not the great medical men of the early nineteenth century.

Across the Atlantic it was a different story. Here is not the place to describe the tragic life of Horace Wells (1815–48). His partner, William Morton, learning about the 'ether jags' medical students revelled in as a cheap, mild intoxicant, decided, quite literally, to 'try it on the dog'; then on himself and, finally, on a patient who rejoiced in the name of Eben Frost. On October 16th 1846, he was granted permission to use ether on a patient at the Massachusetts General Hospital with a host of sceptical spectators watching. In the end those who came to scoff remained to pray. It was a prayer of thanksgiving. Pain had been vanquished. It was the versatile American physician Oliver Wendell Holmes (1809–94) who suggested the names 'anaesthetic' and 'anaesthesia' for the new pain killer and its usage (the word anaesthesia is used both by Plato and Discorides); they were at once adopted.

Back in England the renowned Robert Liston, now of University College Hospital, announced jocosely (December 21st 1846) to his students, one of whom was a young Quaker, Joseph Lister : 'Gentlemen, we are going to try a Yankee dodge to make men insensible.'[3] The 'dodge' was tried on a butler called Churchill, whose leg needed amputating. The new anaesthetic was given by Dr Peter Squire. Liston, operating with his usual speed and skill, found he had done the job in just twenty-eight seconds. A few moments later, Churchill came to, and asked anxiously, 'When are you going to begin?' Liston, virtually speechless, turned to his audience and managed to stammer out : 'This . . . this . . . Yankee dodge, gentlemen, beats mesmerism hollow.'

During this time James Young Simpson, who had followed Liston's work with ether, had emerged from a stormy career with a great reputation. In 1840 he had been elected, but only just, to the Chair of Midwifery at Edinburgh. Here his work on, and interest in, diseases of the uterus led him to publish so many papers that he might be called the father of gynaecology; that is, as a separate subject distinct from, although related to, obstetrics. But his hope of finding something which would relieve the pangs of labour, or any pain, continued unabated. It is a wonder he and his wife survived the toxic concoctions they tried on themselves. In January 1847 he first tried ether, subsequently using it on many patients. But there were disadvantages. Ether had a tendency to irritate the lungs and cause coughing in the initial stages of inhalation. Large amounts were needed in childbirth as it takes a good deal longer for a child to be born than it does to saw off a leg. It required a special form of inhalator. It also had a most persistent and disagreeable smell.

There must be something else, Simpson thought, and went on trying out various mixtures on himself, often with alarming results. It was a Liverpool chemist who suggested he try chloroform. This had been discovered in 1831 by a New York chemist, Samuel Guthrie, and, quite independently about the same time, by Eugène Souberain of Paris and J. von Liebig, the great German chemist. In 1835 it had been given the name 'chloroform' by M. J. Dumas. It was a splendid thing to discover, but no chemist had the remotest idea of what to do with it. The enquiring James Young Simpson had a supply made up for him by Messrs Flockhart of Edinburgh and, with his two assistants plus various members of his family, had a chloroform party. As they began to inhale all sense of fatigue vanished, all became lively and over-talkative; a few seconds later all the lively were dumb and flat on their faces. When Simpson came round he knew at once he had the answer. His assistant, Dr Duncan, was still snoring loudly. Dr Keith was kicking violently to get out from underneath a table. More carefully controlled experiments proved to Simpson that he was right and he began to use it, with great caution, in midwifery. His first patient, a doctor's wife, was so delighted that she had the result of this painless labour christened 'Anaesthesia', which sounds a trifle Russian. Simpson continued using chloroform and also acted as anaesthetist for several surgeons. So the long war against pain was won.

Or rather, it had just begun. One might think medical and lay opinion would be on the side of Professor Simpson and welcome this great stride forward. Far from it. There were surgeons who believed the already high mortality rate which followed all operations would be increased by the use of chloroform. Carefully gathering statistics, Simpson showed that when chloroform was used only one in three died, whereas the average rate was two out of three. No doctor, then, really knew the dangers of post-operative shock any more than he knew about antiseptic procedure.* Here one might hazard a guess that the reduction in mortality rate due to the use of chloroform could have been caused by three things: first, the lessening of pre-operative fear, a form of shock which punishes the adrenals; second, the shortening of the time required to perform an operation since the patient was insensible and quiescent; third, a shortening of the period of post-operative shock caused by pain and exhaustion—always provided the patient didn't die of sepsis, a risk which applied to anaesthetized and unanaesthetized alike. This reduction in the mortality rate, although it still looks appallingly high to us, was a triumph.

Lay critics were less easy to confound and, as usual, such critics included a number of the clergy. These continued to believe that to avert pain, most particularly the travail of childbirth was contrary to God's will as explicitly stated in Genesis 3:6. But Professor Simpson, who knew a good deal of the Bible off by heart, hit these professional theologians by quoting an earlier chapter, Genesis 2:21, where, as he pointed out, the very first operation mentioned in the Bible, the removal of a rib, was not performed until the Great Surgeon had cast the patient into a deep sleep.

Simpson was brilliant at defeating opponents on their own ground, but in the end it was Queen Victoria who put a stop to all this nonsense. By the time the Queen's ninth and last child was born in 1857, chloroform was in general use.

Even to those of us born before the war of 1939–45 who now find ourselves face to face with the complexities of a second scientific revolution, to say nothing of the problems raised by spare-part surgery, it may seem curious that chloroform, dis-

---

* Joseph Lister (1827–1912), founder of antiseptic surgery, did not really begin his great experiments until 1865 and does not come within the scope of this book.

covered in 1831, was not accepted in England until 1853, and if it had not been for Queen Victoria, it would probably have taken another decade of hard fighting before this anaesthetic was generally acknowledged.

But even more astonishing is the fact that as recently as 1832, every anatomist, every physician or surgeon could only become so if he broke the law. The law punished anyone found procuring an 'unlawful' dead body for dissection. Yet the rapidly growing medical schools required every student to have practical knowledge of human anatomy. To steal a corpse, other than a legally permitted one (of which more later), was merely a misdemeanour carrying a sentence of one month in gaol, but if the theft of a body included even one shred of grave clothes this was a felony punishable by transportation for seven years. So every respectable and reputable teacher of anatomy had to acquire, by some means or another, a body or bodies for himself and his students. Few anatomists could, single-handed, 'snatch' the number of bodies needed for the accurate and important study of human anatomy; although the powerfully-built surgeon, Robert Liston, certainly snatched a few.

This absurd, muddled, and unsavoury situation had arisen in England in 1540 when it had been recognized, at last, that a surgeon (not then a man of much status) needed to know how to operate on human beings. An Act was then passed incorporating the Barber-Surgeons.* The new charter was handed to Thomas Vycary, Henry VIII's own Sergeant-Surgeon, who was on the staff of St Bartholomew's Hospital (he was also the author of the first book on anatomy in English), and the newly incorporated company was given the right to dissect four corpses a year, such corpses being the bodies of executed criminals. Presumably, since religion is very mixed up in this, executed criminals could look forward to nothing but Hell on Judgement Day. Thus, in a sense, it was a kindness to cut them to bits, break up their bones,

---

* George II gave royal recognition to the surgeons who had, by then, split away from the ancient Barber-Surgeons Company. In 1745 they were incorporated as the Royal College of Surgeons.

and then the corporeal body could not be resurrected and cast into eternal fire.

Four legal corpses a year are useful but hardly sufficient to promote rapid growth in the study and knowledge of anatomy. By the early eighteenth century demand was exceeding the permitted supply and the Barber-Surgeons had to fine members caught dissecting at home, as it were, instead of in Hall. These earnest enquirers were 'misdeemful members' who bribed the public hangman (these Jack Ketches also received a large Christmas-box from the Company) to deliver the authorized body direct to them, whereas, in law, the body was the property of the Company as a whole. Even without this 'infringement' the Company's own Beadle had a hard fight to get a body from the gallows to the Hall. It then began to be noticed that graves were being violated.

A further complication was that felons due for hanging hated the idea of dissection. It may be they, unlike their judges, thought the Lord to be truly merciful and that He might not condemn them so harshly for eternity. It is more probable they feared, rightly, that the job would be botched and they would be dissected whilst still alive. This very real and universal fear led to terrible rioting at public executions. Relatives and friends of the condemned would deliberately provoke trouble among the thousands of spectators who always enjoyed watching a hanging. By 1751 the government, thoroughly alarmed by the riots no less than by the amount of body snatching taking place, produced an Act (1751) which provided that all murderers executed in London and Middlesex should be either publicly dissected or hung by chains on gibbets. This certainly increased supply, but still demand outpaced it to such an extent that by the end of the century the underworld realized there was money to be made by exhumation.

Irate citizens, well aware of this, laid spring traps among the wreaths, or hired grave protectors, or buried their dead expensively in patented wrought iron coffins. Such precautions were of small use; they did indeed protect graves from the amateurs, who were usually anatomy masters or students, but they delivered grave snatching into the hands of 'resurrection-men' who turned it into a profession.

Profession seems an odd word to use in this connection, but such work required enormous skill, meticulous planning, almost incredible speed, perfect timing and careful organization. These qualities were also necessary to the surgical profession, so grave-snatching can hardly be termed a trade and had not yet turned into a 'business' in our modern use of the word. The professional had to know beforehand a number of details which were difficult to ferret out. The necessary information consisted, among other things, of knowing who was at death's door and exactly when the threshold was crossed. Further, and just as important, a know-ledge of precisely when, where and at what hour the burial would be was essential. To discover all this an organization had to be built up consisting of tramps, hawkers, footmen, barmaids and prostitutes. These were usually reliable sources of information for various reasons. Bad news always travels more swiftly than good. The unregarded and disregarded are usually astute obser-vers who can move about unnoticed. The underpaid are always in need of a few extra pennies. Barmaids, generally, have sharp ears and great discretion. This curious network supplied the vital information about the dead or dying. Footmen and other servants could supply the necessary facts of time and place of burial so that the lie of the land or (rather) the exact burial spot, could be ascertained beforehand. Once all this was accomplished, the elderly prostitute came into her own. Clad in black from top to toe she would hot-foot it to the new grave the instant the mourners had left. There, as a too-late-for-the-obsequies mourner she would linger, drooping with grief, shedding false tears and noting with admirable precision the exact position of the grave, the arrangement of wreaths and flowers, whether there were concealed trip wires or spring traps. Armed with this informa-tion, memory-photographed, she would report back to the chief resurrectionist who, with his trained small corps of assistants, would do his work that night—all the better if it were a moonless night.

Body-snatching

This was no easy task. Wreaths and floral tokens had to be removed, the earth dug out and carefully put on to a large canvas without dropping a crumb, the coffin opened, the body removed and thrust into a large sack; then everything had to be replaced to look as if nothing had been touched. Speed, precision, accurate memory, iron nerve, strength plus necessary and clumsy paraphernalia, were essentials for this and these early professionals were greatly respected by the medical men and anatomists whom they served. They were careful, honest, considerate people. The price of a cadaver was fixed at two guineas and every medical man knew where and how to procure a body from an honest resurrectionist. Hence every doctor or surgeon until 1832 was, in legal terms, an accessory before the fact.

Still there were not enough bodies to go round, nor enough reputable and trustworthy resurrection men. But as money could be made in this way, the profession soon became a racket (and worse). Upstart rival resurrectionist leaders began to indulge in gang-warfare. From their clients they demanded a retainer of fifty pounds, whilst the price of a 'subject' soared until it reached at least ten guineas. Rival gangs bribed and organized undertakers and sextons (alas for the poor tramps, prostitutes and barmaids) and, in a sporting way, a gang might steal a body from Guy's Hospital and sell it to St Thomas's.

Surgeons and anatomists were in a quandary. They had to employ resurrection men no matter how high the retaining fee or the price of a subject. If they refused to pay the increased prices they were in danger of blackmail. The government was also in a dilemma. It knew that the army, no less than the civil population, needed good surgeons and the study of anatomy required the use of more and more bodies; but it was equally aware of the fact that public and religious opinion was strongly against increasing supplies. As usual, when puzzled, the government appointed a Select Committee to enquire into the matter. One of the witnesses called was Sir Astley Paston Cooper (1768–1841), a most eminent physician, brilliant lecturer, demonstrator, surgeon and anatomist, who was questioned about 'the Baronet's

Brigade', the name given to the corps of resurrectionists employed by him—by far the most capable of the lot. When asked what effect the law had on preventing exhumation he answered, firmly, it did nothing to prevent it, it merely raised prices. Another witness, a well-known resurrectionist, who had been in this occupation for many years, said that even as early as 1809 he had sold 305 adults and forty-four children to London medical schools; had shipped a further thirty-seven to Edinburgh,* and 'wastage' amounted to eighteen. But the very fact that a Select Committee was sitting soothed public opinion and allowed the government to sit back and do nothing.

Then the real criminals moved in. It was not until those infamous murderers, Burke and Hare, were caught in Edinburgh (1828), and public wrath vented so violently on public dissecting rooms, on doctors and surgeons all over the country, that the government (1829) introduced a Bill to increase supplies. The Bill passed the Commons, but was defeated in the Lords. Thus the *status quo* remained and might have continued to do so had not two London criminals, Bishop and Williams, been caught for the murder of a fourteen-year-old boy. They tried to sell the body to Dr Richard Partridge (1807–73), then an anatomy lecturer at King's College Hospital. Dr Partridge, with the utmost moral and physical courage, had the salesmen apprehended. Subsequently it appeared that probably as many as sixty people had been murdered by these two. Forty thousand people saw them executed at Newgate on December 5th 1831. Ten days later the Bill of 1829, to regulate the increase of supplies to schools of anatomy, was read. It passed both Houses and on August 1st 1832 received the Royal Assent of the Reform King.

This long-needed Act was a great stride forward. It legally permitted medicine to become a science and, as every tired old schoolboy knows, medicine is a science and an art. Nevertheless,

---

* Shipping 'subjects' from one part of the British Isles to another was common. From London to Edinburgh a van was useful for transporting a water-tight cask which did not contain, say, beer. 'Subjects' were also shipped, when possible and trade was brisk, from Ireland to western ports.

the fact remains that every great early Victorian doctor, and a good many of the later ones too, achieved greatness illegally. Thomas Hood (1799–1845), well aware of this, wrote in verses, considered by many to be in singularly bad taste, of a girl's ghost appearing to her bereaved sweetheart to tell him what happened after her burial in 'Mary-bone'.

> The arm that used to take your arm
> Is took to Dr Vyse;
> And both my legs are gone to walk
> The hospital at Guy's.

Mary's head went somewhere else, her hand was at Dr Bell's 'in spirits and a phial'. Her 'trunk' was 'all packed up to go by Pickford's van' and in the penultimate stanza she exclaims,

> The cock it crows—I must be gone!
> My William, we must part!
> But I'll be yours in death, altho'
> Sir Astley has my heart.[4]

Sir Astley Paston Cooper is one of the key figures in the development of nineteenth-century medicine. Any attempt to mention more than a few of such key figures in a single chapter would be ludicrous. But had it not been for Sir Astley and Sir Benjamin Brodie (1783–1862) the great Medical Act of 1858, which clarified and regulated the position of medicine, and among things, set up a register of 'Qualified Medical Practitioners', would not have come into being. Sir Astley was the patron of the son of the rector of Winterslow, Wilts, Benjamin Brodie, who became one of the most famous surgeons of the era. In the year before the Queen's birth Brodie's treatise on the little-known and difficult subject, *On Diseases of the Joints*, appeared. Later, he became a surgeon to St George's Hospital and, later still, President of the R.C.S. and of the Royal Society. Not only was he a brilliant surgeon with great charm of manner, he was a polymath and distinguished himself in four fields, philosophy, physiology, surgery and administration. He was also surgeon to three monarchs, George IV, William IV, who conferred a baronetcy on him in 1834, and Queen Victoria. His practice was enormous and for some time he earned about £10,000 a year in guinea fees. This was a great sum.

Far less rich but no less important was Charles Bell (1774–1842) to whom *Mary's Ghost* refers. Of Dr Bell, who was knighted in 1830, Müller* has this to say: 'The discoveries of the circulation of the blood and the discoveries of Sir Charles Bell . . . were the two grandest discoveries ever made by physiological science.'[5]

Sir Charles, like Simpson, was a poor Scot; like Sir Astley, a fourth son, whose father, a Church of England clergyman, had the magnificent stipend of £25 per annum. Even so, he managed to give his three elder sons a good education. John became a surgeon; Robert, Writer to the Signet; George Joseph, a professor of Scotch law. Charles was five when his father died and left the family even more impoverished. Of his own education he says: 'I received no education but from my mother, neither reading, writing, cyphering or anything else.'[6] But he had a great natural talent for drawing and painting and, when he became assistant to brother John, he used this talent to make beautiful coloured drawings of anatomical subjects. As there was small opportunity for him in Scotland, he moved to London (1804) and published *On the Anatomy of Expression* (1806), a book intended chiefly for artists. His contention was that artists too often gave animals human expressions of fear, rage and pain. He asserted that the expression on the face of Michaelangelo's David was quite wrong, and gave detailed reasons. The book did not gain him the Chair of Anatomy at the Royal Academy, for which he had hoped, nor did it add to his meagre earnings, but it did establish his reputation as an anatomist and he was able to set up as a teacher in a dilapidated house in Leicester Square. Later, he acquired the Windmill School of Anatomy made famous by the Hunter brothers. Still later, in Belgium after

* Johannes Müller (1801–58) and his pupils came very near to making biology an exclusively German province.

Waterloo he operated night and day, so weary he could have dropped inside his clothing stiffened with blood, but learning as he worked. Somehow he found time to make drawings and paintings of gunshot wounds. Returning, he was appointed surgeon to the Middlesex Hospital, which increased his reputation but did little to augment his finances. The need for money was so great that he sold the specimens from his anatomical museum together with his paintings of gunshot wounds for £3,000 to the Royal College of Surgeons, Edinburgh (they are still there), and began researches on the nervous system. It was Charles Bell who first discovered there were two kinds of nerves, sensory and motor, each with its own special function. His *The Nervous System of the Human Body* appeared in 1830, and most of his research was done on 'illegal' cadavers. This was the first book on modern neurology. In 1835 he published *The Hand, its Mechanism and Vital Endowments as Evincing Design*. It is this work on the complex structure of the hand to which *Mary's Ghost* refers.

Sir Charles was what the Victorians, by 1856, were calling a specialist, a term now dropped in favour of consultant (who is really a consulting-specialist),* and specialization as we know it, really begins in the early nineteenth century. There was Marshall Hall (1790–1857), a physiologist, born near Nottingham, whose great work *On Diagnosis* appeared in 1817. Although a book on the same subject had appeared as early as 1791, most doctors barely knew the meaning of diagnosis. They treated symptoms without thinking about causes. It seems extraordinary to us, accustomed to thinking of diagnostics as a commonplace, that it was Hall who little more than a century and a half ago laid down that the first principle in medicine should be to discover the disorder or disease from which the patient suffered. The way to do this was not by treating symptoms but by observing and

* 'Specialist' is still used in North America today. Our modern term, 'consultant', doubtless derives from later Victorian times when consulting physician, consulting engineer, etc., became popular terminology. Originally, a consultant was a person who consults an oracle.

recording them. In this book he gives a long list of symptoms and argues cogently that correct reasoning and deduction, which is diagnosis, proceeds only from accurate and minute observation. Dr Thomas Sydenham had said this back in the seventeenth century but his advice had been largely ignored. Hall also insisted on the use of the recently-invented stethoscope and condemned the practice of bleeding for diseases such an anaemia or haemorrhage. Leeches alone cost the Nottingham Hospital £50 per annum. He realized that babies, already exhausted from diarrhoea, died more quickly when bled. Hall's disciples, more enthusiastic than their master, refused to use bleeding for any distemper. Thus, after 3,000 years of therapeutic bloodshed, bleeding at last went out of fashion.

Another great discoverer was Thomas Addison (1793–1860). A physician afflicted with that native English condition, melancholy, modest and subject to periods of deep depression, he is known for his description of Addison's Anaemia and Addison's Disease. The first was later called 'pernicious anaemia'. The second, also an anaemia which shows in the deep bronzing of the skin, is caused by a disease of the suprarenal cortex. Addison worked for years on this subject, as well as on many other allied diseases. His paper, *On the Constitutional and Local Effects of Diseases of the Suprarenal Capsule*, did not appear until 1855. Those who, in our own century, are still busy unravelling the mysteries of the adrenal cortex, know the value of Addison's work and this shy, melancholy man's fame is posthumous. What is possibly not so well known, generally, is that Addison was the first clinician to describe appendicitis. How to remove this 'worm' was not then known, but often an incision was made and the pus drained off. Sometimes the patient recovered.

Joseph Toynbee (1815–66) the great social worker, philosopher, and father of Arnold Toynbee, rescued 'aural surgery from the hands of the quacks'.[7] He was the first to try to turn aural pathology into an exact science and to that end made about 2,000 dissections of the human ear. Like John Hunter in the previous century, he died as a result of using himself as a guinea pig.

Thinking that tinnitus might be reduced by inhaling chloroform, followed by inflation of the ear, he tried it on himself in his own consulting room where he was found dead with his notes beside him. Although Toynbee recognized and suggested the possibilities of a mastoid operation, it was his assistant, James Hinton (1822–75) who performed the first one in England but not until 1866. This operation had been done successfully in Paris some time before 1750 by Jean Louis Petit, but no one on either side of the channel had given it much, if any, thought.

It is generally recognized that one of the most difficult branches of medicine, even today, is dermatology. Our first great dermatologist was Robert Willan (1757–1812). Before Willan, it had been thought that skin conditions were merely a matter for self-treatment. Do-it-yourself medical books brought fortunes to many a compiler. Too often such works turned out to be how-to-do-yourself-in manuals. Skin afflictions were as commonplace as their 'cures'. The afflicted would smear themselves with ointments, unguents, liquids, and powders, often containing utterly repulsive ingredients, to say nothing of active poisons. Willan described many morbid skin conditions and noted that some were associated with certain trades—we now call these occupational dermatitis. His book *On Cutaneous Diseases* (1808) was the first to treat the subject on a scientific basis. But the most famous early Victorian dermatologist was Sir Erasmus Wilson (1809–84), a well-known anatomist who, in 1838, published a book with the cheery title of *Dissector's Manual*, and in 1840 *An Anatomist's Vade Mecum*. After this brandishing of saw and scalpel he devoted himself to skin disease which, despite Willan's work, was still a relatively unexplored surface. There was only one thing finer than a healthy skin, he thought, and that was a rare skin disease. He founded a chair of Dermatology at the R.C.S., acquired an enormous practice and became a very rich man indeed. The skin game certainly paid off. Few of us remember him now, yet anyone who walks along the Thames Embankment and notices Cleopatra's Needle might just give him a passing thought. Wilson's hobby was Egyptology and in 1877 he paid around £10,000 to have this famous obelisk, the gift of Mohammed Ali of Egypt, brought to England.

Another physician-Egyptologist-physicist was Thomas Young (1773–1829). He helped interpret the Rosetta Stone, and wrote the pioneer treatise *On the Mechanics of the Eye* wherein he put forward the wave theory of light. Far better known to medical students today is the name Henry Gray (1827–61). His lectures, delivered at St George's Hospital, led to his book *Anatomy, Descriptive and Applied*. First published in 1858, it has been revised time and again, and Gray's *Anatomy* is still a major textbook. Gray was a brilliant anatomist, but must have been careless or so wrapped up in his own subject that, like the true absent-minded professor, he forgot an essential. He permitted himself to die of smallpox, one of the few things we did know how to prevent.

John Cunningham Saunders (1773–1810) was interested in both the eye and the ear. In 1805 this otologist-ophthalmologist founded the London Dispensary for Curing Diseases of the Eye and Ear. Today it is Moorfields Hospital. But the very first hospital to treat the ear only was established by an unqualified ear man, John Harrison Curtis; this enterprise turned into The Royal Ear Hospital. Curtis can have known little about the ear for he treated every condition with an enormous syringe far better suited for use on an African elephant—and a perfectly splendid means of causing irreparable damage to the human ear. James Yearsley (1805–69) pioneered otolaryngology and was one of the earliest to point out that certain kinds of deafness can be caused by a condition of the nose and throat. In 1838 he founded the Metropolitan Ear and Throat Hospital in Fitzroy Square.

So far we have dealt chiefly with diseases of adults and there might have been many more men and women with much to give had it not been for the still giant infant mortality rate. Yet one of the seventeen children of a Yarmouth brewer and ship-builder who did survive was James Paget (1814–99). As Paget père lost all his money, James served a five year apprenticeship to a local practitioner, Charles Costerton. At twenty he entered Bart's and, as a first-year student, discovered *trichinia spiralis* in the human muscle. Every anatomist had noted from time to time these little speckles, but young James showed that each speck was really a minute encapsuled worm, often ingested with insufficiently cooked pork and so responsible for *trichinosis* which can be fatal —and still is in underdeveloped tropical and subtropical countries. Paget, as poor as he was brilliant, which means he was very poor indeed, worked tirelessly and by 1851 as a F.R.S. had become known as a great physiologist-pathologist. His lectures, particularly those concerned with physiology, pushed his fortunes forward and he can be ticketed as the founder of our modern science of physiology. Diagnosis was also a strong point, and among his many discoveries was Paget's disease of the nipple, invariably followed by cancer of the breast, although its relationship to the various types of mammary cancer is, at the time of writing (1971) still obscure.

From these few potted biographies it seems evident that modern specialization began during the first half of the nineteenth century. And if each man, individually and collectively, contributed something to the wellbeing of mankind, the one who should command our greatest sympathy today is one whose name is known to few, simply because so little is known about him. He is one of those great almost anonymous figures who so often come and go leaving no trace of personality behind, save in the work they do. His name is Charles West (1816–98). West was an accoucheur, a word which superseded the older term, man-midwife and which was succeeded by our word obstetrician. Charles West truly deserves that overworked phrase 'the father of'. In his case it applies to modern paediatrics. Again, we must back-track to understand. Anciently, a few medical writers dealt with diseases of children and through medieval times there are a few short treatises on the subject. In England, the first popular work was *De morbis acutis infantum* (1689), written by Walter Harris (1647–1732). This, more a piece of special pleading than a treatise, showed Harris's belief that most diseases of children were due to acid collecting in the body; therefore the correct treatment was to give the child alkaline substances by mouth as often as possible. Sick children on Harris's diet were forced to gag down concoctions of chalk, cuttle-fish bones, eggshells, coral and, best of all, oyster shells powdered and used, separately or combined, in a syrupy base. This may have been useful for calcium deficiency and Harris was certainly on to something in the idea of acid-alkali balance.

After Harris came William Cadogan (1711–97), whose tome, *An Essay upon Nursing and the Management of Children from their Birth to Three Years of Age* (1748) did little to reduce the high mortality rate but at least stated that babies should not be cocoon-wrapped and that even fashionable mothers should suckle their own rather than employ a wet nurse at home or farm the infant out to one. In 1784 Michael Underwood (1736–1820) brought out his *Treatise on the Diseases of Children*, and this remained the standard work for fifty years. In the fourth edition (1799), Underwood discusses the diagnoses and importance of congenital heart disease.

Even earlier (1769), but with a different approach, Dr George Armstrong (fl. 1767) had set up his own Dispensary for the Infant Poor. As he bore most of the cost himself and the poor were so numerous and fertile, he was forced to give up in 1783. In 1818 John Bunnell Davis (1780–1824) founded a smaller Dispensary which later moved to Waterloo Bridge Road. His published enquiry into the infant mortality rate led, eventually, to the establishment of voluntary health visitors who went in to the hovels and tenements of the poor to try to instruct mothers in child care. Then in 1848 came Dr Charles West's great work *Lectures on the Diseases of Infancy and Childhood* and Underwood's book literally 'went west' (this phrase, meaning 'to die out', was in use as early as the sixteenth century). Dr West's book, based on lectures he gave at the Middlesex Hospital, was a compilation of case histories of 600 out of some of the 14,000 children with whom he had dealt, together with his own logical reasoning on each case. The key phrases are 'full case histories' and 'logical reasoning'.

Although his purposeful attempt to make various dispensaries for sick children attach themselves to in-patient hospitals failed, he doggedly turned failure into success when, in 1852, he bought 49 Great Ormond Street where the famous eighteenth-century doctor, Sir Richard Mead, had once lived. By doing much of the administrative work and helping to defray expenses himself, Charles West created the now internationally-known Great Ormond Street Hospital for Sick Children. The accent is securely on the word 'great'.

In the field of orthopaedic surgery other countries were undoubtedly ahead of us. Our Charles I, of unhappy memory, had had to wear iron boots until he was nearly seven. Despite the fine work done by Dr Percivall Pott in the eighteenth century to do away with the cruel iron corsets children with 'weak backs' were forced to wear, we still lagged, until William John Little (1810–94) appeared. Born with a club foot which was successfully operated on by the great German, George F. Ludwig Stromeyer, who divided the tendon, Little determined to make orthopaedics his special concern. Here indeed there was *multum in parvo*, for the London Orthopaedic Hospital was founded by Little when he was but twenty-eight. Later (1853), he wrote the first orthopaedic treatise in this country *On the Nature and Treatment of Deformities of the Human Frame*. There is a type of infantile spastic-paralysis which still bears his name.

But specialization, diagnosis, and other new developments of the time, were not the only branches of medico-science which made the early Victorian era of such significance. In accession year there was no such thing as a public health system; no means of knowing how sanitary information, so painfully acquired during previous centuries, could be collated and usefully applied. For example, there were Commissions of Sewers—but they were local. Their job was, and had been for centuries, to deal with the drainage of low level and marshy ground. On June 6th 1682 a General Session of Sewers was 'holden at Lydd in the county of Kent' to examine the level of 'the Sea Gutt at Dengness' which had 'swerved and topped up with the Beach'.[8] Sewer in the seventeenth century, no less than in early Victorian times, meant a water course or a man-made channel for fresh water. The business of commissions was to see that such courses did not silt up, break down, or fail in any way and cause flooding. So sewers had little to do with what we call sewage disposal.

But one of the near-fatal consequences of the Industrial Revolution was, that with increased urbanization, mere villages became populous, overcrowded towns with unaltered village amenities. Towns exploded into cities, with town amenities. Cities spread their tentacles into their environs and grasped hamlets, villages and the green and pleasant land near them and became still more overcrowded. The trickle of population to the north, first observed in the early eighteenth century, became a stream. Yet, due to the agricultural 'revolution' and the great Enclosure Acts of the reign of George III, the countryside became more depopulated. Those able to stay on the land were often more healthy than their unfortunate contemporaries whom poverty had driven into the towns and cities to find work, and where the filth of tenement or slum life often killed them. Paradoxically, with good land drainage the incidence of malaria fell; whilst the introduction of cheap washable cotton helped reduce the incidence of typhus. Yet, even in the squalor of city slums where death was the only friend of the poor, things had improved a trifle after 1762, when the City of Westminster obtained an Improvement Act. Thus in some cities streets were lighted and paved. Open kennels (channels), which served as drains, were covered over. Sometimes deep pipes were laid, and existing sewer pipes improved. As this had been a matter for local authorities, where such existed, much was left undone and one wonders how successive generations survived in sufficient numbers to become the 'Victorians'.

Water supplies in London, still the largest city in the world, were totally contaminated (this also applied to other cities) as they came chiefly from rivers and surface wells. In London there was still no continuous supply of water even to grand houses with mains. Water was turned on and pumped by various water mills two or three times a week and then for only a few hours. Cesspools were common usage in good homes as late as mid-nineteenth century. Disposal of night soil was done by special 'undertakers'—a filthy, insanitary job—but money could be made by selling the raw night soil as fertilizer. As for sewage, where deep drains were used, the drain debouched into the nearest river and the greatest drain of all was the Thames. It still is. What improvements had been made were due almost entirely to the efforts of private citizens, and it was left to the Utilitarian philosopher, Jeremy Bentham (1748–1832), better known in Europe and the United States than in his own country, to enunciate the fundamental principle that everything which influences or affects the health of a country should be the concern of the legislature. The idea was not new. Imperial Rome was, and is, witness to that. Nevertheless, dilatory as we were, we were ahead of many European countries in public health simply because a number of men came under Bentham's influence, either first or second hand. One was a physician, Neil Arnott (1788–1874) who, among other things invented a smokeless grate with which he hoped to do away with air pollution. Another, the Unitarian minister and physician, Thomas Southwood Smith (1788–1861) whose treatise, *The Use of the Dead to the Living*, had helped forward the Anatomy Act of 1832. Then there was that key figure, the brilliant, difficult Edwin Chadwick (1800–90). He was not a doctor, his profession was the law, but he never practised. His avocation, which became a vocation, was preventive medicine. At twenty-eight he contributed an article to the *Westminster Review* with a most misleading title 'The Means of Insurance against Accidents', but the contents were not of the 'don't come down the ladder, mother, I've taken it away' variety; on the contrary the article suggested that although the average expectation of life had been increased, it could be increased still further if proper attention were paid to 'Sanitation' and 'Hygiene'. This 'sanitary idea', as he called it, was extended when Chadwick (of whom more later), became a member of a commission to investigate the administration of the poor laws and he was the only

The Thames, the sewer of London

member to take into account the health of the pauper population
and the relationship between insanitary housing and illness.
Although temperamentally a difficult man to work with, he and
his co-workers persuaded the government to set up a Sanitary
Commission (1839) which, after many vicissitudes, became the
General Board of Health (1848). It sickened and died at the age
of ten. Yet this premature death gave birth to London's first

Medical Officer of Health. The officer, appointed 1848, was Sir John Simon (1816–1904) of St Thomas's Hospital. But here London lagged behind Liverpool where, the year before, the first Medical Officer of Health in our history, Dr W. H. Duncan, had been appointed.

Other related things also evolved at this time. One was the founding of an Army Hospital Corps, another was the transposition of nursing from the key of G flat for 'Gamp' into F major for Florence. No one can add a note to the Florence Nightingale story. Mrs Cecil Woodham-Smith has written the definitive biography. Neither the Army Hospital Corps nor the nursing profession would have come into being had it not been for Florence Nightingale (1820–1910).

There had never been an Army Medical Corps in England although, from Waterloo on, there was increasing interest in teaching what was known as 'military surgery' (one of the reasons Sir Charles Bell's experiences and drawings were of such value). Army medicine, as such, meant a doctor attached to each regiment, who wore the uniform of his regiment. If he could afford it, he bought an officer's commission and, if rich or influential enough, a combatant commission also. This meant he was paid for both. But the 'Apothecaries to the Forces' were in charge of all medical supplies and equipment, and there seems to have been little, if any, coordination between the various regimental doctors and the Apothecaries. Then there was the question of Army hospitals though this was hardly a question. There were none. If a battlefield happened to be near a city, as was the field of Waterloo, civic hospitals were available but were far too small to cope with the enormous influx of the wounded and dying. Further, there were no Army nurses. There were orderlies, but many of them were pensioners so old and infirm they could scarce lift a stretcher. These are four of the many discrete parts of a single problem which seemed insoluble.

The first venture to bring order into the 'orderly' part of the problem was a well-intentioned attempt to recruit a body of young men and turn them into a Medical Staff Corps. This was a dismal failure, chiefly because most of the young men were totally uneducated and were not given even the simplest instruction as to their duties. One has an uneasy feeling that this good idea went wrong because there was no one with sufficient knowledge to work out a code of instructions; no army official in England who knew enough about the actual conditions the wretched troops had to endure on the battlefield. Florence Nightingale did. She had had much experience of official bumbledom, jealousy and inefficiency when she had gone off to that charnel house, Scutari, and, enraged with pity and compassion, had become 'the Lady of the Lamp'.

Although she went into retirement after the war, she worked behind the scenes and against heavy odds to obtain army reform —in peace and war. Finally, in 1857, she succeeded in having a Royal Commission set up to enquire into the health, housing and diet of soldiers. As she was a woman she could not be a member of this commission, but the members were of her choosing.* This was the first time in history a scientific investigation into the welfare of soldiers in peacetime was undertaken.

In later years she took to her bed and became an influential invalid and an *éminence grise*. 'The Sidney Herberts called yesterday,' the Hon. Emily Eden writes. 'I have not seen him for twelve years, and he is not the least altered in looks. They were going to dine with Florence Nightingale at Hampstead, or rather at her house, for she has come quite to the last days of her useful life and is dying of a disease of the heart. Every breath she draws may be heard through closed doors, but when she can speak she still likes to talk to Mr Herbert of soldiers' hospitals and barracks, and to suggest means of improving them.'[9]

Miss Nightingale was then thirty-nine, and she went on dying until 1910. She used every possible influential friend to press her views. That she drove poor Sidney Herbert nearly demented,

* In 1856 Miss Nightingale printed at her own expense *Matters Affecting the Health, Efficiency and Hospital Administration of the British Army*—a massive book full of facts, figures, tables and statistics. She gave away a few copies of this monumental work to influential people, but it was never published.

was dictatorial, neurotic, demanding, obsessed, morbid, is true. But it is equally true that as a recluse and semi-invalid* she probably accomplished more than she might have done had she become a public figure. Her devotion to improving conditions in military and civic hospitals, to sanitary reforms, to the health of the army at home and abroad, was undiminished. She wrote innumerable reports and pamphlets, carried on a vast correspondence with officials and had enormous influence. Cabinet ministers came to her for advice—she did not go to them. She was noted for her remarkably clear mind, her passion for accuracy, and her brilliance at financial administration. 'She devised a cost-accounting system for the Army Medical Services which was put into operation between 1860 and 1865 and which eighty years later was still in use.'[10]

Many things were masterminded by Miss Nightingale but though essentially very feminine, she was certainly no feminist. It took her until 1877 to acknowledge that women should have the right to study medicine and might even make good doctors. She had been firmly against women doctors and had been scathing about Elizabeth Blackwell (1821–1910), the Bristol-born American who became the first woman doctor in the English-speaking world. In the medical field, she thought, women were merely trying to imitate men and would turn out to be very poor imitations indeed. There were many excellent male physicians and far too few good nurses, therefore it seemed perfectly clear to her that women should become nurses. All the clearer, perhaps, because God had called her to His service in this capacity. External voices, like those heard by Joan of Arc had bidden her to serve God.

It was just as well for our Victorian ancestors that Miss Nightingale had heeded this call, otherwise they might have been left to the tender mercies of Sairy Gamp, the drunken midwife who,

---

* Although her health was certainly undermined by the incredible amount of work she did in the Crimea, nevertheless from late adolescence Miss Nightingale had been subject to various vague maladies whenever emotionally disturbed.

had she been able to afford it, would have laid out all her 'fellow creeturs for nothink . . . such is the love I bear 'em'.[11]

Although we laugh at Sarah, as her creator intended we should, she is no figment of the imagination. She was born in the time of Henry VIII, just about the year 1535 when the dissolution of the monasteries began. Many monasteries had religious orders of women whose vocation was nursing. These orders which took in the sick and the poor and looked after them were swept away also. So where could the sick, who needed care away from home, go? Poor little Edward VI had founded various hospitals, and there was a spate of hospital building after the middle of the eighteenth century, but there was no such thing as a nursing profession; no standard of character, intelligence, education or training was required; anyone could be a nurse, and many disreputable women found it easy to use their 'pickers' in private homes. In hospitals the situation was even worse and small wonder. A hospital nurse might earn a magnificent £5 a year, and was treated as a menial. There was usually but one 'nurse' to a ward who swept, dusted, laid the fire, sifted the ashes, fetched the coal, worked from six in the morning until six at night and had no regular holiday. After the manual labour was done she could care for the sick. Patients able to tip the nurse received, not unnaturally, first attention when dressings needed changing. Those too poor to tip had to wait for days and died in waiting. In most Protestant countries similar conditions prevailed.

The first real reform began in Germany when a young pastor, Theodor Fliedner of Kaiserswerth, visited England, was so impressed by the work done by the Quaker philanthropist, Elizabeth Fry (1780–1845) among prisoners that, on returning to Germany, he devoted himself not only to the spiritual but also to the physical welfare of prisoners. In 1833 he and his wife opened a refuge for discharged female prisoners. Next they realized the needs of the sick poor, so the idea of an organized body of trained helpers became a reality. In 1836 the Fliedners opened a tiny hospital where six young women of good character became 'deaconesses' and performed all the necessary duties on a rota system. In 1840 Elizabeth Fry, who had inspired Pastor Fliedner, went to Kaiserswerth and, reinspired, returned to England to found an Institute of Nursing Sisters, a small group, to work among the poor. These sisters were trained by attending Guy's Hospital every day, to try to pry out of the untrained ward nurses and the student doctors what information could be most useful to the sick. After this local societies of Sisters of Mercy were formed and, in 1848, came the St John's House nurses, trained in the London teaching hospitals. From 1856 to 1885 they nursed at King's College Hospital.

All these and other bodies were groups of hospital nurses formed to help the poor but in 1844 when Florence Nightingale first realized that her vocation was nursing, she did not know where to turn for information. In 1846 she first heard of the Kaiserswerth 'deaconesses'. In 1850 she spent a fortnight in Kaiserswerth, and in 1851 went back for three months. It was the good character of the 'deaconesses', all were peasant women, which most impressed her. Although by 1853 she had become Superintendent of the Establishment for Gentlewomen during Illness in Upper Harley Street, she still longed to train nurses herself, and was just on the point of taking on the job of Superintendent of nurses at King's College Hospital when war broke out and she left for the Crimea. When news reached England of her work there she became a popular heroine and, as a testimonial, £45,000 was raised and put at her disposal. She disposed of it in 1860 by opening the Nightingale training school for nurses at St Thomas's Hospital. Modern nursing began here.*

Back in 1831 when Miss Nightingale was eleven and Princess Drina twelve, a terrible new disease, Asiatic Cholera, reached England. It had taken thirteen years to travel from Jessore to Europe but we had been aware of it and its effects ever since around 1818 when it had ravaged our troops as well as the native population of India.

---

* Her *Notes on Nursing*, 1859, shocked many a Victorian mama, but it became an immensely popular and influential manual both here and on the continent.

On November 11th 1830 Charles Greville notes that a letter
had been received from our Ambassador in Russia, Lord Haytes-
bury, saying, 'there was reason to believe that the disorder now
raging in Russia is a sort of plague, but that they will not admit
it, and that it is impossible to get at the truth'.[12] The truth was
that no one knew anything about the disease or how it was
carried but it spread with such rapidity that soon all the Baltic
ports and most of the capitals of Europe were affected. A very
nasty rumour also broke out among European peasants to the
effect that the aristocracy and the rich—who seemed immune—
were deliberately bribing doctors to spread the disease among
the poor so that they might be more 'conveniently governed'.[13]
This frightened the governing classes almost as much as the
French Revolution had done. Worse, it was also being said that
this horrifying means of thinning population had been very effectively used by the British in India and that the bribed doctors
were really delegates of a central committee with headquarters
in London.

But the only headquarters in London which had anything
to do with cholera was a Board of Health, hastily scrambled up
in June 1831, a purely advisory body with no executive power
at all and responsible to the Privy Council. The Board was asked
to draw up a sanitary code to outline measures to be taken should
cholera come to Great Britain. This code entitled *Instructions and
Regulations Regarding Cholera* was sent off to all local authorities. Each authority was told to set up a Board of Health for its
own area and to enforce strict quarantine measures should the
area become infected.

The instructions were circulated in mid-October. On October
23rd, Dr W. Reid Clanny of Sunderland, a port at the mouth
of the river Wear, diagnosed the first official case of cholera in
England. By November 6th five had died of the disease and
London was informed. By 1833 when the epidemic died out it
had thinned a population of nearly fourteen million by some sixty
thousand. Seven to eight thousand deaths occurred in London
alone, chiefly in the poorest and filthiest districts.

Also by 1833 the 'Reform Government' was at last in power, and Edwin Chadwick, that zealous exponent of the sanitary idea, became chief commissioner for the Poor Law which was a sad jumble of antiquated Acts and measures. In 1834 with the passing of the Poor Law Amendment Act—and Chadwick had been largely responsible for drawing up its measures—he became secretary to the new Poor Law Commissioners. This act in the long run turned out to be of enormous significance in the growth and development of a public health system, but its immediate effect upon the poor was brutal.

Hitherto, poor relief had been a matter for each individual parish and by now there were 15,535 parishes of varying size and population, each with its overseer and poor house, each supporting its paupers out of the rates. So the new Act provided for the union of parishes into much larger administrative areas and parish workhouses became 'Union' workhouses. The Act also cut off all outdoor relief, save to the aged and infirm and decreed that life inside a Union workhouse should be made far more unpleasant than life outside; this effectively killed the old 'Speenhamland System'* where parish aid was given to all those who did not receive a living wage and the ratepayer was taxed accordingly. This old system had had nearly fatal results as it enabled employers to keep wages at a minimum and placed an ever-increasing burden on the ratepayer. Further, it had had a demoralizing effect on the worker; it discouraged thrift, and the desire to work, and killed self-respect. Why work when the parish would support you?

The Act of 1834 was certainly harsh and far too drastic, but at that time there seemed no other way to stop the rot of pauperization, compel the able-bodied to work (always provided there was work and often there was not), and relieve the burden on the ratepayer. But this new Act also set up boards of guardians for each Union and these boards were made responsible for providing medical care for paupers and for appointing paid medical men, as well as inspectors, to see that the Act was enforced. In

* Adopted chiefly in southern and eastern counties.

1836 they were also made responsible for the appointment of local registrars for births and deaths and, in 1840, for public vaccination, which became compulsory in 1853. Thus a centralized machinery for public health was set up and this was the very first central organization for welfare in our history.

A severe outbreak of fever—and 'fever' covered a number of infectious diseases—occurred in the poor quarters of London in 1838 and this gave Chadwick a chance to propose an investigation into the causes of diseases of the poor which, by killing the breadwinner, turned many women into paupers and forced them and their children into workhouses. The investigation was completed in the same year and a report sent to the Home Secretary, Lord John Russell (1792–1878), who had struggled so valiantly to get the Great Reform Bill passed. Lord John did nothing.

Fortunately, Chadwick and his supporters had a staunch champion in Charles James Blomfield (1786–1857), translator of Aeschylus and Bishop of London who, as a parish priest, had seen much of the appalling conditions in which the poor lived. Bishop Blomfield, in 1839, moved in the Upper House that a detailed countrywide enquiry should be made into the cause of diseases of the poor. Reluctantly, the Lords temporal agreed with this Lord Spiritual and thus a very much larger survey was undertaken by the Poor Law Commissioners with Chadwick as chairman. For this survey Chadwick was now able to rely upon reports sent in by the boards of guardians of the new administrative areas. Although the enquiry nearly foundered in 1841 when Lord Normanby, who had other plans, ordered it stopped, luckily the tottering Whig government fell. Lord Melbourne was out and Sir Robert Peel, no doctrinaire Conservative, became Prime Minister. The enquiry continued.

When finished and published in 1842 this *Report on the Sanitary Condition of the Labouring Population* became a best seller, and it horrified all right-thinking people. It was a factual document well illustrated and included a map of Leeds which unequivocally showed that the great cholera epidemic of 1831–3 had been largely confined to the poorest quarters. The report made it quite clear that good sanitation meant good health. It recommended arterial systems for water and sewage with only one local authority to be responsible for this, under the expert advice of those skilled in medicine and engineering. A Royal Commission of 1843, set up to enquire into the health of large towns, confirmed the Chadwick Report. And in 1848, after a heated debate, the Public Health Bill to establish a general Board of Health with authority to create local boards received the Queen's cordial assent.

It was not a minute too soon as in October of that year the second cholera epidemic hit us and we were better able to meet it. If no one knew what caused cholera or how it was spread—and there were dozens of theories, the most popular a belief that it was carried by a miasmatic vapour—we now had a General Board of Health in London which possessed executive power and which could codify all anti-cholera measures and issue them quickly to the new local Boards of Health. As nothing was known about cholera the instructions were, doubtless, of very little real use but at least we had an organization which could move swiftly and was thus able to implement any measures relating to public health.

When in 1849 the epidemic was all but over a National Day of Thanksgiving was proclaimed and the Bishop of London preached in St Paul's. He gave appropriate thanks to God but at the same time pointed out in no uncertain terms that it was a Christian duty to spread the gospel of the necessity for good sanitation. Other clergymen did the same; so did the newspapers and great support was gained for the 'sanitary idea'.

In that same autumn a small pamphlet *On the Mode of Communication of Cholera*, appeared. It was the work of Dr John Snow (1813–58) who had investigated the epidemics in Wandsworth and Southwark. Dr Snow, who was chiefly interested in the new pain killers, ether and chloroform, naturally knew a good deal about inhalation and he had come to the novel conclusion that cholera was not inhaled, as so many doctors believed, but was ingested. Drinking water, contaminated by the excretions of cholera victims was, he tentatively suggested, responsible for spreading cholera. Some doctors felt Snow was right, others thought it nonsense. Snow was a bit of a crank, anyway, what with his interest in new-fangled anaesthetics, his strict vegetarianism and his near teetotalism, it was hardly surprising that he should come up with this nonsensical idea.

Seven years later, in late August 1853, the third cholera epidemic broke out and fell very heavily upon the poor districts of London. Dr Snow, who had in April of that year administered 'blessed chloroform' to the Queen, lived in Soho Square, not far from Broad Street and Gordon Square, where a few cases of cholera were first reported and then, quite suddenly, cases had multiplied with such startling rapidity that the overstrained medical services could not possibly handle them. Dr Snow, convinced that his waterborne theory was correct, managed to persuade the local guardians to remove the handle of the communal pump in Broad Street so that the inhabitants would have to go elsewhere for water. The results were little short of dramatic. Within a few days the nearby Middlesex Hospital, where thirty-three-year-old Miss Nightingale was in charge of the cholera patients, found that the stream of cholera victims had suddenly stopped. In the next year Miss Nightingale and her nurses left for Scutari, where cholera was killing as many soldiers as the enemy.

In 1855 Dr Snow completely rewrote his pamphlet and presented the world with conclusive evidence that cholera was waterborne. Even so, many still refused to believe him and regarded Snow as a reactionary, who was against clean streets and the sanitary idea, simply because he did not believe that cholera was spontaneously generated in rubbish heaps and was diffused on the air. Three years later Dr Snow died of a stroke. He was only forty-four.

It was long before the medical profession in general accepted that cholera was waterborne and although so many improvements took place in medicine, surgery and related fields, and more doctors and apothecaries than ever before were trained, there were still thousands of people who never received medical attention in their lives. For these there were, as there always had been, books on home treatment, many written by doctors.

To know at least the rudiments of first-aid is necessary, but such books went much farther than this and dealt with the treatment and cure of everything from chilblains to cholera. A popular do-it-yourself book of this kind published as late as 1853 was *The Domestic and Surgical Guide for the Nursery, the Cottage and the Bush*, a handy compendium for all *Families, Emigrants, Travellers, Village Clergymen* * *and Sea Captains.*

This death-dealing little volume was produced by Dr Jabez Hogg (1817–99) M.R.C.S., and writer of scientific articles. It might reasonably be supposed that Dr Hogg would be rather well informed on new treatments and new ideas, or at least avoid perpetuating ancient and discredited beliefs. Not a bit of it. Sandwiched between *Astringents* and *Bed Wetting* is the item *Bad Smells* where he contends that, 'privies and drains' are the 'fruitful parents of cholera' which led victims 'quickly to the grave'. This is forgivable but when he adds, 'doubtless much to the gratification of those who prate about redundant population', thus keeping alive an ancient lie, doubts arise as to Dr Hogg's soundness on scientific and medical matters in general.

Certainly he must have helped reduce the population considerably as he recommends extract of henbane, which contains a dangerous alkaloid, as of great use 'to procure quietude', 'to obviate spasm', and for 'irritations of the kidney and bladder'.[14] To do him justice he remarks, in an offhand way, that in cases of henbane poisoning the same treatment may be given as in opium poisoning. As this entailed the use of a stomach pump, it can hardly have been readily available to village clergymen, cottagers or even emigrants. Failing the pump—and more sensibly—the strongest possible emetic is advised.

In Dr Hogg's view, extract of hemlock was the superior

---

* Often the village clergyman in a remote parish was the only person who could read, thus the cure of bodies as well as of souls fell upon him.

anodyne for cancer, rheumatism and nervous afflictions. He refers to it as *Ext-conii* and if this is *conium maculatum* it would certainly, in large enough doses, ease the patient peacefully out of this world. Fortunately minor afflictions such as a black eye, boils, cuts and sprains were nothing. Scraped root of horseradish or Solomon's seal applied to the eye and well bandaged on worked wonders. A more serious eye disease was ophthalmia, so often found in babies and if not treated at once the eyes might easily ulcerate away. This presented small difficulty to Dr Hogg who, later in life, became an ophthalmic surgeon. He advised a wash made of acetic acid, proof spirit, rosewater or nitrate of silver brushed carefully into the infant's eyes with a camel's hair brush and to be used in conjunction with a purge of castor oil or calomel. Adult ophthalmia, happily, responded to a wash of Epsom salts and tartar emetic, a good purge of calomel and jalap, combined with bleeding.

If so unfortunate as to meet with an accident which removed a chunk of flesh, or even a finger or toe, the detached piece should be replaced at once and kept there with sticking plaster, easily made at home by spreading melted resin and soap on stretched silk or calico. Less expensive was pitch smeared on brown paper. 'It is well known', writes one doctor, 'that even a nose, after being nearly, or quite separated from the face has been perfectly united to it again by means of sticking plaster.'[15] A splendid source of sepsis all this sounds.

Sprains were tiresome. Rest and hot fomentations were the cure; but when inflammation set in or the joint was affected, leeches were the answer—and this as late as mid-century. Toothache could be relieved by camphor or opium, but if the tooth were decayed a plug of wool soaked in creosote or chloroform rammed into the cavity was excellent. Better still, destroy the nerve by touching it with strong nitric acid or a red-hot iron.

If troubled with corns, ivy leaves were soothing and easily obtainable. In fact, ivy leaves infused as a clyster were of great use in lockjaw and some forms (unspecified) of insanity. Diabetes, it was recognized, was due to a digestive defect which turned parts of certain foods into sugar, therefore a meat diet, plenty of castor oil and a good deal of opium, taken at night, was necessary. It is difficult to follow this line of thought.

More serious was putrid throat. It had been given a fancy new name, 'diphtheria', by a Frenchman, Pierre Brettoneau, who described it as a clearly defined disease as early as 1826. But we stuck to the old name until 1857. It was, fortunately, recognized as a highly contagious disease and was dealt with by emetics, purges and gargles. Unfortunately, death so often intervened by the seventh day that there was too little time to discover how efficacious the treatment was. Scarlet fever also reduced the population considerably and in its severe form did not differ in nature and treatment from putrid sore throat—or so we are told.

Doctors and books on home treatment were all very well provided one could afford the first or read the second. Happily, neither was an absolute necessity, for as one of the most credulous nations on earth we still dosed ourselves on patent medicines and sovereign remedies. The old quack doctors had not survived to any great extent but the quack remedy and its vendors flourished more strongly than ever. Daffy's Elixir and Dover's Powders were old favourites, invented in the seventeenth century. James's Powder was newer as it had appeared in the mid-eighteenth century. Purl, a medicinal drink made of wormwood and herbs infused in beer or strong ale had also been known for centuries and even as late as 1865 it must have been in use as Dickens mentions it in *Our Mutual Friend*. As for newer remedies, Engels tells us that even in poor districts 'quantities of patent medicines are sold for all conceivable ailments : Morrison's Pills, Parr's Life Pills, Dr Mainwaring's Pills, and a thousand other pills, essences and balsams, all of which have the property of curing all the ills the flesh is heir to'.[16]

James Morrison, who called himself 'the Hygeist', had invented his Universal Pill around 1822. Two taken at bedtime with a glass of lemonade cured everything and made Mr Morrison a fortune. The Universal Pill even restored the infirm minds of the aged, while a young man inadvertently cured himself of insanity by taking a whole box at once thereby, one would have thought, proving his insanity.

Parr's Life Pills were a great favourite for they had the remarkable power to cure both constipation and diarrhoea. Reputedly concocted from a secret recipe belonging to old Parr (d. 1635) who, it was alleged, had lived to be 152 years old, this remedy had been acquired by Herbert Ingram (1811–60) of Nottingham who had such a local success that he removed to London to advertise his pill more widely. This he did by founding *The Illustrated London News* (May 1842) and by buying other newspapers. Parr's Life Pills, due possibly to their dual action, increased the beauty of women, brightened the eye, animated the features and gave fresh vigour to the whole body.

Another famous pill was introduced by Thomas Holloway (1800–83) who went in for an enormous world-wide advertising campaign. His first venture with Holloway's Ointment and Holloway's Pill was not successful. He overspent and landed in a debtors' prison (later he paid all debts in full). The pill was a slow starter and Holloway worked feverishly for four years before it caught on. By mid-century he was making money and had invaded America. His pills were remarkable and one Australian woman testified that after twenty years of complete lassitude and inertia she was, thanks to Holloway's Pills, able to run up mountains.*

But there were other and equally popular nostrums with an all too ready sale. For example, Norris's Drops, which cured colds and fever, consisted of emetic tartar and spirits of wine mixed with a brightly-coloured vegetable dye. Indigestion mixtures containing sulphuric acid were common. Battley's Sedative, so useful in all afflictions, was loaded with opium but was said to be milder than the famous Black Drop. One Black Drop equalled three drops of laudanum. Corrosive sublimate was the active

---

* Later in the century, Holloway, a very rich man, set up a sanitorium for the mentally-handicapped at Virginia Water and endowed Holloway College, Egham, now Royal Holloway College, London University.

ingredient in many medicines which purported to cure rheumatism, diseases of the skin and scrofula. Spilbury's Anti-Scorbutic Drops, Solomon's Anti-Impetigens and Green Drops were based on this poison. Taken internally and immoderately such remedies could easily produce that sure cure for all ailments—death.

Death was such a commonplace that it seems hardly necessary to have paid for it by buying pills or potions. Distinctions between various diseases were still so ill-defined, generally, that for years typhus and typhoid were thought to be much the same and were treated by the same method. Doctors disagreed, then as now, on diagnosis and treatment.

Gout was still a great puzzle and went flying about its victim from joints to head, from head to stomach in a most disconcerting way. It could now, it seems, affect the lungs and produce asthma, which it had not been able to do in the eighteenth century. Poor Emily Eden, at bracing Broadstairs for her health writes, in 1851, that she does not improve. 'They say the last attack a fortnight ago,' she laments, 'was gout in the stomach. I trust God will spare me a recurrence of such suffering, for I am grown very cowardly; but at all events every medical precaution has now been taken, and I am not anxious as to the result though shamefully afraid of the pain.'[17] The Hon. Emily was fifty-four at the time. Despite the doctors she survived to the age of seventy-two.

Although progress had been made in medicine it took a very long time before new discoveries and new treatments seeped down from the top and were received and accepted by most physicians. The art or science of diagnosis as reconstructed by Marshall Hall was still in its infancy. Old methods, old treatments were still in general use. If it seems extraordinary that about one-third of the male population was carried off by fever until well after midcentury, it is less extraordinary when we remember that fevers were generally lumped together under the name 'typhus'.

Typhus fever was the name given to hospital, gaol and gastric fevers as well as to waterborne typhoid and flea-transmitted typhus. Although typhoid had been classified separately early on,

some say by William Jenner (1815–98)* it, like typhus, was a
killer of the day. Queen Victoria had had typhoid when a girl and
had escaped with her life, though not with her hair. But was
she subject to the treatment which, with minor variations, seems
to have been usual until at least 1853?

A mild form was considered to be a low nervous fever. The
more deadly form is what we call typhoid. In either case the
first thing to do was give the patient a good draught of emetic
tartar and ipecacuanha mixed in salt water. This, not surprisingly, unloaded the stomach and for some reason relaxed the
skin. If, after several doses, no improvement was noted, a mild
aperient was given. It was usually a mixture of Epsom and
Glauber's salts plus tincture of senna dissolved in antimonial wine,
which hardly sounds mild. Also during the early days the fevered
one should be stood in a tub and have 'two or three gallons of
cold water thrown briskly over him from head downwards'.[18] All
these simple things could be accomplished at home by the lay-
man but when such measures failed to alleviate the condition then
a doctor or apothecary, if available, should be brought in to
bleed the patient either with lancet or leech.

When debility set in—the treatment thus far seems sufficient
to have caused this state even in the healthy—a tonic of muriatic
(hydrochloric) acid was advised and if combined with 'the bark'
(chincona) was even more useful. Severe debility called for a little
Port or Madeira, such wines were essential when small spots
appeared or gangrene set in. As the disease advanced—and one
does not much care for the idea of gangrene—James's Powder
combined with opium usually helped. Just what it helped other
than pain is not easy to say. Many experienced doctors still advocated pills made of spiders' webs for fevers—they were excellent
for controlling delirium and restlessness (both are characteristic of
typhoid)—yet 'should the patient sink in the advanced stage unexpectedly and suddenly, give wine or even brandy and ammonia'.[19] One might think that after all this there would be

* Created baronet 1868 and not to be confused with Edward Jenner (1749–
1823), the discoverer of vaccination.

nothing left to do but call in the undertaker and order mourning for the relatives. But no. If the patient were not dead by the twenty-first day, recovery was assured, though relapses might be frequent.

Small wonder that Arthur Hugh Clough, the poet, who married Florence Nightingale's cousin, and who was one of Miss Nightingale's devoted workers, should have written as the sixth commandment of *The Latest Decalogue* :

> Thou shalt not kill, but need'st not strive
> Officiously to keep alive.

It was probably better to die quietly without fuss and bother as he did of a stroke in Florence in 1861, for no amount of officiousness by royal physicians could save his exact contemporary the Prince Consort. He too died in 1861, of a 'gastric' fever.

CHAPTER SIX

Recreations

On July 6th 1846 the Rev. Archer Clive and Mrs Clive of the Rectory, Solihull, gave a small evening concert, of local talent, to entertain some guests. It was not a success. Mrs Clive (1801–73), a straightforward woman who wrote indifferent poetry and successful novels, does not deceive herself on this point. With some bitterness she notes in her diary, 'I believe the Solihullians were awed by the presence of strangers, for they were as dull as November. There was too much bad music to-night. A little is all very well, but tonight it was the staple. The wretched Iringhams and Edwards brought their young children, to do them good as they said, not thinking of the harm to us. The Crowthers played something wrong all through the first bar, and then got up a horrid glee for two pianoforte players, one harp and four voices, which was truly dreadful for discord. I sang, as badly as usual, and Archer, who had sung a *cachucha* half a dozen times extremely well, set off on the wrong note and kept steadily wrong all the way.'[1] Small wonder that the guests sat listening in a stiff row, looking 'alarmed and alarming'.

The musical evening was not new to the Victorians but it had become very fashionable indeed and there were now many more of such home entertainments. How far the Queen and Prince Albert set this fashion is difficult to say. Both were musical, the Prince intelligently so. They gave evening concerts at Buckingham Palace and Windsor Castle where, as early as 1840, the Prince completely reorganized the Queen's Private Band, which had consisted then entirely of wind instruments, into a good string orchestra. Famous musicians performed at the royal musical evenings; among them was Mendelssohn, who had a very high opinion of the Prince's musical ability.

A year before the Clives' fatal evening, in May 1847, Sir John Cam Hobhouse (later Lord Broughton de Gyfford; 1786–1869) and his daughter went to a concert at Buckingham Palace: 'I heard Mario, Grisi and Tamburini sing,' he says, which was rather better than hearing the Crowthers or the Clives, but he got into trouble for, 'Lord Ripon talked a good deal with me on Board of Control business until General Bowlby came up and said, "If you please, the Queen wishes you not to talk" '.[2]

Since this was a musical evening and not a *conversazione*—also popular and usually excessively boring—Sir John and Lord Rippon had earned the rebuke, more particularly as the artists were among the best known of the day. Perhaps it was Lord Rippon's fault, as Sir John was fond of music and expressed disappointment that Jenny Lind (1820–87), although asked to come, had begged to be excused since she was due to make her English début next evening at the 'Opera House' and was, she explained, 'extremely nervous'.

But he did hear Jenny Lind on May 25th in Bellini's *La Sonnambula* and was so charmed with her singing and acting that he quite forgot her plainness. He thought her low notes best. The House was crammed to the doors and he sat in a box next to the Royal Box which held, among others, the Queen and the Queen Dowager, who had only one more year to live. The Queen heard Jenny Lind again in June. 'Tonight we are going to the Opera in state', she writes, 'and will hear and see Jenny Lind (who is perfection) in *Norma*, which is considered one of her best parts. Poor Grisi is quite going off, and after the pure angelic voice and extremely quiet, perfect acting of J. Lind, she seems quite *passée*. Poor thing! she is *quite* furious about it, and was excessively impertinent to J. Lind.'[3]

Jenny Lind and other artists of her calibre did not confine themselves to the capital. Indeed, Miss Lind in that same year appeared in opera at Liverpool and Manchester. She also gave concerts in many provincial cities where she was rapturously received. Music was, as it had always been, one of our greatest pleasures. Most cities, towns and even villages had a glee club, a village band or a music society of one sort or another, while the church orchestra, where it still existed in the country, came in handy for more things than playing hymns.

By 1857, ever-growing and very rich, Manchester rivalled London's famous Philharmonic Society, founded in 1813, when Charles Hallé, the German-born pianist and conductor, began to conduct the Gentlemen's Concerts there in 1853. Four years later he started the famous Hallé concerts.

But this love of music was not confined to concertgoers, nor to professionals. There were thousands who could never hope to get near a big concert, or near the great musicians of the day, and these thousands simply took pleasure in playing an instrument or singing at home. It helped pass the long winter evenings. Much of this home-made music must have been decidedly painful, but it provided recreation and amusement for the performers, if not for the listeners. The piano was the favourite instrument and, curiously enough, this symbol of respectability had first become more popular in England than in any other country. Every young lady with any pretensions to being a lady was supposed to know how to play on the pianoforte—though some preferred the angelic harp. Music, if nothing else, was taught at the generally inefficient educational establishments for girls. Every governess was supposed to have a sufficient knowledge of music to teach. But now, for those condemned to long hours of practising in cold rooms and tortured with chilblained fingers, another form of torture had been created by Muzio Clementi (1752–1832), that anglicized Italian composer, performer, music publisher and manufacturer of pianos, who had died at Evesham in reform year but not before he had produced those one hundred indispensable piano studies *Gradus ad Parnassum*. Clementi had developed technique enormously to suit the newer type of pianos. But what girl wanted to slog up Parnassus anyway? Yet if one escaped Clementi, there was his pupil J. B. Cramer (1771–1858) and his

Pianoforte harmonium, 1850–60

pianoforte studies to be reckoned with. Cramer, too, published music and had started his own business in London in 1824. One's music came from him or from Novello & Co. who had been in existence since 1811, or from Chappells, founded in 1812. Many teachers also now favoured a relatively new aid to music, the metronome, which kept the performer to an implacably strict tempo and, in many instances by so doing, turned a living piece of music into a dead one. These things, new to the nineteenth century, were wearisome to the average learner. All that was needed was to play charmingly (and not fumble) the simpler pieces and songs better known to all. Some of the less difficult sonatas by papa Haydn and a few harpsichord pieces by Handel, now transposed for the pianoforte and sounding so much richer and fuller for the transformation—as indeed did all harpsichord or klavichord music. Handel, who was considered British, and Haydn were still great favourites and they had been with us for so long that everyone knew their work.

Unfortunately, there now seemed to be a woeful lack of British composers and in the first half of the nineteenth century what few there were went to the continent to live and work, like the expatriate Irishman, John Field (1782–1837), a pupil of Clementi whose nocturnes for piano are said to have inspired Chopin. But if English composers and musicians fled to the continent, continental composers and musicians came frequently to England. The drawing power of a foreign name was very great. But it was the well-known English pianist, Lucy Anderson (1797–1878), Queen Victoria's teacher, (she played at major concerts from 1818 on), who introduced many of Beethoven's and Hummell's works into England. So that those who were really good at the keyboard braved a Beethoven sonata or two and some of his easier piano pieces. Then there was J. C. Bach—long dead and perhaps a little old-fashioned, dry and unromantic (music too had become a part of the romantic movement) but anything old-fashioned or dry could be offset by a fiery *tarantella*—by the Hungarian, Stephen Heller (1815–88) so electrifying that it was guaranteed to waken any listener who had dropped off for a second.

Heller's music was new. So were many of the piano works composed by Robert Schumann. Schumann and the English musician, William Sterndale Bennett (1816–75) were great friends. In 1854 Sir William Sterndale Bennett gave the first performance in England of Bach's *St Matthew's Passion* and this began the movement for the performance of Bach's choral music in this country. There were also other new composers too whose work was known in England. Chopin, who gave concerts in Manchester, Glasgow, Edinburgh and London in 1848, Mendelssohn, a friend of the Queen and Prince Albert, paid ten visits to England. He conducted the Birmingham Festival in 1837 and 1846 and his oratorio, *St Paul*, in Liverpool as early as 1836. He had written the wonderful *Fingal's Cave* and also his *Scottish Symphony* which he dedicated to the Queen, while his *Songs Without Words* sounded very well on the piano. There was also Ferencz Liszt who never stopped writing piano music, but the music of this virtuoso performer, who visited England in 1824–5 and again in 1840–1, was nearly impossible for an amateur to play—besides, there were now rumours about his morals. Berlioz (1803–69) came in 1851 and Wagner (1813–83) in 1855, both as conductors—and very disagreeable Wagner was too. But the Queen and Prince Albert went to hear the overture to *Tannhäuser*—so dreadfully modern—and liked it so well they went to hear it a second time. In 1856 Clara Schumann (1819–96) appeared in recital, followed the next year by Anton Rubinstein (1829–94). And in May 1861 Adelina Patti (1843–1919) made her début at Covent Garden, also as Amina in Bellini's *La Sonnambula*.

The chief difficulty in knowing about new composers and their works was that only if the works were publicly performed, could they be heard, and then solely by those who attended the performance. The thousands who did not were caught in a backwater and had to wait until some talented concert-goer, friend or relative, came for an evening or on a longer visit and picked out themes on the piano or even brought the printed new music along to be tried over, sometimes to be ordered, or often copied for home use.

Such difficulties did not exist if one were rich enough. In the big aristocratic houses in London, musical evenings were quite different and were rarely home-made. There, the great musicians of the day were hired to come and perform for guests—and were often treated as hirelings. They were frequently made to use the service entrance and when they got upstairs to the drawing-room found themselves cut off from the guests by a cord, doubtless a splendidly ornate one, stretched across the end of the room. In London, too, the Philharmonic Society (not then Royal) gave eight concerts a season in the Hanover Square Rooms, which it shared with the Society for Antient Concerts. A season's ticket cost four guineas, a single ticket, one. These concerts were very fashionable. The orchestra was huge—about seventy members. Its playing was vigorous—and rather ragged. Less fashionable and less expensive were concerts, mainly of Handel's music by the Sacred Harmonic Society, given in the Exeter Hall. These concerts were always enormously successful.

But music at home for the majority of those who indulged in it meant far more than piano solos or duets. The piano was a necessity as the accompanying instrument for singers (or for the occasional gentleman who still played the flute). The old songs like 'Where e'er You Walk' and 'Drink to me only with thine eyes', reputedly set by Henry Harington (1727–1816) whose glees, rounds and catches were a delight, were still favourites. The ballad-operas of Dr Thomas Arne (1710–78), *Love in a Village*, *Thomas and Sally* and others, contained countless singable songs. Samuel Arnold (1740–1802) provided *The Maid of the Mill*, a top favourite, though he turned out dozens of other ballad-operas. William Shield (1748–1829) had an enormous success with *No Song No Supper*, while 'Tom Bowling', from *The Oddities* by Charles Dibdin (1745–1814), is still sung. And who could resist 'Home Sweet Home' by the versatile Henry Bishop (1786–1855) who wrote so much music for the stage and almost specialized in musical settings for stage versions of Sir Walter Scott's novels?

A young man who was to become a novelist also, inadvertently, contributed to home music. This was twenty-four-year-old Charles Dickens (1812–70) who wrote the libretto for a one-act affair in collaboration with his young friend John Hullah (1812–84).* The

* Hullah and Dickens's sister, Fanny, had studied together at the Academy of Music.

piece was called *The Village Coquettes*, performed at the St James's Theatre in 1836, and was intended as a burlesque on the ballad-opera. Alas, the burlesque on sentimentality was too clever for the audience which took it seriously and wept copiously at 'The Ivy Clinging to the Wall'.

But there were other songs, some two thousand, written by James Cooke (1746–1827), to say nothing of the airs from the modern ballad-opera by Michael Balfe (1808–70), *The Bohemian Girl*. It was produced at Drury Lane in 1843 and its wan songs, 'When Other Lips' and 'I Dreamt that I Dwelt in Marble Halls' were considered irresistible. They were sung everywhere with great feeling. The songs of Tom Moore (1779–1852) were also favourites : 'The Last Rose of Summer', which von Flotow liked so well he used it in his 'English' opera *Martha*; and 'The Harp that Once through Tara's Halls', 'The Minstrel Boy' and, most curiously, 'The Canadian Boat Song'* were favourites too. No one could sing like Tom and bring tears to the eyes of the most hardened dowager—but many tried. Moore usually set new words to old tunes.

Then there were glees, which, despite Mrs Clive's unfortunate experience, were enormously popular. Although the glee is a very old type of song (a debased form of the madrigal), not all composers of glees were dead, like the recently defunct Thomas Attwood (1765–1838) who had composed the coronation anthems for both George IV and William IV, but died in the middle of composing the one meant for Queen Victoria. Attwood, a prolific writer of glees, had also been a founder member of the Philharmonic Society. Charles E. Horsley (1822–76), a pupil of Mendelssohn, went on composing a variety of things, including glees, until his death in New York in 1876. While his father (b. 1774), also a founder of the Philharmonic Society, went gleefully on until 1858. He also composed many popular hymns as well as oratorios and anthems. John Callcott (1766–1821), that inspired

* There are two of these. Moore's words are set to an old melody, probably French, which was sung by the *voyageurs*. The second, 'The Lone Shieling', is not a boat song and is barely Canadian.

son of a bricklayer, was certainly no longer making music in this world—but he lived on in many a home for he had had a passion for writing glees and catches.

Glees were popular because more people could participate at once. A glee required at least three male voices (a female voice could be substituted) with musical instruments added, if desired. They were usually cheerful, not to say rollicking, good-tempered music which provided an excellent contrast to the over-sentimental songs which were now in vogue.

If we were low on native composers of note—and they are very scarce after the death of Purcell in 1695—one type of musical composition developed which seems to be peculiarly and typically British in origin—the sea chanty. Sea chanties were working songs. They were not published, they simply grew up in the eighteenth century and the first half of the nineteenth. The words differed from ship to ship, and the words are inferior to the music, but the music remained the same and no one knows how this music originated. Life at sea, in the navy or on the great sailing ships of the East India Company, which lasted for months, sometimes years, produced its own typical folk music. There was usually a chanty man aboard every ship who sang the solo part, the sailors coming in on the chorus. These songs, as working songs, were divided into working categories and the categories bore names such as halyards, capstans and so on. But when steam finally ousted sail, the chanties died and there is no record, as yet, of any being produced later than 1870.

Sea chanties were sung ashore in seaport taverns but whether they ever reached middle-class homes one does not know. Those in which a son had made a long sea voyage, or had entered the navy, may have heard them when the wanderer returned, but doubtless the words were carefully bowdlerized. One could hardly ask the question as to the disposition of the drunken sailor or agree that whisky is the life of man, in the drawing-room and before young ladies. Such songs were better sung in the stables or in a tavern, if at all.

An evening at home with a few friends, particularly if there were young people present and the drawing-room were large enough, very often included dancing. Then some sad young lady, plainer than the others, had the cold consolation of being in demand—at the piano. Or, possibly, an obliging and chaperoning aunt or a governess, who did not dance because she was not permitted to, would provide the music. Dancing at home, in assembly rooms, in taverns, on the village green, at places of amusement, such as Vauxhall and Cremorne Gardens, and at the royal residences, was very popular. 'Went to an evening party at the palace—a family dance. H.M. dances a great deal', Hobhouse notes laconically May 11th 1849. And all who saw her agreed that the Queen danced beautifully—it was one of the things she took great pleasure in. As part of the coronation festivities, Johann Strauss the elder (1804–49) had come to England bringing with him the graceful new Viennese waltz—a great improvement on the earlier German version. Albert waltzed most beautifully, his wife thought.

But there were plenty of other dances to amuse one. The galop, introduced in 1829, was popular, so was the old Sir Roger de Coverley. The newer 'square' dances were, however, more interesting; that is, dances made up of sets of eight dancers or four couples the set. A new one of this type was the Lancers, first danced in Paris in 1836 and very like the Quadrille, but the Lancers held first place in the hearts of the English until around 1840 when, quite suddenly, everyone took to the Polka. This dance was said to have been invented by a Bohemian peasant girl *c.* 1830, and had swept Europe like an epidemic. It became a mania among rich and poor alike and was danced from public house to palace and even in the streets. It is a very lively, simple dance and this may have accounted for its popularity.

It was certainly popular with the labouring classes too. They, for the most part, loved dancing and music. Although they had not room enough to dance in the rabbit warrens in which they lived, and the weather is rarely conducive to dancing in the streets, many a tavern or beer shop had a room for dancing and there were various halls—not all of such incredible squalor as the infamous Enon Chapel in Clements' Lane*—where 'two-penny hops' were regularly held. These were well attended by both sexes between the ages of fourteen and forty-five. In addition to the polka—with local variations—favourite dances were jigs, hornpipes, flash-jigs, country dances and intricate solo dances where the dancer had to keep moving at speed, yet delicately place the toe of his heavy boot into the interstices made by a dozen or more clay pipes arranged in a pattern on the floor, without breaking a pipe. Vigorous dances were best liked and the waltz was unknown, or if known was either not liked or not danced. Known, and rather disapproved of by the men at any rate, was the way in which fashionable women dressed for dances. As one costermonger put it: 'The women doesn't show their necks as I've seen the ladies do in them there pictures of high-life in shop-windows, or on the stage. Their Sunday gowns, which is their dancing-gowns, ain't made that way.'[4]

Twopenny hops were a great source of recreation and were held once or twice a week. Beginning at half-past eight, they went on until midnight or sometimes one or two o'clock in the morning. Rather a lot of drinking took place, particularly among the younger folk because they liked to get their girls drunk, a habit not altogether approved of by some of the older generation. Music was provided, invariably, by a fiddle, occasionally augmented by a harp or a cornopean. This last instrument sounds both astonishing and useless, but it was not an eight-foot reed organ stop; cornopean is merely an old name for the *cornet à pistons*.

In summer there was some outdoor dancing for the 'lower middling' sort, but it bore no resemblance to a twopenny hop. When Nathaniel Hawthorne took his son Julien to the park at Birkenhead, he noted, among other things, 'polka-ing (girls with

* Registered for below-floor burials 1823–42. More than 1,200 buried there. Closed 1842. Bought by a speculator and turned into a dance hall. Advertised as 'Enon Chapel—Dancing on the Dead. Admission threepence. No lady or gentleman admitted unless wearing shoes and stockings.' Bought 1848 by a philanthropic surgeon who had all bodies removed to Norwood Cemetery.

girls) to the music of a hand-organ';[5] but all there was to drink was ginger-beer and British wines. One is a trifle alarmed at the idea of British wines. They were notoriously poor stuff though, probably, by this time the act against adulterating food and drink with poisonous and other materials had made them harmless enough.

The ubiquitous hand-organ* was usually played by Italians who haunted the streets of most large cities, but this was by no means the only street music. Vagabond fiddlers and men playing the fife were plentiful. Even more numerous were ballad singers who roamed the main drags† trying to pick up a penny or two in the richer quarters of cities and towns. Their efforts were not much appreciated. 'The ballad singers are the strangest from the total lack of any kind of music in their cracked voices', Hawthorne notes, June 12th 1854, of ballad singers in Liverpool. There is no reason to believe that cracked voices were exclusive to Liverpool.

Nevertheless, the ballad was at the height of its popularity. Some 700 publishers made a fair to good living out of printing ballad-broadsides. These, usually sold in the streets, were printed on one side of a single sheet of paper only. Some, printed on extra-large paper 'three songs wide' were, in summer, hung from a pole while the seller hawked his wares crying 'Three yards a penny. Songs, songs, songs. Beautiful songs. Newest songs. Popular songs!' There was a ready sale to 'professional' singers and ordinary people or, at least, to those who could read. Those who could, read the ballad to those who could not, so it was memorized and the tune easily picked up from hearing a ballad singer. The ballad had something for everyone since in England (although not on the continent), ballad was an elastic term, musically, and covered various types of song; the old song, or rather the words set to a popular tune, the folk song, the narrative song. It did not, strictly speaking, include the comic or patriotic song.

---

* Hand-organs were sometimes used in small churches which could not afford a real organ and had no orchestra.   †'Drag' was a cockney word for 'street'.

Patriotic songs were very popular and 'Rule Britannia' was a winner, although sometimes the last line was sung 'Britons always shall be slaves'. A further favourite was the Marseillaise (translated), while as late as 1851 the narrative song, 'The Death of Nelson' with its repeating refrain 'Mourn England, mourn, mourn and complain/For the loss of Lord Nelson who died on the main,' was being sung with fervour and feeling although Nelson had been dead for nearly half a century. Rather jollier and quite untinged by patriotism were songs like 'Buffalo Girls Come Out Tonight', 'The Gay Cavalier', 'Jim along Josey', 'There's a Good Time Coming'—which there probably was not—while 'Drink to me only' and 'I Dreamt I Dwelt in Marble Halls' had leaped class barriers and were sung both high and low.

Comic songs were great favourites; some of them now seem to have totally meaningless names. The Victorians of all classes often, and most endearingly, had a taste for nonsense and the titles of some songs may be purely nonsensical. There is 'Chucka-roo-choo-choo-choot-la' which may be nonsense, but also may be an onomatopoeic title, if one thinks of railway trains. However, 'Chokale-roony-ninka-ping-nang' and 'Paga-daway-dusty-kanty-key' do not sound imitative of anything at all. 'Hotty-pie, gunny-pie, China-coo' was alleged to be a Chinese song, which appears most unlikely. More intelligible were 'The Standard Bearer', 'Just Like Love', 'Oh that Kiss', 'I've been Roaming', 'The Policeman'—and policemen, or peelers, were loathed, so the song was immensely popular. There were also parodies and these were also most popular. Several were written on 'The Fine Old English Gentleman', one which dealt sarcastically with the Tories, was composed by Charles Dickens in 1841. A slightly earlier parody 'A Fine Young German Gentleman' dealt with Prince Albert. Songs relating the adventures of Jim Crow were popular during the late thirties and early forties but by mid-century were all but forgotten.

Old favourites such as 'Barbara Allen', 'Cherry Ripe', 'Charley is My Darlin' ', 'Sally in our Alley' were the mainstay of a street singer's repertoire. But new ballads, comic or sad songs, were produced to commemorate important or sensational events, marriages, epidemics, social disturbances or social wrongs; murders, hangings, cabinet ministers. Such songs, encapsuling news in verse and music, were eagerly snapped up by street singers and just as eagerly listened to, for they were a kind of tuneful tabloid of the times for those who could not read.

At the time of the Queen's marriage countless ballads, not always complimentary, were written on the subject. One, to the tune of 'Dusty Miller', began—

> Here I am in rags
> From the land of all Dirt
> To marry England's Queen
> And my name is Prince Albert.

Here the scansion is as bad as the sentiment, but as a general rule this is not so. There were ballads about Jenny Lind, and a new one was written for each new Lord Mayor of London. Hood's 'The Song of a Shirt' was both popular and influential. In 1849 came an elegy, 'On the Death of Queen Adelaide'. This was certainly well known in the shabbiest and most wretched corners of London, for the Queen Dowager had been greatly loved by the poor and the elegy makes this point, 'The friend of the Poor is no more', runs one line.

New words, as we know, were sung to old tunes and the stirring 'The Campbells are Coming' lent itself splendidly both to the bitter 'The Cholera's Coming, oh dear, oh dear', and to the mock-fearful 'The Pope He's a-Coming, Oh! crikey, Oh! dear', which was directed against Cardinal Wiseman.

As for musical evenings at home with friends, it is not easy to hold a musical soirée in a slum room and it is improbable the labouring classes did so. But at least the occupier of the room could sing—if he or she felt like it. For example, an elderly dustie—that is, a man who sifted through the great dust heaps for a contractor and earned half a bull* a day—when asked what he liked best as a recreation in the evening made no mention of twopenny hops or beer-rooms, but answered: 'Vot does

* Half a crown, a good wage for the time.

I care for reading, or anythink of that there kind, ven I gets home arter my work? I tell you vot I likes though! Vy I just likes two or three pipes of baccer; a pot or two of good heavy and a song, and then I tumbles in with my Sall, and I'm as happy as [a] here and there von.'[6]

Sall probably sang while dustie smoked and drank. She was a 'stunner' and also earned half a bull a day, but as she was a 'beggar for lush' that half a bull may have been considerably reduced. Sall and dustie were not married but as he sensibly if ungrammatically put it, 'I sticks to Sall and Sall sticks to I, and there's an end on't—vot is it to anyone?'[7] What indeed! To the early Victorians it was thoroughly immoral and helped explain why the poor were poor—they deserved to be (one differentiated between the deserving and undeserving poor). And it was said, on good authority, that in some of the poorer areas of London only one-tenth of couples living together were married, most could not afford the parson's fee, Mayhew says, and so lived in open concubinage.

Rich men and those of the upper classes—and to the poor, wealth automatically meant upper class or aristocracy—when and if they lived in concubinage—did not do so openly. Married or single, if they kept a woman it was all very private. Open concubinage, as such, had passed with the more raffish side of the eighteenth and early nineteenth centuries and the end product of the new respectability was summed up by the eleventh commandment. The kept woman, Hippolyte Taine tells us, was kept well hidden. Mistresses were usually installed in homes outside central London and visited by their lovers at weekends. Further, the Englishman wanted his mistress to provide a real home for him—not unlike the one he already had. He wanted nothing lively, or gay, or in the least outré, and his light of love must be shy and modest. If not a lady she must learn to behave like one, save in bed. All this sounds more like bigamy than concubinage and deadly dull, too. Small wonder that Hawthorne once commented, 'The English do not appear to have a turn for amusing themselves.'[8]

Although London, in particular, was renowned for its number of prostitutes,* it was not distinguished for its number of courtesans. There were very few women of intelligence and beauty who dressed exquisitely, drove a carriage, held a salon and whose business it was to live, in state, off rich lovers and to be amusing, witty, interesting. To provide good food, wine and sexual as well as intellectual satisfaction. In this, thank heaven, we were unlike the French.

There were, however, innumerable houses of accommodation from the lowest brothels or punch houses, crammed from attic to cellar with gin-sodden prostitutes working on their own, to far more discreet and elegant establishments run by 'madames' who provided hand-picked young ladies and children to suit every taste, whim and aberration. Between these extremes were places like the Argyle Rooms which Taine calls 'lust-casinos', and he found them infinitely depressing. 'The spectacle of debauchery in this country', he says, 'leaves one with a feeling of degradation and misery.' There was, he found, nothing bright, gay or smart about the Argyle Rooms, as in France. Men who looked like prosperous tradesmen, shopkeepers, managers of businesses, middle-class industrialists, sat about glumly and when they wanted to dance were provided with a woman by an 'usher'. Even the dancing was dismal. The couple never spoke, although : 'These poor girls are often beautiful . . . they all dance correctly . . . they are décolletées but, when dancing, keep their capes on.'⁹

The men were well off, visited the rooms for relaxation from their work and liked the 'vulgar display, coloured glass, women in full evening dress'. They paid twelve shillings a bottle for champagne and a full evening cost around six pounds, yet, 'the man and woman both drink—they can do nothing until they are drunk. . . . One comes away . . . with a deep and bitter impression of the helplessness and coarseness of humanity.'¹⁰

---

* In mid-century 10,000 is given as the nucleus, but this is guesswork since no one put down 'prostitution' as a profession on a census form. Taine puts the number at 50,000, but this is merely observation.

Fortunately there were other and less joyless pleasures available to most people. Exhibitions, menageries, panoramas, magic lantern shows, waxworks, fireworks, books, pictures, outdoor sports, indoor games, gambling, the Derby, hangings, the theatre, fairs —all these and many other things provided recreation and entertainment.

The first special fair of the Queen's reign—as opposed to the usual annual fairs held in London and elsewhere—was held in Hyde Park to celebrate her coronation, while smaller fairs, feasts, festivities and illuminations following a church service were held all over the country to mark that day. But the fair in Hyde Park lasting nine days, was the biggest ever seen in England, and attracted thousands. With its tents great and small laid out in rows to form alleys between, each tent decorated with flags, bunting, patriotic slogans and brightly-painted signs announcing the innumerable attractions; with its costumed 'patterers', gilded and painted roundabouts, booths selling hot mutton-pies, sweets and gingerbread, it looked like a strange, enchanted pleasure ground which had sprung up suddenly within the sober confines of Hyde Park.

The best-known names in the fair world had come with their various attractions; animals, acrobats, jugglers, equestrian shows, theatrical groups, tumblers and bogus Red Indians. All the big showmen had taken large areas for their spectacular shows (spectacles always drew the crowd). In between, the smaller showmen had their tents and booths to exhibit a freak, a curiosity, a puppet or a peep show like that of James Sanger. His peep show could accommodate a number of people at once and each spectator stood with an eye glued to a glass set into a large box. Within could be seen in great detail the death bed, lying-in-state and funeral of King William IV, all in brilliant colour with the painted scenes moved by invisible strings. James Sanger's son, 'Lord' George (1825–1911) was not on hand the first few days as he wanted to learn juggling and had joined a pseudo-American juggler, Malibar. Malibar, an Irishman, was given to drink which had a most unsteadying effect upon him. Catastrophe ensued and thirteen-years-old George returned to his father as patterer. He was a very good patterer and they did a roaring trade with 'Britain's Sailor King'.

The Victorians had in them a streak of morbidity. Morbidity and a love of the macabre, like melancholy, were all part of the Englishness of the English; characteristics which foreigners had noted with such surprise for centuries. True to tradition they also loved to look at freaks and the great fair provided freaks aplenty. Innumerable fat men vied with enormously overweight women for the heavyweight championships and were contrasted with living skeletons. There were strangely spotted boys and a brace of Hottentot Venuses. Miss Scott, with her two heads, was there, so were the Misses Cockayne, twin American giantesses. Undoubtedly they were very tall, strapping girls but they were neither American nor twins. Madame Stevens, 'the Pig-Faced Lady', was still a great draw even after eighteen years of travelling with fairs but, by now, some were a trifle suspicious that she was not what she seemed. They were right. Madame Stevens was a bear. With face, arms and paws closely shaved (a bear has a white skin), dressed and wearing a bonnet and gloves with padded fingers, she was invisibly strapped to a chair. With a draped table set before her and in a half light she looked very pig-faced indeed. This was her last year of deception and misery as the authorities stopped the fraud in 1839.

Menageries were always firm favourites. Crowds gawped at performing horses, mind-reading dogs, and loved to see wild and dangerous beasts. It was a pity the young Queen could not have seen them. But if she missed those in Hyde Park in June 1838, she made up for it in the following year when, during the Christmas season, she went off to Drury Lane to see a pantomime, a farce and van Amburg with his lions. Further, she insisted on going backstage to see the lions fed,* 'and has com-

---

* In 1839 the Queen commissioned Sir Edwin Landseer to paint Isaac van Amburg with his animals. The painting, now in The Queen's Collection, shows van Amberg gracefully reclining in a cage with five big cats and a lamb.

manded another performance for Tuesday. This is childish, nothing more,'[11] Sir John Cam Hobhouse comments a trifle sourly.

A year later as part of the festivities attendant on her marriage, the Queen and Prince Albert frequently visited the theatre and six special performances were put on at Covent Garden. But as a whole polite society no longer went to the theatre unless it were to see opera or ballet. Nor did the sober and godly, polite or otherwise, who had been over-influenced by evangelical opinion. Fast, rich young men went, as did those who were unaware or did not care that it was not considered respectable, either morally or socially, to do so, and there were many of these. Audiences also contained a good admixture of toughs, prostitutes and bullies with their bit of muslin. These were prepared at any time to kick up a row, as they had every single night for three solid months in 1809 at Covent Garden when the management had put up the price of admission. Then not one word of any performance had been heard. These well-remembered 'O.P. riots' (Old Price) plus further rioting, drove polite society away from the theatre and it stayed away. This does not make for healthy drama, and the theatre sank to its lowest depths and remained there until mid-century.

By now there were a number of theatres in central London and in the newer, outlying districts, but the two oldest theatres, Covent Garden and Drury Lane, were the only patent or monopoly theatres; that is, they alone had the right to present legitimate drama and they retained this right until the Theatre Regulation Act of 1843. Small good it did them. Few wanted legitimate drama, so they were forced to present all sorts of concoctions to stay alive. Even so, their history is one of successive bankruptcies and in 1843 Covent Garden (it became the Opera House in 1847) was used as a temporary hall for Anti-Corn Law meetings. All the theatres, bar the patent ones, were 'minor' theatres; among them were the Adelphi, the Queen's (formerly King's), the Haymarket—long the traditional house of opera and ballet—the Little Theatre, Haymarket; the Strand, St James's, the Lyceum, the Princess's, all in central London. Astley's, famous for its equestrian shows, had installed a stage and produced an addition, the Olympic. On the Surrey side of the Thames were the Surrey and the Coburg, so named in 1816 in honour of Princess Charlotte's marriage but from 1833, when it was fairly certain to whom the crown would go, rechristened the Royal Victoria—familiarly 'the Vic'—known to us today as the Old Vic. All these and others like them had to compete with the monopoly theatres without infringing their patents which meant managers had to exercise a good deal of ingenuity to provide theatrical entertainment. They put on farces, melodramas, operettas, trained horse and dog acts, harlequinades, extravaganzas, rope dancers, bits of Shakespeare turned comic and livened up with music (all types of audience could be relied upon to recognize Shakespeare, travestied or not) and burlettas. A burletta is not easily defined but it seems, originally, to have been a one-act piece, with five or six songs which had to be an integral part of the piece, and not just interpolations. By around 1830 fifteen songs were held to be good enough to turn a three-acter into a burletta and by 1840 an occasional daredevil chord on the piano crept in.

To capture and hold audiences, who must have had stamina and powers of endurance above the ordinary, no theatrical production consisted of just one work—not even at the patent houses. There might be a three-act burletta, followed by a farce and preceded by a dancer or a singer. Performances usually began at six and lasted three or four hours; at eight admission was dropped to half price. Then too the more spectacular the production the better. Here the theatre at Sadler's Wells pleasure gardens scored. It was near the New river and could feature splendid water spectacles, with real enough ships and splendidly noisy sea-battles.

Other theatres, unable to draw on a cheap natural resource for exciting effects, resorted to a multiplicity of trap doors and elaborate stage machinery as well as lavish scenery to achieve spectacular results which dazzled the eye. The Victorian theatre, much larger than the Georgian theatre, had the box stage instead of the apron stage, and this framed by the proscenium arch and gas lighting brought new and startling effects. As the space above the stage was greater, further theatrical effects could be achieved by having goblins, fairies, and other creatures floating about on wires. When Charles Kean (1811?–68) produced *Henry VIII* at the Princess's in 1855, Catherine of Aragon's death scene was attended by angels overhead. One in particular attracted attention by her beautifully ethereal look. The look, however, was due to the small angel being swayed about on a wire which made her feel very sick indeed. This pallid, heavenly child was Ellen Terry (1847–1928).

Charles Kean and Charles Kemble (1775–1854) were both sticklers for accuracy of detail and costume in historical plays, and poor Kean must have been very vexed when, in *The Winter's Tale*, his wife, Ellen Tree (1805–80), insisted on billowing out Hermione's flowing, classical dress by wearing a crinoline underneath. But it was notoriously difficult to get actresses to appear in historical costume; they wanted to look fashionable on stage as well as off. To appear in a dreary, straight and shapeless classical garment must have seemed to Mrs Kean like appearing in a nightdress—and a not very suitable one at that.

Nevertheless both the Keans were devoted to the nearly hopeless task of trying to raise the standards of the theatre. They restored *Love's Labour Lost* to the stage after an absence of two centuries. They used Shakespeare's own ending to *Romeo and Juliet*, rather than the happy ending which had been fudged up by David Garrick.

In 1850 Kean became manager of the Princess's and opened with *Twelfth Night*. In 1852 he had an enormous success with *The Corsican Brothers*, a play adapted by Dion Boucicault from a story by Dumas *père*. This was, politely, romantic drama which merely meant it was melodrama for polite society. Polite society went to see it. In fact the Politest of all, the Queen, went. This shocked and horrified a number of people. Worse, Her Majesty liked the play. Further, and equally shocking to many, plays were often given at Windsor Castle and 'that' Mr Kean was in charge of producing them.

One of the plays produced in the Rubens Gallery at Windsor in this same year was *King John*, with Kean in the name part and Mrs Kean as Constance. The newly created peer Lord Broughton and Thomas Babington Macaulay (not yet Baron Macaulay) were both there. The unfortunate Arthur was played 'in a very effective and too affecting style by a young girl'. So affecting that both men were in tears. Later the Queen came up and spoke to them about how very moving the scene was and, Lord Broughton adds, 'We applauded a great deal. H.M. is pleased with clapping, no disapprobation is allowed.' As for Mr Macaulay, despite his tears, he found it an agreeable way of passing an evening at court, 'far better than being confined to cards or chess'.[12]

Managers, less fortunately placed than the Queen, could not by icy look or well administered snub reprove audiences for lack of appreciation. They simply struggled on, giving audiences what audiences wanted. Even after 1843 when restrictions were removed they continued to produce plays of little merit by playwrights generally of no note. Although Samuel Phelps (1804–78), an actor who had begun in the provinces, came to London, took over Sadler's Wells, Islington, in 1844, devoted himself to producing Shakespeare for nearly twenty years and made it pay, most theatres put on plays which were merely adaptations of novels by Scott, Harrison Ainsworth (1805–82), Dickens, Pierce Egan (1814–80) and Lytton Bulwer (1803–73). The last-named, later Lord Lytton, also wrote seven plays, three very successful. Mary Russell Mitford (1787–1853), of *Our Village* fame, wrote three, one successful. Robert Browning (1812–89) had a resounding failure with *Stafford*, which he wrote for Macready (1837), while his *Blot in the 'Scutcheon* is the feeblest of melodramas. Charles Reade (1814–84) also wrote plays. His *Masks and Faces* was one of his best known in the first half of the century. Many plays were also translated from the French, chiefly those written by Eugène Scribe, an excellent dramatic craftsman who dominated the Parisian stage. He had a gift for comedy as well as melodrama and his works appealed strongly to the prejudices and tastes of the middle class.

Generally speaking, melodrama was the most popular with audiences since melodrama, like modern soap-opera, makes no demands whatsoever on the mind, so melodramas were churned out by the gross. It is neither possible nor desirable to deal with the dozens of playwrights who did the churning out, nor with their long-forgotten plays, but Tom Taylor (1817–80), Professor of English at London University, 1845, and editor of *Punch* (1874–80) wrote a popular play *Our American Cousin* as well as a number of fashionable romantic melodramas. Several of his plays had an historical background and are well-tailored works. Dion Boucicault (1820–90), in spite of his name an Irishman, was an actor, a one-time manager of Astley's and, as we know, a prolific writer of plays, but these were usually very skilful adaptations of novels, or of other plays. One of his own plays, *London Assurance* (1841) a 'comedy of modern life' was a triumph and, like *The Corsican Brothers*, was recently revived in London. Boucicault's melodramas were not the usually wildly improbable or downright crude stuff which constituted most melodramas. His achievement was to create melodramas fit for gentlemen— and ladies.

Of course playwrights were sadly inhibited by Victorian prudery. Audiences could take any amount of murder, mayhem, torture, violence and villainy but a play entirely about *crim. con.* NO. Poor Marguerite Gautier, heroine of *La Dame aux Camèlias* by Dumas *fils* could never be forgiven the life she led and could appear on the English stage only in English versions (incorrectly entitled *Camille*) so truncated, cleansed and bowdlerized as to be virtually unrecognizable. In 1856, however, Marguerite was allowed to sing herself to death—in Italian—as Violetta in Verdi's *La Traviata*.

Far less polite and thoroughly English were those audiences who packed the gallery of theatres such as the 'Vic' where the heat and smell to one unaccustomed to it were unbearable.

'The odour', says Henry Mayhew with feeling, 'positively prevents respiration.' Here in this hot, stuffy firetrap which had but one staircase, the audience clearly and loudly declared its likes and dislikes. It disliked very much indeed 'touching sentiment'.[13] When, in *Child of the Storm*, the heroine declared she would share her father's death or imprisonment as her duty, the gallery was totally unimpressed. It just thought the girl soft and expressed a disapprobation which would have stunned Queen Victoria.

What the gallery at the 'Vic', the Surrey and similar theatres liked best was a good gruesome murder, vigorous slapstick and the ghost scene from *Hamlet*. *Macbeth* was liked only if confined to 'the witches and the fight'; the 'high words' in a tragedy were called 'jaw-breakers' and, as a costermonger said, 'We can't tumble to that barrakin'.[14] Comic and other songs were popular and the audience roared out the choruses with enormous enthusiasm. Dances of all kinds, the more vigorous the better, were greatly appreciated. A particular favourite was the hornpipe with its many variations. Here, it will be remembered, Mrs Vincent Crummles astonished her husband, who did not even know she could dance, by doing the skipping hornpipe, at her benefit, between those pieces in which she played Juliet and Helen Macgregor. Just why Mr Crummles should have been astonished at this further evidence of Mrs Crummles's versatility is a mystery since, as he confessed, the first time he ever saw his future wife 'she stood upon her head on the butt-end of a spear, surrounded with blazing fireworks'.[15]

The Crummles family, including the pony, were strolling players who performed in the smaller towns, and if not all similar companies were fortunate enough to have among them such a many-sided genius as Mrs Crummles, all presented to their audiences very much the same lengthy olla-podrida produced by London managers before (and after) 1843, but infinitely less well written, set, produced and acted.

Larger provincial cities and towns had stock companies and theatres or halls of their own. For a short season a great-name star would come from London with possibly two or three of his supporting cast; the remaining actors and the scenery were drawn from a stock. G. V. Brooke (1818–66), Barry Sullivan (1821–91) and William Charles Macready (1793–1873), who had made his début as an actor in Birmingham in 1810, were provincial idols. Macready disliked acting intensely and loathed melodrama, yet became a splendid actor who reached the top by 1819. He acted in Paris and several times in the U.S.A. where, in 1848, a quarrel with the difficult American actor, Edwin Forrest, turned into a riot in which twenty-two people were killed and thirty-six injured by the militia. Macready managed at different times, Covent Garden, Drury Lane and the Haymarket, and did everything possible to improve standards of drama, stagecraft and production. He is, perhaps, the most important figure of the nineteenth century in the development of the technique of acting and production. Sullivan was far better known and more popular in the north of England than in London.

Considering the woeful respectability of the times, it seems incongruous that the music-hall should have been born just then. It was less of a birth than an evolution as it crawled out of semi-basement dens and tap rooms in the poorer quarters of London, where rakish young men about town had always sought raffish amusement, and became a special kind of entertainment in its own right. With its own building or hall, which catered chiefly for the working man, music-halls also drew in the less attractive and more violent element from theatre audiences and this helped make the theatre fit for polite society again.

There were, however, still those who thought the theatre the high road to Hell, and to amuse these Thomas German Reed (1817–88), a musician, and his actress wife, Priscilla (1818–95), set up their innocent 'Entertainments' in St Martin's Hall in 1855. The 'Entertainments' consisted of readings, impersonations, music, ballads, all carefully chosen. It sounds deadly and yet it also sounds as if their 'Entertainments' were the pious and genteel equivalent of the music-hall.

The first music-hall, as such, was reputedly built at the Canterbury Arms, Lambeth, in 1852, by the publican Charles Morton, who liked his songs operatic, and his comedians well dressed, although Sam Collins, an ex-chimney sweep and singer of Irish songs, founded Collins' Music Hall around the same time. So that wonderful, now vanished, typically English institution began with the early Victorians.

Another thing which began then, but in the first year of the Queen's reign, was what has been called 'Bozomania'. This was caused by the appearance in monthly parts of *The Posthumous Papers of the Pickwick Club* by 'Boz' who had previously written sketches for the *Morning Chronicle*. 'Bozomania', which persisted for years and can still be found today, did not really settle in until Sam Weller made his entry in the fifteenth monthly number. Overnight, to the gratification and embarrassment of the publishers, the circulation shot up from around 400 to 40,000 and 'Mr Boz', as that gallant and unfortunate devotee Captain Brown called him, was made, and began his career as a novelist.

Today, when Charles Dickens (1812–70) is probably the best known and most widely read of the great Victorian novelists, it is surprising to read a comment made only twenty-seven years after his death that, 'the England of 1837 was so different from the England we now behold, that the *Pickwick Papers*, belonging to that date, require explanatory notes for the benefit of a young generation'.[16]

It was certainly different in a great many ways but one would not have thought *Pickwick* needed a gloss in the year of the Queen's Diamond Jubilee, any more than we need a gloss for, say, *The Spoils of Poynton, The Nigger of the Narcissus* or *The Invisible Man*. All three were written in 1897, and so are further away, in time, from us than *Pickwick* was in the 1890s. Yet one thing is certain, the whole of the nineteenth century is undoubtedly the great era for the growth and development of the novel.

It is impossible to deal with the Victorian novel here. Even within the limit set by the years 1837–61, a cursory and inadequate glance must suffice, for even by 1837 the novel was rapidly establishing itself as the prime literary form of the century—and the most popular one. The Victorians liked to read, their diversions were fewer than ours and books were a major one. As the middle classes had increasingly risen (and continued to rise) in importance, power and wealth, novelists and the novel, essentially a middle-class form, also increased in numbers to supply the demand of a new, large, literate public. Lending libraries proliferated, the number of publishers grew, and even newspapers and periodicals catering for all tastes and shades of political or religious opinion totalled around five hundred by mid-century.

What the typical reader wanted from a novel was, not unpredictably, escape, amusement and excitement. He was not interested in abstract ideas, philosophical undertones or the psychological motivation of character. He was interested in people of all sorts and kinds, in what happened to them, and in social contrasts. He wanted to know about life, ordinary, everyday life as he imagined it but freed by plot, adventure and melodrama and heightened sentimentality (for he liked to shed tears) from the dullness of everyday life as he knew it. He liked tales of horror and of the occult. He still read Scott with pleasure and excitement, but those eighteenth-century novelists Fielding and Smollett were coarse. What he preferred was the sensational married to the genteel.

With the coming of a vast new class of people who were moderately well off or rich, who would like to have mingled with the aristocracy and gained acceptance, a new type of novel sprang up—the society novel which, allegedly, mirrored the life of the beau-monde in all its aspects. It was not a new idea, but the method of handling was. These 'silver fork' novels went into exhaustive detail on dress, food, furniture, stately homes, conversation and behaviour on all occasions. Their appeal lay in their apparent accuracy, their true to 'high life' tone.

Often such a novel was published anonymously so that the publisher could suggest its author was a man of the beau-monde. The market was gratifyingly wide. The 'ins' liked to read about themselves almost as much as the 'outs' liked to read about the 'ins'. Probably the very first of this new kind of society novel was *Tremaine, or the Man of Refinement* (1825), its anonymous author was Robert Ward (1765–1846) and this began the vogue. Edward Bulwer-Lytton (1803–73), Theodore Hook (1788–1841), (the 'Mr Wagg' of Thackeray's *Vanity Fair*) and Mrs Charles Gore (1799–1861) who wrote more than seventy works (and was also parodied by Thackeray) plus many lesser writers all produced society novels as well as other kinds of fiction. So, for a short time, did Benjamin Disraeli (1804–81), that 'Jew d'esprit' as the cockneys called him. His first novel, *Vivian Grey* (1826), written when he was twenty-one was an instant *succés de scandal* because a number of its characters were well-known thinly disguised and this created much discussion in society. The book, however, was full of social solecisms* which is not surprising as the anonymous author had never in his life moved in the circles he wrote about. The 'ins' knew this. The 'outs' did not. Disraeli is by no means a great novelist, but he did write our first political novel, *Coningsby* (1844). This, with *Tancred* (1847) which is about religious issues, and *Sybil* (1845), form a trilogy. Of the three *Sybil* is one of the first and most famous of social (not society) novels. It contrasts the two nations, that is the rich and the poor, the employer and the employed and there is true feeling in the book which seems to spring from a first-hand knowledge of industrial and agricultural misery and squalor, cruelty to children, and the turning of men into savages, brutal creatures due to social abuses. This is contrasted with rich society. Just as the wretched town of Mowbray is contrasted with the almost too dazzling splendour of Mowbray Castle. In *Sybil* the reader got both societies, the high and the humble.

But the 'silver fork' novel, popular though it was, could satisfy neither the increasing demand for novels nor meet all the requirements of readers. Thus, the demand created a supply of long-forgotten hacks who spawned ephemeral books to feed the market. It also produced those novelists whose work we still read and enjoy today, although from this distance possibly from a different point of view. Had the typical early Victorian reader

* For the 1853 edition, Disraeli removed the gaffes.

been told when he read, say, Dickens, Thackeray, Currer, Acton or Ellis Bell* or Mrs Gaskell, that he was reading Literature with a capital 'L' he would have been as astonished as was M. Jourdain when he learned he had been speaking prose all his life.

No less than playwrights, Victorian novelists were hampered by the conventional morality of the time. Evil must be punished. Virtue rewarded. Heroines had to be as innocent as a new-born babe—innocence and downright ignorance often seem synonymous. Thus heroines, with but few exceptions, tend to be so deadly dull as to appear almost half-witted.

Not dull is the eponymous heroine of Charlotte Brontë's *Jane Eyre* (1847) who horrified a number of Victorians—but not Queen Victoria. She found the book fascinating and read it aloud to 'dear Albert'. Not so Miss Elizabeth Rigby† who, in 1848, attacked the book in the December *Quarterly* and stated that if the author were a woman, she had 'forfeited the society of her sex'. But Miss Rigby was not always so hard upon her sex. Some years after her marriage she seems to have had sense enough to advise Euphemia Gray to leave her impotent, parent-consumed, author, artist and social reformer husband, John Ruskin. As a social reformer it is more than possible the novels of Dickens had a greater effect upon the average reader than the works of Ruskin.

Just after mid-century two very different kinds of novelists appeared and brought something new to the novel. The first, George Meredith (1828–1909), broke new ground by combining brilliance, irony and romanticism. His first two novels, *The Shaving of Shagpat* (1855) was an oriental fantasy, while *Farina* (1857) reduces popular romantic supernaturalism to an absurdity. The third, *The Ordeal of Richard Feverel* (1859) displays a subtlety and wit which the already established novelists lacked.

* The anonymity of the Brontë sisters was never officially broken in their lifetime; Currer was Charlotte (1816–55); Acton, Anne (1820–49), and Ellis, Emily (1818–48).

† Miss Rigby (1809–93) author and contributor to the influential *Quarterly Review*, married 1849 Charles Lock Eastlake (1793–1865), painter and president of Royal Academy 1850–65. Knighted 1850.

His best work, however, does not begin until the mid-60s. The second novelist, and entirely different from Meredith, is Mary Anne Evans (1819–80) (George Eliot) who did not begin to write novels until 1857. A radical, an idealist, an agnostic with a powerful brain, she was one of the Victorian sages and cut herself off from polite society—which was just as well—by her irregular union with George Henry Lewes. She tried to lift fiction onto a higher plane and this resulted in novels which are uncompromising. Mrs Gaskell, Dickens, Charles Kingsley, when using the novel to point out injustice and social inequalities, gilded the pill. George Eliot refuses to gild. Her characters emerge as real and three-dimensional—the added dimension was unusual then. Further, no one before her had ever taken a man's occupation as a serious and integral part of his life, and in doing so George Eliot enlarged the novel form. Her plots evolved around a moral purpose, not around conventional morality; which, again, enlarges the novel. She seems to say that those whose motives are selfish and mean become morally degraded; moral regeneration can be achieved only by absolute selflessness and love. And she manages to express this through her characters, without sanctimoniousness for she brought psychological subtlety to the novel. With George Eliot holding the pen, the novel developed from entertainment into a highly intellectual art.

The Prince Consort was an ardent and early devotee of her work. He read *Adam Bede* (1859) which was a notable success, and in 1861 *The Mill on the Floss* (1860). Other novels which he read in that agitated year were *The Woman in White* (1860) by Wilkie Collins (1824–89) and Charles Kingsley's *Hypatia* (1853), the novel in which Goths, Jews, pagans and heretics come out rather better than the early Christians. As he lay dying in December, he wanted to be read to and asked for Trollope's *The Warden*, Charles Lever's *The Dodd Family* and George Eliot's *Silas Marner*, but he was too restless to listen. Later, his daughter Princess Alice read him *The Talisman*, and finally the Queen read him *Peveril of the Peak*. He had always loved the works of Sir Walter Scott.

There was also poetry and verse to be read, preferably aloud. Arthur Hugh Clough (1819–61) was not popular with the average reader, nor was his friend Matthew Arnold (1822–88). Both men wrote during the early years of their lives, but Clough's work seemed indecisive, torn by doubt and anxiety, while Arnold's sensitive, intellectual and melancholy brooding upon the meaning of life was too full of despair for most people. Most people, however, were besotted with *Festus* by Philip James Bailey (1816–1902), an interminable poem about universal salvation. First published in 1839 it was so popular that with each new edition published, Bailey added extra lines until he finally reached a total of some 40,000 which seems a trifle excessive even for a man who complacently saw himself as a second Milton.*

Edward Fitzgerald (1809–83), a scholarly recluse and friend of Carlyle, Thackeray and Tennyson, published, anonymously, a free poetic translation from the Persian of *The Rubáiyát* of Omar Khayyám in 1859. It was completely ignored until Dante Gabriel Rossetti—how outrageously he painted and wrote!—discovered it and started a cult for the poem. The cult grew, slowly, and did not reach its peak until late Victorian times when the *Rubáiyát* became a first favourite and quite inescapable.

There was also, until mid-century, Mr Wordsworth (1770–1850), who had succeeded Robert Southey as poet laureate in 1843. He was long past his prime, still there was his exciting *Grace Darling* (1843) and many of the older generation must have felt he had expressed their own feelings exactly with, 'Is there no nook of English ground secure/From rash assault?', a question which opens his short poem *On the Projected Kendal and Windermere Railway* published during the year in which he reluctantly accepted the laureateship. Doubtless his only laureate work, *Ode on the Installation of his Royal Highness Prince Albert as Chancellor of the University of Cambridge*, July 1847, was appreciated by the Queen but it is sad stuff. Poor William

* Bailey's poem, admired by Tennyson, Browning and certain pre-Raphaelites, is unreadable today. He also wrote other poems and was satirized as one of the 'Spasmodic' school by Prof W. E. Ayrton (1813–65) in *Firmilian: a Spasmodic Tragedy* (1854).

Wordsworth, the great poet could not even finish the poem and most of it was ghosted by his nephew, Christopher Wordsworth (1807–85), Bishop of Lincoln, who as a young man had discovered the site of Dodona. That is, possibly, the most pleasant thing one can say for him. He was, at bottom, a very bigoted bishop.

There was Robert Browning (1812–89), who was quite unintelligible to the average reader; and his wife, Elizabeth Barrett (1806–61) who was not. Their runaway marriage had been one of the sensations of 1846, but as early as 1844 Miss Barrett had already made a deep impression with a volume of poems whereas in 1835 her husband had had an unqualified failure with *Paracelsus*—though well thought of by Dickens, Leigh Hunt and Wordsworth. And what could one make of *Sordello* (1840) or those eight pamphlets produced between 1841–6 entitled *Bells and Pomegranates*?

Mrs Clive, above average intelligence herself, knew exactly what: 'Browning . . . is a man that has published a sort of poem called *Bells and Pomegranates* in which there is no meaning at all,' she writes. *Pippa Passes* cannot have been totally meaningless to Mrs Clive, but as she wrote poetry and novels perhaps she was a thought jealous. She goes on to say of Miss Mitford, with whom she was having luncheon, that she is 'priggy and talks entirely of books and too much of their titles and not of their contents.' Miss Mitford also referred to her friend, Mrs Browning, as 'the great poetess.' 'Which,' Mrs Clive remarks acidly, 'she plainly is not or there would be no necessity to call her so.'[17]

Mrs Browning was certainly not great but, equally certainly, she was very well known and much read. She shook her readers into thinking about social conditions with *The Cry of the Children* (1843) and again in 1857 with *Aurora Leigh*, a plea for the rights of women and the lower classes. With this she achieved immense and immediate popularity. Although the plot is highly complex, the wild melodrama must have suited the taste of the time. Aurora is herself, the author, not very well disguised. Mrs

Browning's poetry is fluent, undisciplined and impetuous (she began writing at the age of eight) and her second volume of poems, in 1844, caught the imagination of the public here and in the United States—and the heart of Robert Browning. After the publication of her *Sonnets from the Portuguese* (1850), she became one of the most widely read and highly thought of poets in England. Romantic love, controlled only by the sonnet form, could not fail to be a winner. Today, with one or two exceptions, these sonnets cannot be read without giving the reader a feeling of uneasiness and embarrassment and this illuminates our own taste as much as it does that of the early Victorians.

In an entirely different class was Mr Alfred Tennyson (1809–92), a shy, moody man, who thought everyone stared at him wherever he went—even in his own garden—or so the Anglo-Irish poet William Allingham (1824–89) told Nathaniel Hawthorne. His 1842 volume of poems was very popular and *The Princess* (1847) was considered a very gentlemanly work, no matter what some people thought. *In Memoriam* published 1850, the year in which he became poet laureate, was liked enormously by the public, which was sounder in judgement than the critics, many of whom disparaged it dreadfully. His *Charge of the Light Brigade* (1854) said what many thought; but no one thought anything of *Maud* (1855); in fact, it was universally unpopular. Poor Mr Tennyson was on a seesaw. Then came *Idylls of the King* (1859) and from then on his popularity and fame grew rapidly. The *Idylls* were so much admired by the Prince Consort, who read the poem in April 1860, that he wrote Tennyson praising the work. He also wrote in the same letter 'will you forgive me if I intrude . . . with a request which I have thought some little time in making, viz. that you would be good enough to write your name in the accompanying volume of *Idylls of the King*?'[18]

If the Prince liked Tennyson, then so did the Queen, but she was no judge of poets or poetry on her own, for a real favourite of hers—and millions of others—was, regrettably, Martin Tupper (1810–89). Tupper began his interminable career as an author in reform year with *Sacra Poesis*. In 1838 came *Geraldine and*

Other Poems and the first part of an endless didactic, moralizing so-called blank verse poem, *Proverbial Philosophy*. Tupper went on producing dreary part after dreary part of this poem until 1867. With its plenitude of the most deadly commonplaces it achieved world fame. Nothing could stop Mr Tupper and he continued to produce floods of edifying verse and prose of no merit for years.

A foreign writer who visited Mr Tupper at his home noted that, 'in the dining-room there are six fine lithographic prints of the Queen's children, as large as life, and all taken at the same age; so that they would appear to have been littered at the same birth, like kittens'. The Queen had sent them to the author and 'he is the only person who has been thus honoured. The Queen is a great admirer of the *Proverbial Philosophy* and gives it to each of her children as they arrive at the proper age for comprehending the depth of its wisdom.' One detects sarcasm in that, 'depths of its wisdom', because the visitor privately thought Tupper 'the ass of asses'.[19]

There were other recreations of a more interesting if less uplifting kind than reading Mr Tupper. The kaleidoscope was still a craze even if it had been invented as long ago as 1816. According to its inventor, the natural philosopher Sir David Brewster (1781–1868), the object of the kaleidoscope was not solely amusement but rather to show and create beautiful forms and patterns which could be used in ornamental art. Amusement linked to instruction was greatly favoured by Victorians. Whether the zoetope, invented by the mathematician and schoolmaster W. G. Horner (1786–1837) combined these two qualities, is doubtful. The zoetrope, a slotted drum, had drawings of figures or animals in different phases of movement arranged about the inside. When the drum revolved swiftly the figure became animated into a moving picture. Much later, Brewster improved upon an invention of Sir Charles Wheatstone (1802–75)* and produced a

---

* Inventor, maker of musical instruments, oculist, chiefly remembered for work in electric telegraphy in collaboration with Sir William Fothergill Cooke (1806–79).

workable stereoscope. Unable to interest English opticians, he took his invention to Paris where J. Dubosq began to make stereoscopes in 1850—just in time for the Great Exhibition. When shown, the Queen expressed such interest that the stereoscope became an instant success and Dubosq was swamped with orders. It was the optical wonder of the age, even better, it could be made so cheaply that it could be bought by the poorer people and provide them with home amusement. In fact the stereoscope was the television of the time.

The stereoscope had been made cheap and possible by the invention of photography, but there were other pictures to be seen at home which helped pass the time. There were prints, drawings, watercolours, usually unframed and kept in a portfolio, to be taken out and admired. Of the last two types of artists' efforts many were the products of the often sadly untalented daughters of the house, as all young ladies had to learn drawing or painting whether or not they had an atom of talent. The Queen did both—and rather better than average. Even when adult she had taken lessons in watercolour* from Edward Lear (1812–88) whose delightful *Book of Nonsense* appeared in 1846.

Then there were cards, as there had always been, but the cards themselves were changing. The full-length court card was disappearing and the double-headed card coming in. Many disapproved of this novel idea and in some old-fashioned clubs in London the full-length card remained until the third quarter of the century.

Favourite games were old ones such as whist, Pope Joan, loo and piquet. Preference and cribbage were much favoured by the ladies of Cranford for whom cards 'was the most earnest and serious business they ever engaged in'.[20] A new game was *écarté* which had been introduced during the 1820s, but of all games whist was the most-played by the middling and upper classes, as it had been ever since its invention in the seventeenth century.

* Her enormous paint box is in the Royal Academy, but not on exhibition.

After a dinner party or merely after family dinner, if there were enough players, a table of whist passed the evening.

The Duchess of Kent was an inveterate whist player and those condemned to dine at court when the Duchess was present were mercilessly pressed to her whist table by the Queen, who rarely seems to have played with her mother although she certainly played cards, spillikins and round games such as *nain jaune* and *mouche*.

'Played at *écarté* last night,' Lady Lyttelton writes from Windsor. 'It is now for money, and I won six pence, which the Queen paid very honestly. A round game was played lately, after which Miss Paget had to pay Prince Albert two pence stiring[*sic*], which she did, first washing them with yellow soap for the royal hands.'[21] One cannot take the scrubbed two pence too seriously. Miss Paget, doubtless, was trying to be amusing and to relieve the tedium of the evening.

The labouring folk and those who had a few pence to spare also played cards; rarely at home, but more often in an ale house where the landlord supplied the pack of cards free, and drink at the usual price. In such circles *écarté* had never been heard of and whist was disliked as being too dull and slow. Usual games were all-fives, all-fours (very like seven up), cribbage and put (or putt), a very old game similar to nap. The house cards were so worn, dirty and greasy as to be nearly illegible but, Mayhew tells us, many a sporting costermonger carried his own pack with him which, needless to say, had rarely been stamped. Play was usually for beer but the game became far more exciting when bets were laid. A penny was the lowest sum and five shillings the highest; the average was about a shilling, rather more than the sums won or lost at court.

When playing amongst themselves, the ale house men were perfectly honest but if a stranger came in and wanted to join the game he was most welcome and cheating became the order of the day. Strangers were made to be fleeced.

So, indeed, were rich young men who frequented the many gaming houses in larger cities, although an Act of 1839 gave the police additional powers toward suppressing gambling. A favourite London haunt was The Cottage in Jermyn Street and there were many others in Leicester Square; all were often raided by the police. The district around St James's Palace also swarmed with gaming houses which openly vied with each other for victims. Effie Bond's 'infamous Hell' was known to Disraeli and the young Henry Stanley, a younger son of the thirteenth earl of Derby, who once hid there for a fortnight. Yet these houses seemed to escape the vigilance of the police, whereas those in unfashionable areas did not. 'Thus the Leviathans in crime were allowed to continue their nightly course of profligacy and plunder with impunity.'[22] These Leviathans continued, happily, in their wicked ways until 1853 when it was made a punishable offence to keep a gaming house.

In the poorer quarters there were as many desperate gamblers as in prosperous and fashionable areas. Here, three-up was the favoured game and even spectators bet on the outcome. If a player lost his money and could borrow no more, having no estates to pledge, he gambled away his clothing—hardly sensible in winter. Gambling in these districts was a Sunday recreation, thus Sabbath-breaking was added to the offence. Against this the constant efforts of the police were of no avail.

At fashionable clubs such as Crockfords, where food, company and surroundings were of the highest quality, there was nothing to fear from the police. Here gambling—hazard was a favourite game—could go on in complete security. Most of the aristocracy were members of 'Crockey's', so were a number of bishops, Ministers of the Crown, and M.Ps. The Duke of Wellington belonged, so did the immaculate dandy Count d'Orsay—Lady Blessington's quondam lover and now her home-pet. Poor d'Orsay was trying, unsuccessfully, to mend his broken fortunes at the tables. Disraeli and Bulwer-Lytton also frequented Crockfords,*

---

* William Crockford (1775–1844), a fishmonger, started a club in 1827 and employed the great French chef Ude. The club was expensive and impeccable and soon became famous. Crockford, it is said, made a fortune of more than £1 million.

to watch many a nobleman lose his money or his estates. Disraeli may have gambled but he may have been too deeply in debt to do so. George Anson, who became personal private secretary to Prince Albert in 1840, was also a member. Of this Prince Albert would not have approved.

But the Prince did approve of billiards and played whenever possible. The billiard room at Osborne House contains a full-size table on eight monstrous square white legs. These are painted in a rather pseudo-Pompeiian style to a design by the Prince. The pockets are also white and over the table is a movable double light which bears two enormous ruched, frilled and now mercifully faded, mustard-coloured silk shades. The ceiling, with its bright blue cornice, is lavishly decorated with plasterwork painted in gold, blue, pink and green. In each corner the cypher V.A. is set in an ornate circle.

But the game must have been a blessed relief to the Prince at times for, as the governess to the royal children writes; 'So dull a dining down I never performed, the silences were so dead, so long. Till at last, when the Prince and the gentlemen had withdrawn to a noisy game of billiards, very enviably, the Queen began to talk over her wild Highland life . . . Scotch air, Scotch people, Scotch words, are all far preferable to those of any other nation in or out of this world; thus deer stalking is the most charming of amusements, etc. etc. The chief support to my spirits is that I shall never see, hear or witness their various charms. This soothing thought helps me to smile on happily.'[23]

Billiards, an ever-popular game, had changed considerably but it was not until the nineteenth century it was improved and developed into very much the same game we play today. Brand new was the leather cue tip, invented around 1806, and the prepared chalk which allowed the player to strike the cue ball off centre giving it 'side'.* Before the use of prepared chalk, it is said, players would rub their cue tips on the whitewashed ceiling, which would have made rather a mess of a ceiling such as that of Osborne.

* 'Side' = 'English' in the United States.

Two other major improvements were made in the mid 1830s. In 1835 John Thurston (1777–1850) introduced the India rubber cushion which replaced the old cloth-stuffed cushion. This was splendid during our week or ten days of summer, but the rubber hardened in cold weather and this fault was not overcome until 1842 when a process of vulcanization was discovered. Thurston smartly took out a patent permitting him to apply the process to billiard cushions. In 1836 or 37 Thurston and Jonathan Kentfield together introduced the perfectly flat slate bed. This replaced the old wood bed with its tendency to warp, shrink or crack. On a slate bed the elephant-tusk ivory balls ran smoothly, swiftly and accurately over the close-woven cloth and the game, therefore, required smoother cueing, crisper striking and greater sensitivity of touch. In 1838 Thurston made a table for the Queen which is still in constant use at the Conservative Club, Hounslow, Middlesex. He also made the table which is a show piece at Osborne House.

Billiards was not merely for the rich, and never had been. There were public rooms, some very simple, others less so, where devotees could play or watch the play. This was not new either, as since the seventeenth century few large towns had been without a 'Public Billiard-Table'.[24] But in this century there were many more rooms and in smaller towns too. Billiards had become a professional as well as amateur game.

The first outstanding professional was probably Jonathan (real name, Edwin) Kentfield who had his own Subscription Rooms at Brighton, and when Kentfield played crowds came to see him. Women watched, too. 'I can hardly help going to a billiard table in town,' the Countess Granville writes from Brighton to her brother, the Duke of Devonshire, 'to see the great performer [Kentfield] at that game, of whose play . . . Harriet raves.'[25] Kentfield was challenged in 1849 by John Roberts Sr, but as he was getting on in years, refused. Roberts became champion and remained so until 1870.

There were many more outdoor sports, games and recreations for men than for women. Lawn tennis had not yet been invented and real tennis was still a man's game. Men went shooting, fishing, deer stalking and coursing the wretched hare, as they had always done, but archery had crept back into favour. Limply revived by Sir Ashton Lever (1729–88) in 1780, the Royal Toxophilite Society was founded in the following year to small effect, and archery languished until the Prince of Wales (later George IV) became a patron of the 'Tox' and instituted the 'prince's lengths'—one hundred, eighty and sixty yards. After that a very real if somewhat limited revival took place and as an outdoor sport archery became one of the few open to both sexes—there was a medieval flavour about it which appealed to the early Victorians. The Queen practised it and on a visit to Belgium in 1843 was created a member of the Ancient St Sebastian Society of Archers. A portrait of her shows she wore a slim skirt, bonnet hat turned up on one side, and totally inadequate shoes. Doubtless this was the correct dress for women archers—a hoop would have been hopeless. She also wears a very elegant bracer on the bow arm and, correctly, holds the arm absolutely rigid, having obviously just loosed the arrow.

Another game which by 1850 had become immensely popular with both sexes was croquet. It apparently came over from Ireland in 1850. Although a form of croquet, *paille maille*, had arrived from France with the restoration of Charles II, it bore no resemblance to the Irish game. Lord Lonsdale (1787–1872) was one of the first to lay out a croquet lawn and soon croquet became a craze. There was no settled form of play or shape of hoop, and there were as many variations of the game as there were courts.* It was a wonderful game for everyone, men, women and children. All it needed was a fairly level lawn, which most people had, and a croquet set. Further, a woman did not have to change to play and so she could cheat like mad. A crinolined player had a superb advantage, she could quietly, underneath

---

* By 1867 the first ever all-comers meeting was held at Moreton-in-Marsh. The next year, rules were standardized. In 1870 the All England Croquet Club was formed. Its annual contest was held in its own grounds at Wimbledon. In 1875 it allocated one of its lawns for the new game of Lawn Tennis.

or within the ample folds of her skirt move the ball to a preferred position before driving it off. Even in winter one could play, as miniature indoor croquet sets were soon made and table, parlour, or carpet croquet added to the amusement of rainy days or dull eveninngs.

Very young women also played the child's game, battledore and shuttlecock, from which badminton developed in the 1870s. Women also walked, sometimes botanizing, sometimes collecting geological specimens and often just walking for walking's sake— Victorians, men and women, were prodigious walkers. Daring women also hunted and even the most timid rode, at least when young. The Queen was an excellent horsewoman but even in her beloved Highlands was not like Lady Elgin, 'a strange character in Scotland—never out of a riding habit (horses being her passion), and wearing a beard'. Yet, 'shaved and in chip bonnets, she still looks marvellous . . . I think her excellent, interesting from her zest, energy and simplicity and more agreeable in *tête-à-tête* than almost anybody'.[26]

Lady Elgin, bearded or clean shaven, might have played cricket, a few daring women now did, and this centuries-old game which had come to the fore among the upper classes in Kent, Surrey and Hampshire in the eighteenth century, had become increasingly popular among all classes and extended well into the north. The Marylebone Cricket Club (M.C.C.), founded 1787, with its home at Lord's, was the great matchmaker. It invited subscriptions from members to meet match expenses and the first North and South match was played in 1836. Ten years later the All England Cricket Club began to take cricket to all parts of the country and gained adherents, supporters and players.

Cricket improved, too. The invention of the lawn mower in the 1830s and the heavy roller now kept the pitch flat. Round-arm bowling, despite a fierce dispute in 1835, remained illegal until 1864. Bowling was fast, and 'Long Bob' (Robert) Robinson (1765–1822) the cricketer with a mutilated hand, first invented pads for batsmen's legs. They were thin wooden boards set at an angle and acted as shinguards. Unfortunately, when struck by a fast ball they emitted such a loud crack it sent spectators into gales of laughter. Robinson also thought up spikes—but for one shoe only and of such great length as to keep the player rooted, stork like, to the spot. Nevertheless these ideas were subsequently improved on and pads, spiked shoes and even gloves soon became an essential part of cricketing equipment. Cricket, like billiards, became 'modern' in the first half of the century.

Football, for centuries a game played chiefly by working people who did not care a whit about numerical inequality of sides, fractured skulls, broken arms, legs, jaws, noses, or copious bloodshed, crept into the public schools where the boys at first happily imitated the rowdy play of the skull bashers—no nonsense either about equality of sides. Westminster, it is said, first developed orderly play; other schools followed, although many had their own rules* and variations of the game—and still have. Rugby first produced its famous version in 1823 when William Webb Ellis caught the ball from an opponent's kick and astonished everyone by running with it—either by accident or design—in the direction of the opponent's goal. This startling innovation in, or violation of, rules was not recognized in school rules until 1841. Ellis became a hero, 'Rugby' a new game.

Rugby boys took their game up to Oxford and Cambridge with them, just as boys from other schools took theirs. As early as 1840 old boys were already forming clubs, and within the next decade and a half independent clubs were being established. Football had been cleaned up, it no longer looked more like a riot or a battle than a game and although it was chiefly an affair of the old boys' brigade, by the end of the century it had become a game which attracted all classes and had spread around the world.

A few so-called amusements were, finally, prohibited by law. Bull and bear baiting were proscribed in 1835 and many a bear garden was turned into a ring for pugilists. Cock-fighting was not prohibited until 1849, and illegal cock-pits survived and flourished for years after this date. Badger baiting was not made illegal

* A regular set of rules for the Association game dates from 1863.

until 1850, just why so late it as difficult to understand as it is
to understand how anyone could watch a badger being baited
—or any animal for that matter. Still, we were, at last, becoming
a shade less brutal, less savage—at least to animals—than we
had been in previous centuries.

But there were still rat-pits—London had at least forty. Rat
catchers would supply rats for about 2s 6d per dozen to a dealer
who resold them to a pit proprietor. The rats were hemmed
into the pit by a large wire cage, then were chased, caught and
killed by terriers. Great fun for everyone, bar the rat.

In poor quarters skittles was a great recreation, as was sparring
or boxing. Again, this took place in ale houses where the landlord supplied the gloves at a penny or twopence a night. Sparring
rarely went on for longer than fifteen minutes at a time because,
as only two antagonists were concerned, the onlookers quickly
became bored. The winner was he who first gave his opponent a
bloody scent-box.

This was not usual. In professional boxing, under the new rules
of 1839 (revised 1853), when a fighter went down the round ended
for thirty seconds. Then the fighter was allowed eight seconds to
get to the centre of the ring again and if he failed he was declared
'not up to scratch'. By these new rules biting, butting with the
head, low blows, kicking and gouging were all declared fouls.
Also, it was no longer permitted to seize an opponent by the hair
with one hand and clout him with the other, but as bare-knuckle
fighting—hitherto the only form of fighting—had all but gone
out in favour of gloves, one could not seize one's opponent anywhere, anyway.

The sport was favoured, both to watch and practise, by the
middle and upper classes. Sons of noblemen and gentlemen
attended boxing schools to be taught by professionals. It was a
great sport and useful too, particularly late at night when the
streets were not safe. Or it could be fun to fell a peeler who
interfered with one's little game of twisting knockers off doors
at night—a fashionable pastime in 1837 with certain well-bred
young men. Much mischief of this sort was done by a group of

upper class hoodlums led by the Marquis of Waterford, a keen boxer and a keener prankster.

Well-bred young men also enjoyed larking at Vauxhall and Cremorne pleasure gardens, but well-bred young women did not. Vauxhall, the oldest of London's pleasure gardens, opened in 1661 and became extremely fashionable in the eighteenth and early nineteenth centuries, but it was now slipping quietly downhill. One could still eat, drink, dance, listen to music and chase women down the Dark Walk; see firework displays, pantomimes, representations of famous battles and recently added attractions, such as rope climbers, or Mr Grew and the intrepid Mrs Graham making balloon ascents. Yet no matter how many new attractions were added to the programme nothing could save the Gardens. No longer favoured by the general public and only sporadically by rich and fashionable young men who were up to no good anyway, Vauxhall died. It was closed, after nearly three hundred years, in 1859 and on the site countless streets of tenements and houses were built and covered the whole area.

Ranelagh, its close rival as a fashionable resort, had closed in 1805. Marylebone in 1778. White Conduit House in once rural Islington, a small pleasure garden two hundred years old, had always catered for family parties, but it, too, began to slide, and its billiard room now attracted young men who were as noisy as they were seedy. In 1849 it was demolished.

The new Cremorne Gardens, Chelsea, had been a riverside farm and was transformed into a pleasure garden in 1843 when other gardens had fallen into disrepute. It had all the usual attractions, trees, lawns, grass plots, booths, temples, a monster platform for dancing, pavilions tucked away discreetly and magnificent gas lighting where it was wanted and not where it was not. It also had the added attraction of being in a more salubrious part of London. At first, Cremorne attracted all classes, but shortly after mid-century it, too, became unfit for gentlewomen—although not for gentlemen or Bohemians such as Rossetti and his brother artists. The gardens now swarmed with prostitutes and Dr William Acton (1813–75) tells us: 'On and around that

Cremorne Pleasure Gardens

platform waltzed, strolled and fed, some thousand souls—perhaps seven hundred of them men of the upper and middle class, the remainder prostitutes, more or less *prononcées.* . . . Lemonade and sherry seemed to please the dancers. . . . A strongish party of undergraduates in drinking—all males—were deepening their native dullness in a corner. . . . Of the character of the female visitors, I could have little moral doubt, but . . . self proclamation by any great number of them was out of the question. It was open to the male visitor to invite attention and solicit acquaintance.'[27]

H. A. Taine, however, when he visited the gardens was openly solicited—perhaps because he was a foreigner—and the whole place depressed him, as much as it did Acton who found it dull, lacking in natural vivacity and merriment.

No lack of natural vivacity, merriment, noise, bustle and confusion was apparent on Derby Day, and all roads to Epsom were blocked with every conceivable type of vehicle and mode of conveyance; farm carts, gipsy wagons, ancient coaches, smart new equipages, push barrows, men on horseback, wagons and pedestrians. The Derby was the one event where all classes mixed. Derby week was both a race week and a fair, as fairground people always set up their attractions nearby, while vendors of food and drink with their trays slung about their necks catered for the mass appetite. In 1840, the Queen was 'rapturously received' at this greatest of all races. This rapture, according to the *Morning Post*, was 'because Lord Melbourne was not with her'.[28]

Derby Day was the great holiday for all who could manage to get to Epsom. On a fine day in May or June it was a colourful, exciting and splendid event. Rain, if not too severe, was no deterrent but, to everyone's horror, snow fell in 1839 before and during the race which was won by Bloomsbury, the only time in history snow has fallen during the Derby. Many who came from a distance always stayed for the whole week to see the Oaks run on Friday, and Epsom was packed out; not a bed to be had. Those unable to afford a bed anyway, rigged up some kind of tent or sought shelter in the hedgerows. Other races were also very popular, but did not attract Derby crowds. The Thousand Guineas at Newmarket and the St Leger at Doncaster were the most famous, but all over the country during spring and summer there was racing which drew festive crowds in each locality. Racing, the sport of kings, was the delight of the people.

In London one of the main attractions was, as always, the Thames. But now, with the coming of steam, steamer trips up and down the river—which stank dreadfully in hot weather— were available to everyone. On Sundays, in particular, Battersea Fields was crammed with apprentices, mechanics, small tradesmen with their sweethearts or their wives and children waiting to crowd into river steamers, which had first appeared in small numbers on the Thames in the 1820s. So great was the number of people that not all could get aboard, but there were inns and beershops nearby to provide, in this case, second-best amuse-ment.

Those with more leisure and more money took a rather different kind of trip. 'Went up and down the river in steamboats, up to see the new Houses of Parliament and down to eat dinner at Greenwich', writes a clergyman's wife, who was spending a few days in London with her husband in 1844. 'Nothing is more amusing than the river', she continues, 'nor more full of beautiful views. New London Bridge is the finest of all bridges.' Arrived at Greenwich, they dined at the *Ship* on 'water-suchet, whitebait, lamb chops and iced champagne'. And, she adds, 'we sat in a window and got very jolly indeed over that good fare'.[29] As the dinner cost but twelve and sixpence, there was more than one reason for jollity. But they were not too gay not to notice that twenty-one steam boats passed in one hour whilst they dined.

If the Thames was an attraction so now was the seaside, and fishing villages all round the coast were turned, or turned them-selves, into seaside resorts. Brighton had long been a favourite, fashionable and exclusive health resort, and Weymouth too, ever since George III had gone there to recuperate from his illness of 1788–9 by sea-bathing from a machine painted to resemble the flag. Now going to the seaside was more for a holiday than for health. Ramsgate, Pegwell Bay, Broadstairs, Margate, Black-pool, Bournemouth, Southport, Weston-super-Mare, to say noth-ing of Ventnor and Ryde—for the Queen had made the Isle of Wight fashionable—became resorts. Not all were fashionable, but all provided sea air, damp lodgings, bad food, and two lots of bathing machines separated by a good stretch of shore : one for women bathers, the other for men. There was no mixed bathing. Men bathed naked but women made up for this by wearing either a voluminous, sleeved bathing dress tied at the ankles by string, or a heavy all-enveloping, tent-like cloak. Neither was con-ducive to swimming but women did not swim anway, they just dipped with the assistance of an attendant. The Queen had the first dip of her life on July 30th 1847 in Osborne Bay from her

own larger than usual bathing machine.* She thought it delightful until she put her head under, then feared she would be stifled.

In the better resorts there were many forms of amusement :
lending libraries, assembly rooms, halls where lectures and
scientific demonstrations were given. There were bands of varying quality (German bands were the noisiest) and, since shell work
was so popular, everyone could look for shells or buy them from
local shell gatherers. There was also, at some resorts, that daring
new thing a pier. Brighton pioneered the pier in 1820. It was
chiefly for ships, but at the shoreward end was a promenade for
visitors who cared to pay an entrance fee. Here a bench or two,
a sundial, a brace of cannon, a camera obscura and a mineral
water booth provided amusement, and in 1839 a weighing
machine was added to these startling attractions. In 1841 the
London to Brighton railway was opened; by 1843 excursion
trains were being run and Brighton became a very popular resort. To the dismay of its aristocratic inhabitants and guests, and
the delight of its shopkeepers, the trippers had come.

Indeed, the opening up of more and more railways meant,
among other things, more diversions available to nearly everyone. The railways could carry so many more people at once, and in
so much less time than stage coaches that, all round, they provided cheaper travel facilities. The working classes could take
advantage of this and get away for a day out of the smoke and
grime of towns or cities, into the country, or to the sea, or even
into the different smoke and grime of another city. It was beginning to be thought, by an enlightened few, that labouring
folk were improved by the occasional holiday. It was good for
them and for their work.

Possibly the first man to realize that diversion and recreation
for the working classes could be procured cheaply through using
the railways was the ex wood turner, printer, Baptist missionary
and temperance man, Thomas Cook (1808–92). In 1841 he
persuaded the Midland Counties Railway to run a special train

* Still to be seen at Osborne near the 'Swiss Cottage', the play (and work)
house for the children.

from Leicester to Loughborough so that workers could attend a temperance meeting there. Cook advertised this publicly and for a shilling took his party there and back. The success of this excursion led him to think about making the organization of excursions, at home and abroad, a full-time job. In 1844 he entered into a permanent agreement with the Midland Railway to put trains at his disposal for which he would provide the passengers. The next year he personally conducted his first pleasure trip from Leicester to Liverpool. He had had guide books printed, hotel accommodation guaranteed and he advertised—first class 14s, second 10s. So many people turned up at the station that there was a near riot. The excursion to Liverpool was the greatest success. Thomas Cook never looked back. From 1846 he issued a popular magazine *The Excursionist* (our first travel-agent literature), and he continued to improve his service, run excursions and build up the organization which still bears his name. In 1855 he took the first excursion from Leicester to Calais for the Paris Exhibition, and in 1856 came his first grand circular tour of Europe. But in 1851, before Paris, before the circular tour, Thomas Cook was busy bringing trainloads of people of all classes into London to see the Great Exhibition or, to give it its correct title, *The Great Exhibition of the Works of Industry of all Nations.*

There was nothing very new about exhibitions. Already there had been several in Germany, France, Ireland and in this country, and they had been well enough attended; but there were a number of entirely new things about this exhibition which made it quite different. It was the first International Exhibition ever held. Its purpose, as declared by Prince Albert (whose idea it was), was not merely that of a trade fair, but was to help international understanding and brotherhood and thus promote peace. The Exhibition was housed in a great, three-tiered, glass winterpalace, dubbed by *Punch*, 'The Crystal Palace'. No one had seen anything like it before because, thanks to Joseph Paxton, there never had been anything like it. Glittering, gay, improbable and ephemeral, it covered eighteen acres of Hyde Park and enclosed within the soaring arch of the transept three full-grown elm trees.

A season ticket holder, who attended the opening on May 11th, writes, 'I took my stand with my colleagues on the right of the throne. The Queen came in exactly at twelve and took her seat. I shall not attempt to describe the scene or ceremony; they were indescribable. I was much affected by them, so were others of a far sterner nature. The Lord Chancellor could not refrain from tears. . . . The grandeur and vast expanse of the fairy palace, the multitudes within, almost lost in the distance . . . the gorgeous display of all productions of art and industry from all corners of the globe, there with the young Queen, her children, her husband—the real creator of this wonderful scene—produced an effect such as I have never witnessed before and never shall again.'[30]

Millions, during the 141 days of the Exhibition, agreed with him and many must have agreed with Charles Greville (never noted for enthusiasm) who comments that outside the building, 'it was a wonderful spectacle to see the countless multitudes streaming along in every direction, and congregated on each bank of the Serpentine down to the water's edge; no soldiers, hardly any policemen to be seen, and yet all so orderly and good humoured'.[31]

Inside there were 13,937 exhibitors; 6,556 foreign and 7,381 British and colonial. The exhibits totalled 100,000 and their estimated value (excluding the Koh-i-Noor) was £2 million. The Queen went to the Exhibition nearly every other morning during May, June and July, methodically visiting every section and mingling with the crowds to the utter astonishment of foreign visitors. The Duke of Wellington, now eighty-two, was also a frequent visitor. Early in the morning he would arrive, hoping to escape notice, but invariably parties of schoolboys would recognize the bent, beak-nosed figure and cheer wildly. Nearly everybody who was anybody visited the Crystal Palace; so did the 'nobodies'—in hordes—and they thoroughly enjoyed it. School children came from all over, which delighted the Prince; whole parishes from country districts came in parties led by the vicar and his wife; one woman walked from Cornwall. Visitors, important and unimportant, came from overseas and, very wisely, admission prices varied on different days. Season tickets cost three guineas for a man, two for a woman, and there were £1 days, 5s days, 2s 6d days and 1s days. On one shilling day, the place was packed out, in fact nearly four and a half million shillings were taken and a good proportion of these were paid by what were called 'the Industrial Classes'. Much to the surprise of many, they were orderly, good tempered, and decently dressed people who took an enormous interest in everything.

To those who had never been out of England or, indeed farther than the next big town, it was as good as a foreign tour, what with guide books printed in different languages, and religious tracts to point out the moral of each exhibit and, predictably, Martin Tupper's *Exhibition Hymn*, translated into thirty languages and with music by Sebastian Wesley. These were on sale, but nothing else, other than food and drink, was sold. The whole thing was an unqualified success. It provided entertainment, but more, instruction, not only about what we could produce but about other countries—some so far away and strange—India, Turkey, China, Tunis, Canada, Trinidad, New Zealand. How very different they all were from England. But, really, when it came down to it, our industry and art manufactures were infinitely superior to those of any other country in the world. It was a very pleasant thought.

Visitors to London sometimes tired of the Exhibition and sought other diversions. There were plenty of them. The Tower did a roaring trade, so did other places such as the various Panoramas, Dioramas, the Hippodrome, Madame Tussaud's in Baker Street, the Zoological Gardens, the Egyptian Hall and trips on the Thames. London cab drivers made a small fortune overcharging foreigners until, to the vast amusement of the cockneys, polyglot policemen were provided to prevent non-English-speaking guests from being cheated.

When the Exhibition closed to the public on October 11th

Thames pleasure steamers

more than six million had seen it. To the discomfort of those who had predicted it would be a fiasco, it made a clear profit of £138,000. On the advice of Prince Albert and with extra money from the government (repaid), the Exhibition Commissioners bought eighty-seven acres in South Kensington as a site for a centre to encourage science and art. Here the South Kensington (now the Victoria and Albert), the Science, the Natural History and the Geological Museums etc. now stand, as does the Royal College of Music.

On the day the Queen opened the Exhibition she confessed to her journal that the Park presented a wonderful spectacle. With the crowds, carriages, troops, bustle and excitement it was, she thought, quite like the coronation.

Perhaps, the crowds and troops suggested this but certainly the great glass building enclosing all the man-made wonders of the world bore no resemblance to that unsophisticated Great Fair —the biggest ever—which had been held back in 1838.

Yet nearby, on some wasteland at Knightsbridge, a fair had been set up, and many of the same showmen who had taken part in the Coronation Fair in Hyde Park were hopefully there.

It was not a success.

CHAPTER SEVEN

Gardens

Prince Albert was knowledgeable about gardens and trees. His bride of eight months knew nothing, but, writes Lady Lyttelton from Windsor, 'she is learning trees and plants; and in a very pretty and childlike manner, when last we walked, told me gravely and low, half-shy, "That, Lady L. is a tulip-tree, you see—a rare tree but yet hardy—we hope it may succeed, though it is rather large to be transplanted." Last year she did not know an elm from an oak. Love rules the Court, the Camp, the Grove.'[1]

The Queen, now awaiting the birth of her first child,* had, until her marriage, infinitely preferred town to country life, but the Prince preferred the country. He loved simple country pursuits—planting trees and designing gardens made him happy. He loved Windsor and the clear air, free of the smoke and grime of London, and he had started to improve the gardens at the castle in August 1840. Here he had had taste and sense enough not to let the Fishing Temple and the George IV cottages be destroyed, although they were scheduled for demolition. Even as early as May of that year he had begun improving the gardens at Buckingham Palace, and subsequently he laid out the grounds, terraces and gardens at Osborne House where he was his own master. Osborne was a private house, whereas Windsor Castle and Buckingham Palace were under the control of the Office of

---

* Princess Victoria (Pussy), the Princess Royal, born November 1840, died 1901. Married Frederick III (Fritz) German Emperor and King of Prussia. Mother of William II, German Kaiser (1859–1941).

Works. At Osborne he could, and did over the years, plant thousands of trees, and much of his work remains.

To him gardening was a three-dimensional art, comparable to, if not better than, modelling. 'We have an art', he writes in answer to a letter from the Princess Imperial of Prussia, 'in which this third element of creation—inward force and growth—is present, and which has, therefore, an extraordinary attraction for me of late years, indeed I may say from earliest childhood, viz. the art of gardening. In this the artist who lays out the work, and devises a garment for a piece of ground, has the delight of seeing his work live and grow hour by hour; and, while it is growing, he is able to polish, to cut and carve, to fill up here and there, to hope and to love.'[2]

Although the Prince was so often accused of being stiff, formal, humourless and, worst of all, un-English, in his very real love of gardens and gardening he might have been mistaken for an Englishman. And the Englishman, according to Taine, revealed himself better in gardens than in any other creative work. In a garden he could make his poetic dream come true—or nearly true.

The poetic dream may have been beautiful to look at, but it was sheer hard work, physical and mental, to achieve and there was probably no harder worker than John Claudius Loudon (1783–1843). He, one of the two most famous gardeners of the era—the other was Joseph Paxton (1801–65)—was a Scot, the son of a Lanark farmer. At school he learned writing, drawing, chemistry, botany and the rudiments of Latin and French—a rather more comprehensive and practical education than was obtainable in England at that time. Knowing what he wanted to do, he became apprenticed to an Edinburgh nursery firm and when he had served his apprenticeship came to London. He was only twenty but soon made the acquaintance of Sir Joseph Banks (1743–1820), explorer, naturalist and President of the Royal Society. Banks's wonderful library and herbarium—now in the British Museum—as well as his gardens at Spring Green, Isleworth, were open to Loudon and the older man soon had the younger made a member of the Linnaean Society.

One of the first things Loudon noticed when he came to London was its public squares all planted with the more dismal evergreens—pines, yews, spruces—and, it seems, wrote an article, *Observations on Laying Out Public Squares*, no one knows quite when, in which he advocated the use of plane trees, sycamores and almond trees rather than dank and dreary conifers. How soon his advice was taken, I do not know, but certainly plane trees and sycamores seem to have been planted in London squares during his lifetime. A keen arboriculturalist he also advocated breathing zones of unoccupied space around the capital. This was not new. John Evelyn (1620–1706) had recommended something very similar in his book *Fumifugium* published in 1661. With our usual celerity we accepted the idea in the twentieth century and introduced the green-belt system.

Loudon was a man of prodigious energy, industry and many talents. He became landscape gardener, architect, painter (exhibiting at the Royal Academy), botanist, writer, editor, encyclopaedist, agronomist and natural historian. Possibly he was too many-sided as his health broke down and he went to convalesce at rural and agricultural Pinner. While there, he observed the outmoded and inefficient methods of English farming as compared with farming in Scotland, so he took Tew Park, Oxfordshire, and set up a school to teach Scots methods of husbandry. By 1812 he was so successful that he sold out, invested the proceeds and travelled in northern Europe where he made notes on every garden possible, as well as on the ravages of war. Unfortunately, when he returned he found his investments were rather worse than English farming; the crop had all but failed. At this point he began his first great book, *An Encyclopaedia of Gardening** and finished it during travels in southern Europe. When published it was an instant success.

'Improvement is the characteristic of civilized man, and implies progressive advances. Men rest satisfied with what they have, when they know of nothing better,'[3] he writes. This sounds

---

* Published 1824. Revised editions 1850, 1878. I have used the 1850 edition, revised by his wife, throughout.

uncommonly like Mrs Beeton with her 'leading lesson of progress' and 'privilege of civilization'. For Mrs Beeton, civilization and good cookery went hand in hand. For Mr Loudon, civilization and gardening are synonymous and he maintains that 'one of the chief sources of improvement in the taste of patrons of gardening . . . is the increase of knowledge'.[4] Indeed, from the *Encyclopaedia* alone, with its hundreds of original illustrations and 1,278 pages of miniscule print no one could fail to gain information, knowledge and eye strain.

Around 1825 Loudon, much afflicted by rheumatism in his arm, put himself in the hands of bone-setters who by yanking and pulling were successful in breaking his right arm and then, presumably because infection had set in, proceeded to amputate it. This cured the right arm but the rheumatism moved into his left and soon he had but three usable fingers. For a landscape gardener and prolific writer this could have been a tragedy. That it was not was due to his wife, Jane Webb (1807–58), whom he married in 1830 when he was forty-seven and she twenty-three. Miss Webb had published, with some success, a science fiction novel entitled *The Mummy: A Tale of the Twenty-Second Century*, as well as a small volume of verse, and she devoted herself entirely to her husband and to learning as much as possible about his profession. He was her teacher but she also attended Professor Lindley's lectures on botany. She soon became her husband's right hand—and his left. He wrote at length and she was his amanuensis; she also went with him to watch or assist as he directed his work on a new site. Her first job after marriage was to take down, at his dictation, his *Encyclopaedia of Cottage, Farm and Villa Architecture* (1832) which runs to 1,150 closely printed pages. She must have been a remarkably courageous bride. From then on they became a team and it would be proper to speak of work done by Mr and Mrs Loudon—certainly Loudon could not have accomplished what he did without his wife.

When Loudon first started his career the great gardener Humphry Repton (1752–1818) was still alive and in demand, but in 1811 he went into semi-retirement because of ill-health. Loudon, although he disagreed with some of Repton's tenets, admired the man and his work. Repton had succeeded Lancelot 'Capability' Brown (1715–83) as the landscape gardener for the great and fashionable of his era, and he lived and worked during a time when opinion was sharply divided over what a garden, pleasure ground and park should look like.

A typical Brownian garden had the house—usually classical—set rather nakedly in a vast smooth sea of lawn which divorced it from its surroundings. A nearby lake, with an island—if the lake were large enough—added calm interest. A stream snaked its way to and from the lake to disappear in the woodland. The middle distance was broken by clumps of trees and shrubs; beyond, lay the park while a belt of trees circumferenced the whole. If there were hills, Brown plumed them with a stand of trees and left the sides bare. He also completely banished flowers from the garden—which was singularly un-English of him. His gardens were 'natural'—and natural is a key-word of the time—although in nature tree-topped hills rarely have naked flanks, brambles, nettles and various weeds flourish in stretches of grass, whilst small lakes become silted up and ragged with reeds and sedges. Brown idealized nature. His gardens were poetic, beautiful, calm, pastoral and like a landscape painting complete with statues, temples and the occasional melancholy ruin. In time Brown was accused by his detractors of clumping and belting, of creating monotony. Repton defended Brown against these charges and claimed the damage had been done, not by Brown, but by his illiterate followers.

Nevertheless, fashions in gardens were changing, as they always have done in England, and the 'picturesque' school sprang up. Its chief progenitors were two country gentlemen, Richard Payne Knight (1750–1824) and Sir Uvedale Price (1747–1829) who wrote essays and poems on the picturesque; and what they meant by the word was not what the eighteenth century had meant by it. The eighteenth century, almost from its earliest years, had considered that a garden should look like a landscape painting, preferably one by Claude Gellée de Lorraine and his disciples. But the new interpretation of the word meant that a garden should be created to look like a suitable subject for a landscape painting—the wilder and more untamed the subject the better. This was considered more natural—which indeed, in a sense, it was, but it too had its excesses. A beautiful tree was an ancient and gnarled one, outcrops of rock should be jagged and patterned with lichen and fern; a blasted oak was far more picturesque than an unblasted ash. It was not the kind of tree, it was the blasting which made the difference. All this and more was a reaction to the Brownian pastoral garden and also a part of the Romantic movement with Gothic overtones. Gardens no less than nature must have the power to move the spectator to intense feelings of rapture, gloom, exaltation, melancholy, wonder, awe; although the 'mere jargon' used to describe the beauties of a garden or of nature were not to everyone's taste.

'Remember,' Edward Ferrars tells Marianne Dashwood, whose sensibility was all too potent, 'I have no knowledge of the picturesque, and I shall offend you by my ignorance and want of taste if we come to particulars. I shall call hills steep, which ought to be bold; surfaces strange and uncouth, which ought to be irregular and rugged; and distant objects out of sight, which ought only to be indistinct through the soft medium of a hazy atmosphere; you must be satisfied with such admiration as I can honestly give. I call it very fine country—the hills are steep, the woods seem full of timber and the valley looks comfortable and snug—with rich meadows and several neat farmhouses scattered here and there. It exactly answers my idea of a fine country, because it unites beauty with utility—and I daresay it is a picturesque one too, because you admire it; I can easily believe it to be full of rocks and promontories, grey moss and brushwood but these are all lost on me. I know nothing of the picturesque.'[5]

Repton did not indulge in picturesque excesses any more than he slavishly imitated Brown. More important, he defined very clearly the differences between a landscape in nature and one set down on canvas by a painter. Briefly, the chief differences were that the spectator saw a landscape painting from one point of view only—the painter's, and the light was forever fixed at a particular time of day; whereas, in a real landscape the spectator moved within it and saw it from ever-changing points of view and thus had a much larger and more varied field of vision. In addition, the light changed constantly from hour to hour. Landscape-painting and landscape-gardening were totally different and should not be confused. Art could not imitate nature and nature in the hands of man could not be shaped as a subject matter for painting.

Nor did Repton believe in divorcing a house from its environment in a Brownian manner. House and surroundings should be a unity. He reintroduced the terrace—which the late eighteenth century had got rid of—in front of the house. The terrace was often balustraded and set with urns to add interest to the foreground and it married the house to the lawn. He did not banish outbuildings or the kitchen garden to an unhandy distance, but left them close to the house and masked them with trees and bushes. He introduced or reintroduced flower-beds and has this to say : 'A flower garden should be an object detached and distinct from the general scenery of the place; and, whether large or small, whether varied or formal, it ought to be protected from hares and smaller animals by an inner fence. Within this enclosure rare plants of every description should be encouraged, and provision made of soil and aspect for every different class. Beds of bog-earth should be prepared for the American plants; the aquatic plants, some of which are particularly beautiful, should grow on the surface, or near the edges, of water. The numerous class of rock plants should have beds of rugged stone provided for their reception, without the affectation of such stones being the natural production of the soil; but above all there should be poles or hoops for those kinds of creeping plants which spontaneously form themselves into graceful festoons, when encouraged and supported by art. Yet, with all these circumstances, the flower garden, except where it is annexed to the house, should not be visible from the roads or general walks about the place. It may therefore be of a character totally different from the rest of the scenery and its decorations should be as much those of art as of nature.'[6]

Repton held the view that different classes of plants each formed a different feature of a garden and should be treated as such, or that a garden should consist of one particular class of plant only. This was an entirely new idea and testifies to our growing knowledge of, and interest in, botany. New, too, was his theory that the pleasure ground could differ entirely in character from the park. Ultimately this led to pleasure grounds* becoming larger and parks smaller and there was no relation in size or scale between the two. It was this which, carried to extremes, became the pattern for the great Victorian gardens and there was really very little change in the theory of landscape gardening from then until 1870 when William Robinson (1838–1935) began his work.†

Repton, also, had no objection to avenues of trees leading to a house—and avenues of trees had been consistently destroyed by the 'natural' school. His concern was not with the Claudian landscape—although at first it had been—nor with the picturesque, as such. He was after the beautiful, which he believed could be achieved in a variety of ways and was not to be limited by any formula. His importance should not be underestimated. Humphry Repton was a liberator. He was also the father of Victorian gardens and his mantle fell on the shoulders of J. C. Loudon.

Loudon, unlike Repton, did not confine himself exclusively to landscape gardening, which he defines briefly as 'the art of laying out grounds'. Further, he believed that the taste for land-

* A pleasure garden or pleasure ground, according to Loudon, consisted of the kept grounds and walks, but should contain flowering shrubs, a maze, an American, French or Dutch flower garden. To Cobbett it was a shrubbery with walks and flowers.
† The last two decades of the century saw the rise of a new landscape school headed by Robinson, which had little in common with what had gone before. Together with Miss Gertrude Jekyll (1843–1935) he completely altered ideas of gardening, freed them from rigidity and bedding-out.

scape gardening 'had been comparatively dormant in England for the past thirty years',[7] which takes us back to Repton's day. But Loudon's range was very much wider than landscape gardening. Under the blanket term 'Gardening' he includes 'Horticulture, or anything that relates to the kitchen garden or orchard; Floriculture, or all that relates to the flower garden, the botanic garden, the shrubbery and the culture of flowers or ornamental shrubs or trees; Arboriculture, or the formation of useful and ornamental plantations, and the culture of the most valuable timber trees'.[8]

Gardening, for him, was a science as well as an art. Gardens should be beautiful—and he coined the hideous word 'gardenesque'—but they should also be useful. He was as interested in the vegetable garden and its proper management as he was in Arboretums,* Pinetums, or the growing of exotics under glass. 'Every man who does not limit the vegetable part of his dinner to bread and potatoes', he says, 'is a patron of gardening, by creating a demand for its productions. The more valuable patrons are those who regularly have dessert on their tables after dinner, or who maintain throughout the year beautiful nosegays and pots of flowers in their lobbies and drawing rooms.'[9]

If one were rich enough, a variety of vegetables, fruits and flowers all the year round from one's own garden was no problem. For this was the age of the glasshouse or greenhouse (and the beginning of commercial growing under glass). The rich 'patron of gardening' had his own special house for forcing vegetables, pinepits for producing pineapples (the growing time had been shortened from three years to eighteen months), vineries for grapes, houses for early strawberries and other fruit, and vast conservatories for all sorts of exotic trees and plants—just to delight eye and senses as the other houses pleased the palate.

The reason for this plethora of glasshouses may have been an interest in food, or in exotic plants but it may also have been a way to *épater les bourgeois* or to outdo one's equals. Equally,

---

* In 1839 he began to lay out the Arboretum at Derby given to the city by Joseph Strutt (1765-1844). It is still to be seen, although much altered.

it may have been that as more explorers and botanists were sent out by botanic and horticultural societies to collect and bring back new plants, our interest in growing these strangers increased. In the years between 1650 and 1750 perhaps only one thousand types of non-indigenous plants had been brought back to England and grown, not privately, but in the Physic Gardens of Oxford, Chelsea and Lambeth. But since then there had been such an enormous upsurge of interest in the scientific and aesthetic value of plants that by about 1850 more than six thousand had been introduced.

Since so many of these came from tropical countries, they could be grown only in the right temperatures, atmosphere and soil. The rich could provide this and also get plants from the Botanic Society in Regent's Park, or from Kew—once Kew had been set on its feet again after a long period of desuetude during the reigns of George IV and William IV—and so the rearing of strange new plants in conservatories became for some an education, for others a hobby and a craze.

'It is impossible to live without a conservatory', Ferdinand Armine tells Mr Temple; and when he and his beloved Henrietta leave Mr Temple behind, prosaically chewing a pasty, to enter her conservatory, complete with fountains and birds, Ferdinand remarks casually : 'These orange groves remind me of Palermo.' Although orangeries were common enough in England, groves of oranges seems a trifle exaggerated. Even more unusual was a rare flower growing among the other exotics which Henrietta confides 'is the most singular thing in the world . . . if it be tended by any other person than myself it withers. Is it not droll?'[10]

This vast conservatory at Ducie with its orange groves, singular flowers, and tropical birds, must have exceeded in size and content that Great Conservatory at Chatsworth which Joseph Paxton, a man of extraordinary abilities began for the sixth Duke of Devonshire in 1836 and completed in 1840–1. This was an entirely new type of building, curvilinear in design with a great curved central span roughly seventy feet high flanked by side aisles of lesser height. It was 277 feet long, 123 feet wide and cost

Circular conservatory with Elizabethan detail, 1853

£33,099 10*s* 11*d*, an enormous sum for a conservatory in those days and prohibitive today. Beneath this great stove house was a heating chamber with eight boilers to feed seven miles of piping which heated the conservatory and kept the water in the tanks the right temperature for aquatics. The conservatory, which also had a gallery, probably contained every tropical plant and tree then known, as well as tropical birds to bejewel the trees with their vivid plumage, and fish to flash gold and silver in the pools. The main pool or tank was thirty-three feet in circumference and the floor was raised three feet six inches to give it sufficient depth. Crystals of various formations and mineral ores glittered in the filtered light and at night 12,000 lamps sparkled like giant motionless fireflies. The Conservatory* was so large that when the Queen and Prince Albert with their entourage visited the Duke in December 1843 they drove around inside in open carriages.

The Great Conservatory was a triumph, a wonder. There was no other privately built and owned conservatory to equal it in England, and although Decimus Burton, the architect, claimed to have designed it, this is not so. The work was entirely that of Joseph Paxton. It is often thought that Paxton originated the idea, new to the era, of building greenhouses of iron and glass, simply because he used iron and glass so successfully in the Crystal Palace, but he did not. The Great Conservatory was only partially iron. Paxton preferred wood and used it. Loudon advocated a cast iron framework for greenhouses and Repton before him had suggested it for a pheasantry in the grounds of the Brighton Pavilion. What Paxton did originate, to the great benefit of kitchen gardens in particular, was the ridge and furrow roof, which caught on very quickly.† This, together with iron framing and curvilinear design, meant that greenhouses and conservatories could be built in entirely new shapes; they could be architecturally effective and the old square or rectangular house was doomed. Greenhouses and conservatories of circular or elliptical shape with domes, bays and convex sides stood apart in pleasure grounds, were added as a winter garden wing to an old house, or built as an integral part of a new one. When Loudon designed and built his villa in Porchester Terrace in suburban Bayswater

---

* Demolished after the 1914–18 war. The area it once occupied is planted with lupins on the south side; Michaelmas daisies and dahlias on the north, and a maze of yew was planted in the central space in 1961. It is not yet grown enough to admit the public.

† Probably the best place to see the ridge and furrow roof today is Paddington Station.

in 1823 he had a 'domical-conservatory' as the main feature of the western front. It rose from ground to between the first and second floors and the verandah which ran around the square 'double' house gave access to it at ground floor level. These verandahs had also another purpose,—they ended in conveniently placed water-closets! They may have been conveniently placed but can hardly have added to the beauty of the verandah. In his kitchen garden he had various greenhouses and these had flat, slooping roofs but they were built before Paxton invented the ridge and furrow roof which Loudon later advocated enthusiastically.

Paxton was no novice at building greenhouses (it was just one of the many things he did supremely well), and among other greenhouses he built at Chatsworth were four large houses for pines (built around 1833), one for strawberries, three vineries, a mushroom house, a cucumber and melon house, and no fewer than three houses for orchids. These last were built around 1834, and in 1837 he produced a specimen of *Cattleya crispa* with seven flowers on one stem. This was unheard of, although by then growing orchids had become a very popular and fashionable thing to do. This is hardly surprising as more than fifty different species of orchid were introduced into England between 1800 and 1850,* and orchid houses multiplied exceedingly. A suitable orchid house for the fancier was expensive, but a single orchid could be grown in its own bijou glasshouse or 'Wardian Case'.

The Wardian Case was accidentally invented by the medical practitioner, botanist, plant cultivator and F.R.S., Nathaniel Bagshaw Ward (1791–1868) when one day he put some damp earth into a bottle, added a moth chrysalis, corked it and absent-mindedly forgot about it. When he finally remembered to look, he found flourishing in the bottle, not a moth but a plant which had grown from a seed in the moist soil and had gone on growing

---

* *The Encyclopaedia of Gardening* by T. W. Sanders, as revised by A. J. Macself, lists fifty-six for this period. There were doubtless more, as it is probable the number of species of the orchid family exceeds that of any other flower. It is believed to contain 10,000 to 15,000 species in 450 to 600 generae.

happily despite its unusual environment. The principle was scientifically investigated and the Wardian Case was adapted and adopted for the bulk transportation of tropical plants. But such an interesting and novel invention could not be left to serve merely scientific purposes, and the Wardian Case was produced in much smaller sizes, in quantity, and sold commercially. It was outstandingly successful and soon no home of any pretentions was complete without this airtight, transparent ornament adding to the general clutter of drawing room or boudoir. Orchids were a first favourite for this earliest of bottle gardens, but ferns ran them a close second for the Victorians also had a passion for ferns.

Loudon wrote much on greenhouses and their management, not only for the production of exotics and ferns but for the raising of flowers. As early as 1833 William Cobbett, M.P. for Oldham, had complained that the making of pretty gardens was 'a taste which, I am sorry to say, has been declining in England for a great many years', and that 'the present taste seems to be on the side of irregularity: straight walks, straight pieces of water, straight rows of trees, seem to be out of fashion; but it is also true that neatness, that really fine shrubberies and flower gardens have [has] gone out of fashion at the same time'.[11] He does not seem to have known that regularity and the re-introduction of flowers into gardens was well under way, so that by the late thirties the era of great bedding and carpet bedding was firmly established and became a fashion which lasted well on into the sixties.

It may be that Joseph Paxton first saw the possibilities of using glasshouses to raise bedding plants, we do not know, but the idea was quickly followed by all gardeners, and plants were taken straight from the greenhouse and bedded out in their pots. The minute one faded it was removed and another replaced it, so beds were kept in a state of perfection, and each bed could also show, overnight if necessary, the passing of one season and the coming of the next in the type of flowers bedded out. This was an old Chinese custom but new to England, and it required acres of glasshouses and countless pots to keep the beds always filled.

Those who had glasshouses could raise their own plants, those without could buy them from nurserymen, and nurserymen had multiplied exceedingly, as had seed firms. Prices were low, for example twopence to fourpence for a dozen half-hardy perennials. Anyone who could afford a garden at all could afford dozens at this price. And if one could not afford a landscape gardener or to employ a head gardener there were innumerable pattern books which showed how to lay out an astonishing variety of gardens of all shapes and sizes. Armed with a pattern book, a willing gardener or gardener's boy, and an honest nurseryman, anyone could produce a tolerably good garden of the do-it-yourself variety, and the keen amateur could always consult Mr Loudon, or rather Mr Loudon's various encyclopaedias.

Loudon had his own very decided theories on how flowers and shrubs should be planted. In addition to geometric beds he advocated the mingled border or garden. In these, flowers were to be planted in rows, good straight, regimented rows which would have delighted Cobbett's heart. No irregularity was permitted—which sounds and is absolutely deadly. Nothing must look crowded, wild, confused or 'natural' because this was an 'artificial' flower bed. Not that Loudon opposed the natural style; indeed he believed 'man's handiwork should be seen as much in *gardens laid out in the natural style* as in the most formal geometric garden, because both are equally intended to show they are works of art, and to display the taste and wealth of the possessor'.[12]

Mrs Loudon explains, for the benefit of ladies, and rather more simply, the difference between a natural and a geometric garden. The first is planted 'without any regard to regularity' and is known abroad as 'the English style'. The natural is beautiful in pleasure grounds but 'very ill-adapted to a flower garden which is essentially artificial'. The beauty of the second, that is the artificial or geometric garden, lies in 'the elegance with which it has been arranged and the neatness with which it is kept or, in other words, in the evidence it affords of the art employed in forming it'. No nonsense here about the art which conceals art as, 'an artificial mode of arrangement is more suitable . . . than any other', and when a garden is large enough 'to show a formal figure to advantage, the artificial mode of arrangement should be adopted'. Small gardens had to make do without beds, flowers could be planted singly or in patches and be mingled in a natural style, mixing annuals and perennials to make an ornamental botanic garden which would flower for the whole season. Such a garden would be 'not merely a source of elegant amusement, but also actually of scientific knowledge without any appearance of formal arrangement'.[13] Again, the combination of pleasure with the virtues of learning proved irresistible.

Ladies with large gardens made them 'Geometrical', which necessitated their drawing plans made up of 'angular, circular or serpentine forms to represent beds' arranged 'so as to form a whole'. This, understandably, required 'much taste and ingenuity' as each form had to be handsome in itself and 'harmonize with the others'. Grotesque shapes were suitable for a small area, where the eye could apprehend the whole garden at once, but were totally unfit for a large area where 'the beds should be simply formed', and the uniform shapes could be looked at either singly or together 'without forming any disagreeable impression on the mind'.[14] This paper plan was painted in with the colours of the flowers required and was then translated into the real thing. One cannot but feel that this kind of garden must have resembled a monstrous and untalented version of the small Elizabethan knot garden.

Both the Loudons—and everyone else—agreed on artifice, and Loudon when it came to colour in the garden held some very artificial views on the colour grouping of flowers. He believed flowers should be so arranged that a compound colour came next to a simple one which, and this sounds rather more difficult, was not contained in it. Hence, since the simple or primary colours blue and red when mixed produced purple, purple flowers must be set next to yellow ones. Red and yellow produce orange, so orange should stand next to blue, and as blue and yellow make green, green should be contrasted with red. This may have been effective, we do not know, but it sounds a bit on the dazzling and obvious side.

Another Victorian fancy, and for this we cannot blame Loudon, since it had been suggested sometime in the late 1770s, was the Cone bed, which sounds singularly unattractive. The centre of a bed was planted with tall flowers of one colour which ranged from eight to ten feet in height. This core was then enclosed by half a dozen or more widening circles of progressively shorter stemmed flowers—each circle in monochrome until the outer circle was reached where the flowers were but eight inches to a foot tall. In this fashion varicoloured concentric circles rose step by step, or band by band and colour by colour, in a huge cone like a gigantic, coarse Victorian nosegay. So far from approving was Loudon that he thought this kind of gardening fit only for remote districts, the colonies, young children and 'females'—which puts women in their place. Fortunately, Mrs. Loudon wrote her books on gardening for ladies; and perhaps they were read by females too.

Another fancy was the clock or dial garden planted with flowers which opened or closed at approximately regular and successive hours, and by which one could, equally approximately, tell the time of day, provided the sun obliged. To tell the hours, say, from 6 a.m. to 6 p.m., the sectionalized dial might be planted with Shrubby Hawkweed or Spotted Cat's Ear which opened at six, followed by African Marigold, Scarlet Pimpernel, Field Marigold, Red Sandwort and Star of Bethlehem which opened at succeeding hours until midday, which was the Ice Plant hour. Common Purslane reputedly opened at one o'clock and from two until four Purple Sandwort, Dandelion and White Spiderwort successively closed. At five Jalap opened, and at 6 p.m. Dark Crane's Bill. This boring and weedy little clock could be made just as inaccurately with other flowers.

What were known as select flower gardens, which limited each bed to a particular kind of plant, were more popular than ever.

All American plants in one, florist's flowers* in another, bulbs in another, which is fair enough and might even be interesting, but when it came to roses, a great and tortured ingenuity was often displayed to produce something novel. A bed with outcurving or gently scalloped sides and convex ends was cut in the turf; in this, rose bushes were planted and the outline enclosed with shaped sections of heavy wire or wood in a lattice or other open-work pattern and finished with little curved or pointed arches around the top to imitate basketwork. A handle of wire completed the framework and supported a climbing rose. The end result was that the bushes were contained within a sweetly pretty ornamental basket—rather like an outsize sweetmeat dish minus its glass liner. When the roses bloomed there, to please the eye and cause exclamations of wonder and delight, was a huge basket of roses sitting flat and naked on the lawn as if carelessly set down by Gog the head gardener. Roses could also be planted in shrubberies or borders or in simple geometric beds edged with common box —and common box was the wearisome favourite edging for flower beds, walks and kitchen gardens, albeit it was never clipped with shears but pruned with a knife. A rosery was also considered an effective way of displaying roses. This had a rock-work centre covered with creeping roses and all around this hub, roses were compartmented, that is, placed in radiating separate spoke-like beds. In one compartment a rose of any kind was put together with the varieties most like it, in another compartment another kind of rose with its similar varieties and so on. Nothing could have been more geometrical or artificial. Standard roses, 'now so common' had been 'unknown until about 1803',[15] and pre-sented a problem. They were best in a flower border or set singly

---

*Florist's flowers were first developed in the seventeenth century by amateurs, chiefly in East Anglia. They specialized in growing and breeding auriculas, tulips and carnations, and held shows and competitions. Florists' shows were popular and the custom spread from East Anglia to the Midlands and elsewhere. The amateur who grew these flowers was a florist. There was no commercial meaning attached to the word 'florist' at first. In 1832 Queen Adelaide became first patroness to the newly formed Metropolitan Society of Florists and Amateurs.

in a lawn because their similarity of form, which Loudon calls 'compact and lumpish', did not allow them to be grouped well. Their real beauty lay in their singularity.

Most gardeners held that no rose, and there were said to be 2,000 varieties, did well in or near a large town because of the smoke and the 'confined air'. Here they echoed the great seventeenth-century gardener, John Parkinson (1567–1650) who, as early as 1629, had complained that smoke-filled atmospheres were the most 'unwholesome ayres' and that the worst smoke came from sea-coal, 'as our Citie of London can give proof . . . wherein neither herbe nor tree will long prosper, nor hath done ever since the use of sea-coales beganne to be frequent there'.[16]

Over the two centuries since Parkinson's day the use of coal had increased greatly in London, and in the past fifty years had spread to the Midlands and the North to such an extent that the smoke-burdened and polluted air had so enveloped the surrounding countryside that even vegetables from market gardens tasted of soot. Smoke, once localized around London, had, with the growth and spread of industry, become almost a nationwide menace and there was nothing to be done about this new pest. Belching factory chimneys spelled prosperity. They also meant blackened towns, stunted vegetation and respiratory diseases.

Other natural pests we had always had with us and could fight. Plant-lice or aphids were a familiar curse to all. More honest than many, Loudon admits there is no known method of eradicating them completely and presents his readers with the discouraging and useless information that Réamur had calculated one aphid could be the progenitor of 5,904,900,000 descendants in five generations, and that there were ten generations in nine months! This was enough to make any rose grower give up in despair, but he must not. He could do nothing about smoke, soot, confined air and noxious fumes but he could, with incessant labour, control the ulta-prolific aphid. Hand-watering the bushes with lime water and then dusting them with powdered tobacco leaves or snuff was one method, although large quantities of snuff came expensive. Smoking the bushes with tobacco and moxa (a

Garden watering machines

cone made of the leaf-down of wormwood which has cauterizing properties), or Spanish tinder was also useful and the moxa used alone positively stupefied caterpillars, snails and slugs which, in their unconscious state, could then be gathered up by hand. One of the surest ways to clear bushes of aphids was to brush every single bud clean with a soft brush even if this took days. But nature herself had provided a remedy in the lady-cow (lady-bird) which should never be destroyed but encouraged to inhabit the garden. How to encourage lady-cows is not mentioned. A further preventive against ravages by aphids was to spray all bushes with water at a temperature of 100°F after the leaves had fallen, or with strong tobacco water. A lather of good soft soap just might prove useful but this was expensive in the early years of the century as the tax on soap was nearly 100 per cent. It was halved in 1833 and finally abolished by W. E. Gladstone in 1853.

K *

Roses were also a prey to the caterpillars of several small moths whose life cycle was then unknown. These injured buds and shoots; one kind even sewed up leaves and then sewed itself up in a leaf. These were monstrously difficult to get at. The only sure way to rid roses—or anything else, for that matter—of caterpillars was to pick them off by hand, a job 'which may be performed by poor women who are incapable of more severe labour'.[17]

Snails and slugs, ruinous to any garden, had to be trapped and this could be done by laying down slices of raw potato and cabbage leaves at night and 'examining them before the dew is off the plants' in the morning, but as this required 'very early rising', ladies were advised by Mrs Loudon that a more convenient method was to lay a few flower-pots on their sides 'near the places where the snails have committed their ravages' and 'the snails will generally be found to have taken refuge in the flower-pots from the heat of the sun'.

For moles, mice and birds several varieties of trap were required, while coping with wireworms and maggots must have been a tedious and lengthy job as the earth had to be removed from the roots of affected plants, the offenders removed by hand and destroyed. Wasps were to be smothered in their nests or scalded to death with boiling water, which sounds a terrifyingly inefficient and dangerous way of dealing with them. Earwigs and woodlice were trapped in the hollow stalks of vegetables or in beetle-traps, or enticed to destruction in pots inverted over a handful of hay or moss.

New to the era, and disseminating useful knowledge on how to plant trees, grow plants, slaughter pests, build glasshouses and plan gardens were magazines for gardeners. There had been, and still were, numbers of botanical journals for specialist readers but the first-ever gardeners' magazine, as such, was launched in 1826. Its founder was J. C. Loudon and it was so successful that it was soon earning him a clear £750 a year. It was quickly followed by other magazines including Joseph Paxton's short-lived *Horticultural Register* (1831) and *Paxton's Magazine of*

Botany and Register of Flowering Plants (1835) which put Loudon's *Gardeners' Magazine* out of business. The first number of *Paxton's Magazine* was dedicated to his patron and friend the Duke of Devonshire, but in time Paxton flew higher. In 1843 it was dedicated to the Queen, in 1844 to the Emperor of Russia and in 1845 to Prince Albert.

Paxton, later Sir Joseph Paxton, is best remembered for the Crystal Palace and is often forgotten as the great gardener he was.* The seventh son of a Bedfordshire farmer he became, at fifteen, garden-boy to Sir Gregory Page-Turner at Battesdene, near Woburn, moved to Woodhall, Herts, returned to Battesdene for a bit and then went to the Duke of Somerset and, subsequently, to the newly-opened gardens of the Royal Horticultural Society near Chiswick House. Chiswick House belonged to the Duke of Devonshire, who needed a new gardener at Chatsworth. Paxton caught his eye and in 1826, instead of emigrating to America as he had been thinking of doing, Paxton went to Chatsworth, Derbyshire, and in a short time became head gardener. He travelled in Europe with the Duke and subsequently became his very able man of affairs. Unlike Repton or Loudon he was not in business himself and he was certainly not so well known to the middle classes as Loudon. Probably the first startling success for which he became famous was his flowering of the great lily *Victoria regia* in 1849. Had he not been an expert in glasshouses, an excellent botanist and a superb gardener he could not have succeeded.

This enormous water-lily, now called *Victoria amazonica*, was discovered by Robert Schlomburgk in what was then British Guiana in 1837. Schlomburgk sent full notes, excellent drawings and specimens back to England; asked, and was granted, permission to name it after the Queen. Other foreign explorers claimed prior knowledge of the lily but Schlomburgk was the first to describe and draw it in detail. Seeds were sent to England in 1846 but did not flourish at Kew and it was not until spring

* R. W. Emerson (1803–82) in *English Traits* (Chapter X) cites only two early Victorians as creators of beautiful things, Loudon and Paxton.

1849 that seeds finally germinated there. From Kew's director, Sir William Hooker,* Paxton got a tiny plant with leaves six inches in diameter. He had already built a heated tank and house for the lily and in August 1849 he installed the small plantlet. Two months later its bright green, nearly circular leaves, with their turned-up margins showing the crimson underside, measured four feet in circumference. In November, *Victoria* flowered for the first time. The flowering caused the greatest excitement (Paxton had beaten Kew) and the event was noted by newspapers and journals as a wonder, which indeed it was. An engraving of Paxton's nine-year-old daughter, Annie, standing primly on one of the great leaves as it floated on the water, appeared in November in *The Illustrated London News* and showed the size and strength of the leaves. No one in England had ever seen anything like the huge flowers either, with their white to rose-coloured petals the whole measuring ten inches to a foot in diameter. On Wednesday November 14th Mr Paxton presented a leaf and flower of *Victoria regia* to Victoria regina and Prince Albert at Windsor Castle. Within a year *Victoria* showed herself to be enormously prolific and had produced 112 flowers, 140 leaves and innumerable seeds. She had also twice outgrown her tank, and new buildings had had to be especially built for her. Mr Paxton was indeed 'quite a genius', as the Queen had once termed him.

Mr Paxton was also very able, which geniuses often are not. Although he was the Duke's man, he did undertake a few private commissions. More important, he, together with Professor Lindley and another gardener, a Mr Wilson, saved the Royal Botanic Gardens at Kew. A Treasury Committee asked these three to report on the gardens, which many felt should be given up. The report made a strong plea for the revival of Kew as a National Botanic Garden and for its extension by thirty acres. The recom-

* Sir William Jackson Hooker (1785–1865) Regius Professor of Botany, Glasgow, 1820, became director of Kew Gardens 1841. He extended the gardens and opened them to the public. Succeeded by his son, Sir Joseph Dalton Hooker (1817–1911) who discovered the Sikkim rhododendrons during his expedition of 1847.

mendations were adopted. Paxton also reported on other Royal gardens and parks in 1838 and found Windsor in a state of 'excellent wretchedness'.[18] He also designed Prince's Park, Liverpool, in 1842 and Upton Park, Slough, in 1843, as well as the first park ever provided by public funds for public use at Birkenhead (opened 1847) where he transformed a virtually useless piece of land into something beautiful and useful.* He was also clever enough to make a good deal of money out of railways and was not caught in the crash of 1849 as so many were.

Loudon disapproved of the great changes Paxton was making at Chatsworth and said so in his magazine. Paxton defended himself in his and a certain hostility existed between them for a time, but later they became friends. Paxton made money in railways. Loudon ran up a debt of £10,000 on his classic *Arboretum Brittanicum*† (1835–8). He could not pay the money and although he had given up active landscape gardening for writing, he went back to it at five guineas for an eight-hour visit. He also had several commissions for designing cemeteries or in undertaking the 'horticulture of graveyards'. In 1843, while engaged in laying out a cemetery at Southampton, he died.

Loudon's importance can now be gauged only from his written work, but it is probably safe to say he was the first landscape gardener who realized that suburbs and surburban villas needed planned gardens as much as, or even more than, great estates. Many more people were making money and becoming middle class and one suspects the bulk of the readership of his *Gardeners' Magazine* to have been among the middle classes. The new prosperous competitive class which, on its various levels, was doing

* Among other things he laid out the cemetery, Coventry, 1845; Manchester Royal Infirmary grounds, 1854; Halifax People's Park, 1856. Knighted 1851, he became M.P. for Coventry, 1854.

† After the failure of the *Gardeners' Magazine*, Loudon founded the *Architectural Magazine*, the first in our history, and *The Magazine of Natural History*. Under the pseudonym 'Kataphusin' the young Ruskin contributed an article to the *Architectural Magazine* in November 1837. Its title was *Introduction to the Poetry of Architecture; or, The Architecture of the Nations of Europe considered in its Association with Natural Scenery and National Character*.

very well indeed out of our new, booming industry, and which bought or built grand or not so grand houses on much or little land depending on the prosperity of the individual. If the amount of land were large, it had to be turned into park, pleasure ground and gardens. If small, its ten acres or so needed lawns, flower beds, gravel walks, trees, urns and—had there been gnomes—gnomes.

Rapidly expanding towns had sprawled into suburbs with their villas, each villa surrounded by some land and requiring a garden. It was on designing gardens for suburban villas in and around London that Loudon very wisely concentrated his efforts early in his career and by 1838 he had already written his *The Suburban Gardener and Villa Companion.** Those who could not employ Loudon in person, could read his detailed advice and follow it or instruct their head gardeners to do so.

Curiously enough, this book rather belies its name as it grades houses from first to fourth rate. And the first rate has nothing to do with suburbs and villas, since such houses require not less than from fifty to one hundred acres of land—several thousand acres was more desirable—a park, a dairy and so on. Some of this acreage would, of course, be farmland but, Loudon warns, it is well known that many owners of large estates more often than not lose money if they farm the land themselves, therefore farmland should be let to a working farmer. It is not until the fourth grade, which admittedly comprises the largest section of the book, that we arrive at those houses and villas which form a part of a row or street and stand in grounds of from one perch to an acre. Into this category Loudon's own 'double detached' villa and garden in Porchester Terrace, Bayswater, fell.

His carefully planted garden looked like a single garden but it was divided by a low brick wall in the back and a low fence of wrought iron palings, ornamented midway by an urn, in front. Here he grew two thousand different plant species exclusive of varieties. He had a tiny moss-garden and even a seaweed garden

---

* It is probable that Loudon stopped active work not long after his marriage and devoted himself to writing. But he also designed the Birmingham Botanic Garden.

in a salt-water tank. His alpine house contained some six hundred specimens and he had a wonderful collection of hot-house plants. The lawn was planted with three to four hundred different kinds of bulb. His flower borders, his vines, his *Lonicera flexuosa* and his favourite trees all made what he called a 'veritable paradise' for him when he came home to Bayswater from busy, filthy London. This garden of such great variety occupied only a quarter of an acre and cost £250 a year in upkeep.

What Loudon did for himself he did for others and in so doing altered the conception of what could be done with very small gardens and thus gave to them a hitherto unknown importance.

Small gardens, naturally, had no pleasure grounds, no parks, no great flower beds or other of the adjuncts belonging to large gardens such as fountains, statues, gravel walks, innumerable garden ornaments and new types of garden house and furniture. Great gardens were well equipped with all these. Popular furniture was often of cast iron with gigantic fern leaves forming the backs of chairs and benches. Stone benches set at either end of a terrace were greatly favoured; failing stone, the bench could be run up in cement and if sprinkled with sand while the cement was still wet, a passable imitation of stone was achieved —or so we are told. Also useful were the new folding wooden seats which were imported from Norway and cost only 3*s* 6*d* each. These could easily be carried about the garden and placed where desired. The chair back folded over the seat and so both remained dry in wet weather. Garden houses and seats were called 'Convenient Decorations' and varied in design from a simple rustic wooden seat to the 'Prospect Tower'. The latter was, 'agreeable to the eye and convenient for the purpose of recreation or culture',[19] which sounds a bit ambiguous. Then there was the 'kiosque' or Chinese tower of 'peculiar construction'. It had many storeys, each with its projecting roof, and was merely a near replica of the Pagoda at Kew. The once dearly-loved temple-like garden houses of the eighteenth century had by now been 'brought into contempt' by too frequent use and were replaced by porticoes and porches which were considered to be the most admirable kind of shelter. Porches and porticoes were usually just garden houses made to look rustic. Alcoves, that is small sentry-box-like houses, to keep off the winter wind and trap the summer sun were musts, while arbours, overgrown with ivy, clematis or everlasting pea and further shaded by encircling trees and shrubs were strictly for summer use. A favourite was the so-called Italian Arbour. Spacious and generally with a dome of thick meshed copper wire, for climbing plants, it could be as simple or elaborate as desired. Then there were moss houses.

Moss houses were new and popular and afforded great scope for artistic effort, particularly to ladies who could collect the moss, work out the patterns, and even complete the building when the wooden framework was ready. This framework consisted of eight to a dozen rustic pillars—straight stout branches with the bark left on or sapling larches or firs—which supported the roof. Between these, laths or rods were nailed close together and on these the design was roughly drawn in chalk. Then the mosses which had been collected, and it must have required a mountain of moss, were sorted into kinds and colours and, according to design were pushed in between the rods, roots first, with a wooden wedge. Arabesque patterns were charming, and as mosses range in colour from white to dark brown, when done sufficiently well an arabesque pattern gave the effect of a Turkey carpet—which sounds a trifle surprising as a design for a garden house. Or the house could be of monochrome moss with only the family crest in a contrasting coloured moss set up above the door. Failing a crest (but few failed) the designer's initials would do. The roof was thatched or shingled and a pretty touch was a circle of pine cones fixed as a cornice. If the house were large enough for windows, coloured glass gave a rich and pleasing effect.

But pushing moss into a framework was not the only thing a lady could do in a garden. There were any number of other things to be done. She could, by a little attention to the 'principles of mechanics and the laws of motion', dig or stir the soil, were the spade small enough, although digging might appear 'a very laborious employment and one particularly unfitted to small delicately formed hands and feet'. She could also sow seeds properly and 'steeping seeds in oxalic acid to make them vegetate' is recommended by Mrs Loudon, but not by me.

She could water seedlings with a watering-pot; pond water was best as it contained air. Grafting could be undertaken with every hope of success; and pruning, which appeared to be, 'a most laborious and unfeminine undertaking', could be easily accomplished 'with the aid of a small, most elegant pair of pruning shears . . . procured from Mr Forrest of Kensington Nursery'.[20]

Some ladies went so far as to keep bees. 'Lady Peel is about making a flower garden', her husband writes, 'and told a country neighbour not skilled in derivation that she had a great mind to have *an apiary*. "Lord ma'am, where will you get your apes from? For my part I could never 'bide a monkey." '[21]

What a lady could not do was mow the lawn, unless she had the strength to use one of Mr Budding's new mowing machines, which she probably had not. But until Edwin Budding—an engineer in a cloth factory near Stroud, Glos.—adapted a small machine for cutting pile on cloth to a large machine for cutting grass on lawns, all mowing was done early in the morning by scythe. Budding patented his machine for cropping or shearing the 'vegetable surface of lawns' as early as 1830 and he used to practise mowing his own lawn after dark to test the machine for imperfections, which the neighbours thought rather sinister. By 1831 the machine was perfected and was manufactured by John Ferrabee at the Phoenix Foundry near Stroud. By 1832 similar machines were being made by James Ransome of Ipswich. Most gardeners welcomed and praised the machine. Even so, at the Great Exhibition Ferrabee and Ransome were the only two exhibitors of lawn mowers and the machines were virtually the same as the original. Mr Budding had thought his machine would prove amusing to gentlemen and give them healthful exercise, but it took some time to persuade gentlemen of this. This first-ever lawn mower came in two sizes and prices. Small for gentlemen, wider for workmen, and was priced at seven and ten guineas respectively. This was one of the newest and most useful of garden tools, and once it caught on laborious scythe-mowing went out of fashion.

Other things of a quite different order also went out of fashion. Caves and caverns were no longer contrived to lend enchantment and mystery to a garden, and if they existed naturally, should be regarded as picturesque and not for use. Our climate was now thought too bad to use a cave or a cavern as a real part of a garden. Grottoes too were all but out. These enchanting, wonderful and imaginative creations, so dear to the eighteenth century that no great garden was complete without one, are given cavalier treatment in the nineteenth as 'resting places in recluse situations, rudely covered externally and within furnished with shells, corals, spars, crystallizations and marine and mineral productions according to fancy'.[22] To add to this insult, if one must have a grotto bits of looking-glass stuck about at pleasure was a clever idea.

The grotto as a work of art had ceased to exist in Victorian gardens but happily the tiny portable grottoes of shells which for centuries had been used to celebrate St James's Day were still made by children who sat beside them in the streets on July 25th asking for a 'penny for the grotto'. This centuries' old custom, dying out in the rest of the country, was prevalent in the East End of London throughout the last century and continued into our own. These grottoes, usually built of oyster shells, stood about eighteen inches high, were roofed and had a front entrance. The children made them with great care and were by no means slum children who begged purely for themselves. The begging-bowl was a shell and with the money collected—which was never much—the children bought candles to put inside the grotto to light it as it was regarded almost as a sacred duty to light the candles at dusk. If any money were left over this went on sweetmeats, but candles came first.

There were several begging rhymes or songs used in the Tower Hamlets. One, from the Parish of St Mary Stratford Bow, runs :

Please to remember the grotto.
Only once a year,
Father's gone to sea,
Mother's gone to fetch him back,
Please remember me.[23]

So grottoes, though unfashionable in a garden, were still made in miniature, often very beautifully, by children.

But if rocky caves, caverns and grottoes were out, rock-work was definitely in. Rock-work, new to the era, was hardly what we would call a rock garden. Paxton began building a rock-work in 1842 at Chatsworth on a bare slope where he cemented together great boulders and hunks of rock to imitate picturesque groups of natural rock, copying the wild form and planting it with the right kind of vegetation.

At Blenheim the Duke of Marlborough had a rock-work admired by many but not by Mrs Loudon. It was magnificent but could never be taken for a natural outcrop of rock and its chief interest lay in the plants grown in it. Formed in a scar in the natural rock, which was hewn into zig-zag paths, there were niches on each side of the path and in these were plants so carefully tended that they grew luxuriously and hid the rock-work so effectively that at a distance it looked like a bank of flowers— which is not what rock-work was intended to look like. Where there were no flowers, mosses grew and the whole, although not 'natural', had a peculiarly 'rich and sparkling effect'.[24]

Syon House had a splendid terrace with geometric flower gardens at its base, and these quite overpowered the adjacent rock-work made of masses and masses of granite mixed with the broken capitals and other bits of marble columns, 'all thrown together in a natural manner', Mrs Loudon says, which sounds rather as if an earthquake had done the job. This mixture was planted with ornamental plants, chiefly exotic.

Of innumerable rock-works the most impressive was that created by Lady Boughton at the Hoole near Chester. This was indeed a mountain, or rather a mountain range in miniature, as it was a model of the mountains of the Savoy complete with the

Iron fountain with rock-work base

valley of Chamonix. The rocks used to make the mountains were
enormous and Lady Boughton had had the greatest difficulty in
getting them in the right colours and shapes. Further, the rain
washed away the soil in a muddy avalanche, the frost cracked the
stones and, on several occasions, the main wall collapsed under

the sheer weight. The main wall and foundations—rock-works had to have solid foundations to prevent them sinking into the ground—were of local red sandstone, as was the outer circle of rocks. These rocks were planted with alpines. The rest of the mountainous range was composed of rocks chiefly from Wales and the whole work was carefully planted with trees and shrubs of dwarf species or slow growth to keep up the Alpine illusion. The illusion was heightened by the *Mer de Glace*, made of quartz, spar, and grey limestone with fragments of white marble cunningly inserted to imitate snow, just as the spar and quartz imitated ice. The whole work took from six to eight years to create and the rocks were large enough 'to give a person walking among them an idea of their [the mountains'] reality'.[25] It sounds perfectly appalling but at least it must have been the epitome of the artificial aping the natural.

Rock-work seems to have become a passion, and Nathaniel Hawthorne out walking with his wife near Birkenhead gives us his view of this new fashion when he saw the new villas which had sprung up there with their gardens and, 'heaps of curious rock-work, which the English are ridiculously fond of adorning their front yards with'.[26]

Not everyone was going in for new villas, rock-work, glass-houses, geometric gardens and vast shrubberies. There were still small country and cottage gardens, as there had always been, which went on unworried and relatively untouched by new-fangled ideas of planning and laying out. Here, all the old dearly loved flowers and roses were grown in a manner which no one could call artificial and which depended entirely on the taste of the individual. Occasionally new flowers were introduced, but for the most part cottage gardens expressed the love and the artless artistry of their owners. Some were neat and tidy and prim, some sprawled in a wild tangle of roses, hollyhocks, pinks, sweet williams, lavender, crown-imperial, honeysuckle and hearts-ease—but heartsease, long loved by cottagers, became at this time a most fashionable Victorian flower and many new and splendid varieties were produced to grace larger gardens. Nevertheless, throughout rural areas, 'the very labourer, with his thatched cottage and narrow slip of ground, attends to their embellishment. The trim hedge, the grass-plot before the door, the little flower bed bordered with snug box, the woodbine trained up against the wall, and hanging its blossoms about the lattice, the pot of flowers in the window, the holly, providentially planted about the house . . . all bespeak the influence of taste, flowing down from high sources, and pervading the lowest levels of the public mind. If ever Love, as poets sing, delights to visit a cottage, it must be the cottage of an English peasant.'[27]

This pretty and glutinously sentimental picture of the English 'peasant', happily living in such charming surroundings, due largely to the influence of high sources may be partially true, but, if so, 'high sources' must also bear the responsibility for 'old stone cottages, of the rudest structure and doubtless hundreds of years old, with thatched roofs, into which the grass has rooted itself and now look verdant. These cottages are in themselves as ugly as possible, resembling a larger kind of pig-stye; but often by dint of verdure on the thatch and the shrubbery clustering around them, they look picturesque.'[28] Poverty, not love, had visited these cottages and there were too many of them.

Miss Mitford, who lived at Three Mile End, near Twyford, Middlesex, inhabited a 'wretched cottage on the turnpike road', with 'a wretched dark London-looking garden behind'; but 'behind that is another light garden full of flowers and geraniums'. Further, 'she raised a seedling dahlia which she exchanged with a nurseryman for £15 worth of fuchsias'.[29] Miss Mitford was not a typical cottager and hardly a typical Victorian, despite her love of geraniums. She was, however, in her love of gardens typically English and when Daniel Webster,* the great American lawyer, called on Miss Mitford they walked together in her garden and discussed 'the different indigenous flowers of our country and the United States'. They also 'talked naturally of

---

* Daniel Webster (1782–1852), a man of overwhelming eloquence, bitterly opposed to the war of 1812, visited England in 1839. He was an abolitionist, Member of the House of Representatives and later a Senator.

the roses and pinks that surround us', and of 'the primrose and cowslip, immortalized by Shakespeare and by Milton; and the sweet-scented violet, both white and purple, of our hedgerows and our lanes'. When Mr Webster returned to America he took the trouble to send her seeds of the 'scarlet lily of New York and of the Canadian woods', and the 'fringed gentian of Niagara', which she had never seen and which were known to her only 'by the vivid descriptions of Miss Martineau'.[30]

No stranger who visited England even then, when gardens with their geometric designs, their dank ever-increasing shrubberies, their rigid walks and unprepossessing convenient decorations, were going through an ugly phase, was other than delighted or amazed by our genuine love of gardens and gardening, as well as our deep affection for the countryside. To some it seemed that it was only in the country Englishmen became real.

'It is in the country', Washington Irving wrote, 'that the Englishman gives scope to his natural feelings. He breaks loose gladly from the cold formalities and negative civilities of town; throws off his habit of shy reserve and becomes joyous and free-hearted . . . the taste of the English in the cultivation of land, and in what is called landscape gardening is unrivalled.'[31]

CHAPTER EIGHT

'Der Tod das ist die kühle Nacht'

In August 1861 the Queen and the Prince Consort, aboard the royal yacht, went from the Isle of Wight to Ireland *en route* to Balmoral. On the 23rd the Prince rode over from Dublin to the Curragh camp to see how the Prince of Wales was getting on with his military studies there. The young prince, on his seventeenth birthday, November 9th 1858, had been gazetted colonel in the army, unattached, and now at nearly nineteen he had joined the second battalion Grenadier Guards for a month's training at Curragh.

On the 24th, the Queen went over and reviewed the troops. 'Bertie marched past with his company, and did not look at all so very small',[1] she writes, for Bertie's height was held against him as well as a good many other things. As a child he had had a stammer and was also considered backward. Certainly he was no good at book learning, as was his father, and never would be. He could not master Latin, his spelling was bad and his deficiencies were constantly being rammed home to him so that he developed an outsize sense of inferiority which led to constant squabbles with his brothers and sisters and to temper tantrums. Later, when he went up to Oxford and Cambridge for an undistinguished career, he was not permitted to live as an undergraduate in college for fear he might make unsuitable friends. He had his own dull establishment. Even his personal appearance did not escape denigrating comment from his mother. His Coburg nose was too large, his head too small. His hair grew in such a strange way. He was knock-kneed and too short. His father, terri-

fied of the hereditary factors which might affect his son—those
wicked, lax Hanoverian uncles of the Queen (and what of both
the boy's grandfathers?)—sought to shield the heir to the throne
from temptation of any sort by constant vigilance. Yet this dis-
appointing boy had a genuine interest in English history and
in the army. He also had a warm affectionate nature. His parents
might be forgiven for thinking him incapable of learning what
they wished him to learn, but not for failing to realize his good
qualities and his need to give and receive affection. The Queen's
remark on reviewing the troops at Curragh camp that the prince
did not look 'so very small' seems to indicate that she regarded
him as a child. She did. And continued to regard him as such
for the next forty years.

But the Queen was feeling very depressed at the time. 'I have
felt weak and very nervous and so low at times;' she writes. 'I
think so much of dearest mama and miss her love and interest
and solicitude *dreadfully*; I feel as if we were no longer cared
for, and miss writing to her and telling her everything, dreadfully. At the Review they played one of her marches, which
entirely upset me.'[2]

The Duchess of Kent had died the previous March at Frogmore after an operation for an abscess of the arm, and the Queen's
grief for her mother had been excessive and prolonged. Remem-
bering on what bad terms she and her mother had once been,
this overwhelming grief for 'dearest mama' cannot be un-
associated with some feelings of guilt—even though the Duchess
had been greatly at fault. The Queen recognized this but was
inclined to blame their estrangement on the once 'dearest, dearest
Lehzen' and Sir John Conroy. That there had soon been a total
reconciliation was due to Albert who loved his Aunt Kent and
could not bear divisions in the family. Credit must also be given
the Duchess. Perhaps the alienation from her daughter, the
Queen of England, had taught her a lesson. She ceased to be
domineering, arrogant, self-assertive, rude and ambitious, and
turned herself into the perfect mother, grandmother and mother-
in-law. She became her daughter's confidante. They talked over

the children, baby clothes, confinements, teething troubles, nurses, diets and 'baby's' funny little ways—whichever of the nine babies it happened to be. She was her son-in-law's friend and admirer and a loving grandmother to the royal children. The change seems incredible, but possibly the Duchess was one of those women who take their colouring from the men in their lives. And the men in her life had been a rude and disagreeable first husband, a pompous, self-satisfied martinet of a second husband, the dishonest and ambitious Conroy, and finally Albert who was loving, kind and gentle and who expected her to be the same and become a loving mother and a comfortable, not to say cosy, grandmother.

At this point it is tempting to think that Albert succeeded too well. Had the Duchess and her daughter not been so completely reconciled, not been on such intimate terms, her death might not have been such a blow to the Queen; she might not have felt 'no longer cared for'. As it was, she was thrown completely off balance and undoubtedly had some sort of nervous breakdown, as by May, when she celebrated her forty-second birthday, it was known she was suffering from what was called 'nervous prostration' and rumours went flying about—not for the first time—that she was mad. The ghost of George III was always at hand to lend this kind of rumour the mask of truth. Still, the Queen could hardly transact business, so more and more fell upon Albert—but she did manage to hold two dismal Drawing Rooms and two Investitures in June.

Yet bouts of recurring depression and wild grief continued to afflict her for months. She had no one to talk to now mama was dead. Albert never stopped working. It was a mania with him. He was disturbed by reports that French agents were intriguing with revolutionary parties in Poland, Hungary and the Danubian provinces. Italy was far from settled—there was the question of Venice to trouble the new king, Vittorio Emmanuele and, more important, what did that ambitious Napoleon III plan to do in Italy? He had annexed the Savoy. What next? Belgium?—and war in Europe? Russia was restive, there was trouble in Turkey;

and civil war in the United States. Where would it all lead? What could be done? All these matters and many others, foreign and domestic, had to be totally assimilated and understood by the sovereign. Every ministerial despatch had to be read and approved and when advice could be given it should be given. Albert never stopped working. His memoranda went, as always, to the Queen, but she was unable to work herself and he bore an increasingly heavy burden. In addition, there were always speeches to be made, journeys to be taken. He never stopped. Hence he had too little time to spend comforting and encouraging his wife. He did what he could but she was incapable of pulling herself together without his constant help.

If only Vicky could have been with her. Vicky was her father's favourite—they were very alike—but Vicky would have understood. However, Vicky could not leave her children. Charlotte was only an infant and William 'such a little love' was barely two. Besides, Vicky had just become Crown Princess of Prussia and had, in consequence, heavier duties of her own. Albert really did not understand—no man understood—that a woman needed a woman to talk to at certain times. Albert kept on trying to persuade her to take an interest in outside things and to control her grief. She tried very hard but she could not. Albert, she must have felt, had never known what it was like to lose a mother.

Balmoral, fortunately, brought relief. There were walks, rides, picnics and mountain expeditions. During one golden week in October the Queen and Prince Consort went out every day 'taking luncheon with us, carried in a basket on the back of a Highlander, served by an *invaluable* Highland servant I have, who is *my factotum here*, and takes the most wonderful care of me, combining the offices of groom, footman, page, and *maid*, I might almost say, as he is *so* handy about cloaks and shawls, etc. He always leads my pony, and always attends me out of doors, and *such* a good, handy, *faithful*, attached servant I have nowhere; it is quite a sorrow for me to leave him behind.'[3]

However, she still had that invaluable, good, handy, faithful, attached servant, Albert, to take back with her. But Albert had

Balmoral

changed. At forty-two he was no longer the handsome knight in shining armour. He had put on a lot of weight. His hair had receded in front and had been heavily tonsured by age at the back so that he had to wear a wig at breakfast to keep his head warm as the Queen did not believe in unhealthy fires and hot rooms. He was—and had been since the age of twenty-six—frequently racked with rheumatic pains which a few fires might have helped. He took cold easily, was a bad colour and his weak stomach was too often out of sorts. He tired easily, too, but even as a young man he had been unable to bear late nights and was dropping with fatigue by eleven o'clock. He rose at seven, worked two hours before breakfast and afterwards began his working day. Small wonder that at forty-two Albert was prematurely aged, worn out by overwork (and unable to stop working) and by his own nature—for he was a perfectionist—and by coping with the Queen. His will to live was not robust and he had often explained to his wife that he, unlike she, did not cling to life and although happy in his lot if he were attacked by some severe illness he would not struggle. From this it has been deduced that the Prince suffered from a death wish and that this was caused by the Queen. But this assumption does not take into account the Prince's basic melancholy nature, nor the fact that this wish, if it existed, might equally well have been due to the traumatic experience of being left by his mother at the age of four.

Early in November news reached the court that the whole Portuguese royal family had typhoid. Prince Ferdinand died on the 6th and was swiftly followed by his brother King Pedro V, who was only twenty-five. Albert was very attached to the young king whom he regarded almost as a son. His death depressed him greatly and he suffered from insomnia. It further depressed the already depressed Queen. 'Dear Pedro was so good, so clever, so distinguished!' she writes to her uncle. 'He was so attached to my beloved Albert, and the character and tastes suited so well, and he had such confidence in Albert! *All, all gone!*'[4] To her diary she confided, 'The only thought which has comfort in it is that he—dear, pure, excellent Pedro—is united to his darling angelic Stéphanie, and that he is spared the pang and sacrifice of having to marry again.'[5] This could hardly be more unhappily phrased as it sounds as if the Queen considered death preferable for a young man of twenty-five to a second marriage.

On the same day which brought the news of the death of Prince Ferdinand and King Pedro, the Prince Consort received a letter from Stockmar. It was a shocking letter as it revealed that while at Curragh camp, the Prince of Wales had indulged in an amorous adventure or escapade, and that the news was seeping through all the courts of Europe. Apart from the fact that amorous adventures were just what Albert detested and most feared for his son—given the boy's heredity and lack of intellect—both he and the Queen were fearful that this might stand in the way of Bertie's engagement to Princess Alexandra, daughter of Prince Christian* of Schleswig-Holstein-Sonderburg-Glücksburg, a beautiful, modest, eminently suitable girl—though as poor as a

* Later King Christian of Denmark.

low church mouse. The Prince and the Queen discussed the affair and Albert, to his credit, wrote his son a long, patient and understanding letter—at what cost we shall never know. He also wrote to Stockmar. 'I am fearfully in need of a true friend and counsellor,' he said, 'and I think that *you* are the counsellor and friend I want, you will readily understand why.'[6]

Shortly afterwards the Prince took cold, but on November 22nd went off to inspect the new Staff College and Royal Military College at Sandhurst, a job he did in the pouring rain. He returned to Windsor soaked through, chilled to the bone and shivering violently. He had, it was thought, caught a chill on top of his cold. It was, however, a social weekend at Windsor and for Albert a miserable one. His insomnia persisted and he was tortured by 'rheumatic' pains which can occur in the first stages of typhoid fever. Yet on Saturday he went out shooting with Prince Ernest of Leiningen and on Sunday walked with the Queen to Frogmore to visit 'mama's' mausoleum. On Monday 25th he went by rail to Cambridge to talk out the Curragh affair with Bertie. He did not tell the young prince that his mother knew. Instead, to save embarrassment, he said that she did not know and must never know. Very probably the Queen would never again have thought of the horrid business had Albert lived. As it was she held her son responsible for his father's death.

Albert returned to Windsor on the 26th feeling so ill he could not go walking with the Queen until the afternoon. Dr William Jenner, the new Physician Extraordinary to the Queen and an expert in continued fevers had been brought in by Sir James Clark, now retired and he pronounced the Prince better. On the same day the Queen wrote to her uncle : 'Albert is a little rheumatic, which is a plague—but it is very difficult not to have something or other of this kind at this season with the rapid changes of temperature; *unberufen, unberufen,* he is much better this winter than he was the preceding years.'[7]

It was difficult for anyone not to catch something at any time at Old Windsor. The place, due to its appalling drainage, was notorious for a recurring ailment known as 'Windsor fever'. It is reported that the Prince's faithful valet Löhlein, well aware of this, said to the Prince when he was ill, 'Living here will kill your Royal Highness. You must leave Windsor and go to Germany for a time to recover health and strength.'[8]

By the 27th it was obvious to even the healthiest—and the Queen was physically very healthy—that the Prince was ill, but on this day news arrived of the *Trent* affair and by the next day the country was in an uproar. Very briefly, what had happened was that the *Trent*, an English ship, had sailed from Havana on November 7th carrying passengers and mail. Among the passengers were Mr James M. Mason and Mr John Slidell, envoys appointed to London and Paris respectively by the Confederate President, Jefferson Davis.* These gentlemen had succeeded in running the blockade and getting to a neutral port to embark in a neutral ship.

News that the *Trent* was carrying Confederate commissioners reached the ears of Captain Charles Wilkes of the United States warship, *San Jacinto*, which was searching for the Confederate cruiser *Sumter*. Wilkes determined to intercept the *Trent* and arrest the envoys and their secretaries, Eustis and McFarland. His second-in-command, Lieutenant Macneil Fairfax, was against such action, feeling it might lead to war with Britain. But on November 8th, Wilkes sighted the *Trent* and as she came closer the *San Jacinto* fired across her bows and then fired again at closer ranger. Captain Moir of the *Trent* knew resistance was useless. An armed boarding party led by Lieutenant Fairfax—who had been instructed to take the *Trent* as a prize but did not—came aboard the *Trent* and, over the vehement protests of Captain Moir and the Royal Mail agent Commander Williams, removed under armed guard Messrs Mason, Slidell, Eustis and McFarland with their luggage to the *San Jacinto*.

* Jefferson Davis (1808–89), army officer, cotton planter, member of the House of Representatives, Senator and a reluctant secessionist, was inaugurated first and only president of the Confederated States February 18th 1861 and tried, unsuccessfully, to prevent armed conflict with the Northern States. After the Civil War he was accused of treason, imprisoned 1865–7, but good sense ultimately prevailed and the treason case was dropped.

Mrs Slidell, who had concealed important documents in her crinoline, Miss Slidell and Mrs Eustis were left behind and the *Trent* proceeded to Liverpool. The prisoners were taken to New York and ultimately to Boston and the Northern States went mad with joy at their capture. Mad is the correct word. What Wilkes had done was in total violation of international law; further, he had insulted the British flag. His action could easily have led to war—and with England on the Confederate side, the Northern States would have been forced to fight on two fronts. Wilkes, however, was rather proud of himself. He had acted off his own bat and not on orders from Washington. Fortunately, this story was later confirmed by Mrs Slidell, for when the Government first received news of the *Trent* affair and when people heard of it—and the newspapers were vituperative—the chief emotion was intense anger and a desire for prompt retaliatory action. We prepared at once to mobilize the fleet and send eight thousand troops to Canada.

By November 30th the draft of our proposed note to Washington was sent to the Queen. The Prince sat up all night reading it and related papers although the previous day he had been able to eat nothing, yet had pleased the Queen by walking with her while she inspected two hundred Eton volunteers. There were visitors that weekend too; the Duc de Nemours, Mr and Mrs Gladstone and Lord Carlisle. The Prince had sat at table with them but could not eat. He had a foul, dry, leathery tongue—a sympton of typhoid. Even so, Dr Jenner (he had taken the place of Dr Baly, killed in a railway accident in January) thought him much better. There was no cause for alarm nor any need for a physician to sleep at the castle.

The Prince worked doggedly at Lord Russell's* draft to Washington and ended by writing a memorandum suggesting that another line should be taken with the United States for he had found the draft brusque, blunt and belligerent. He felt the Government should express hope that the incident was due to

* Lord John Russell, foreign secretary, was created Earl Russell and Viscount Amberley, 1861.

Captain Wilkes's misunderstanding of his instructions (a face-saver). That while we could not allow the flag to be insulted nor the security of the mail jeopardized, Her Majesty's Government was most unwilling to believe that the Government of the United States of America would wantonly put an insult upon this country. He expressed the additional hope that the United States Government would spontaneously offer such redress as alone could satisfy this country, namely, the restoration of the unfortunate passengers plus a suitable apology. In fact the Prince removed from the ministerial draft all the hamfisted sentences and threats which would have given great offence to 'a proud and sensitive nation'.[9] It was a temperate, conciliatory memorandum and it was the last he was ever to write. When he had finished he took it to the Queen at eight o'clock in the morning and said to her: *'Ich bin so schwach, ich habe kaum die Feder halten können.'*[10] The Government accepted his revisions and put them into formal language. War was avoided. *Die Feder* had proved to be, as the Prince always hoped, mightier than *der Säbel*.

On December 2nd the anxious Queen sent for Sir James Clark, now seventy-three. Dr Jenner, who had returned, said the Prince had no fever but that one might develop. However, there was no cause for alarm. Lord Palmerston, who was at Windsor, was wild with anxiety and suggested that another doctor be called in but the Queen refused. Albert did not like doctors and too many would worry him. By the following night he was so restless that he walked ceaselessly about the castle and had to be given opiates. Next morning he seemed better, rose, dressed—but the improvement was shortlived.

What seems so extraordinary to us is that anyone so obviously ill as the Prince should have been allowed out of bed at all, and should have had no nursing other than that done by his equerries. But the Prince's illness had made him stubborn; he refused to stay in bed, he would lie on a sofa in the Blue Room, where George IV and William IV had died, but to go to bed and be ill—no. One wonders if he were subconsiously afraid that this would be giving in and therefore cowardly, or if his habitual routine of

Windsor Castle

rising at dawn, dressing, reading drafts and correspondence,
breakfasting at nine and then settling to the day's work had not
impressed itself like an iron corset on him and held him upright.
Certainly he knew he was ill but kept on asking how long his
illness would last which sounds as if he did not realize, because
no one had told him, how ill he was.

By December 6th Dr Jenner told the Queen the complaint was gastric bowel fever, another of the numerous names for typhoid, but no one dared call it typhoid in view of the recent deaths of Prince Ferdinand and King Pedro; further, the Prince was terrified of fever. The doctors assured the Queen that this enteric fever, as it was often called, was what they had expected but that they knew how to treat it and it would all be over in a month dating from November 22nd.

If they knew how to treat it, which is more than doubtful, they did not do so for on December 8th the Prince was still allowed to wander about although woefully weak. His mind wandered, too. Lord Palmerston was in an agony of apprehension. He had suggested other doctors a week before and been refused by the Queen but by now she, too, was agonized by fear and on the 9th Sir Henry Holland (1788–1873) and Dr Thomas Watson (1792–1882) were sent for. The Prince, who had become listless and disinterested and very troubled with his cough, liked Watson on sight and thought him the right man.

But on the evening of the 11th even the doctors were uneasy as the Prince's breathing had become difficult. On the 12th he was worse yet on that day the Queen wrote her uncle a favourable report on his condition. 'He maintains his ground well—had another good night—takes plenty of nourishment, and shows surprising strength. I am constantly in and out of his room, but since the *first four dreadful* nights, *last* week, before they had declared it to be *gastric fever*— I do not sit up with him at night as I could be of no use; and there is nothing to cause alarm. . . . I cannot sufficiently praise . . . Dr Jenner, who is the *first fever* doctor in Europe . . . and good old Clark is here every day. . . . We have got Dr Watson . . . and Sir H. Holland. . . . But I have kept clear of these two.'[11] The doctors had not told her how seriously ill the Prince was and she was deceived into false hope.

By December 13th, however, Dr Jenner saw fit to warn the Queen that congestion of the lungs was a possibility. Yet all that night comforting reports on his condition were brought to the wretched woman, and on the 14th Mr Brown, the Royal

Apothecary from Windsor, told her the Prince had passed the crisis. Mr Brown was right.

The Prince of Wales had arrived in the early hours of that morning. His sister, Princess Alice, had written to him of their father's illness but with such tact or lack of information that Bertie had not thought it serious and had fulfilled a dinner engagement before setting out for Windsor, where he arrived cheerful and unprepared.

The Queen, believing the crisis over, went to Albert's room early, 'and never can I forget how beautiful my darling looked,' she wrote later, 'lying there with his face lit up by the rising sun, his eyes unusually bright, gazing as it were on unseen objects and taking no notice of me'.[12] Hour after hour she waited near him and in the afternoon he knew her. About 5.30 his face grew dusky and the Queen went to him. His breathing was laboured. This was the end and she knew it. *'Gutes Frauchen,'* he managed to murmur and kissed her. She left. He grew worse and she returned to whisper in his ear, *'Es ist kleine Frauchen'*. He moved his lips faintly in a kiss and fell into a doze.

At 10.45 he died. An era died with him.

BIBLIOGRAPHY

Ashton, J., *Gossip in the First Decade of Victoria's Reign.*

Bamford, S., *Passages: Early Days.*
Beeton, Mrs I., *Book of Household Management* (1861).
Bell, Sir C., *The Letters of Sir Charles Bell,* ed. Lady Bell.
Blake, R., *Disraeli.*
Bolitho, H., *Albert the Good.*
Briggs, A., *Victorian People.*
— *Victorian Cities.*
Brinton, W., *On Food* (1861).
Broughton, Lord, *Recollections of a Long Life,* ed. Lady Dorchester, vols. v and vi.
Burnett, J., *Plenty and Want.*

Carlyle, T., *Past and Present.*
Chadwick, G. F., *The Works of Sir Joseph Paxton.*
Chadwick, O., *The Victorian Church,* vol. i.
Clark, K., *The Gothic Revival.*
Clive, M., ed., *Caroline Clive: Diary and Family Papers of Mrs Archer Clive.*
Cobbett, W., *The English Garden* (1833).
Codmore, F., *Life of Robert Owen.*
Cole, M., *Robert Owen of New Lanark.*
Christie, O. F., *The Transition from Aristocracy.*
Croker, J. W., *Correspondence and Diaries,* ed. L. J. Jennings, 3 vols.

Drummond, J. and Wilbraham, A., *The Englishman's Food.*
Dickinson, V., ed., *The Letters of Emily Eden.*

315

Engels, F., *Conditions of the Working Class in England* (1844), trans. Mrs Kelley Wischnewetzky.

Eyck, F., *The Prince Consort.*

Fulford, R., *Royal Dukes.*

George, D. M., *England in Transition.*

Gore Allen, W., *King William the Fourth.*

Graham, T. S., *Modern Domestic Medicine* (1837).

Greville, C. C. F., *Memoirs,* ed., Henry Reeve, pt. ii, vols. i–v.

Halévy, E., *A History of the English People in the Nineteenth Century,* trans. E. I. Watkin, 4 vols.

Hammond, J. L. and Hammond, B., *The Life of Lord Shaftesbury.*

— *The Rise of Modern Industry.*

Hogg, Jabez, *Medical and Surgical Guide.*

Hogg, James, *The Habits of Good Society* (1860).

Hopkirk, M., *Queen Adelaide.*

Huish, R., *William the Fourth.*

Jaeger, M., *Before Victoria.*

Kitson Clark, J., *The Making of Victorian England.*

Laing, G. H., *Sir James Young Simpson.*

Lambert, M., *When Victoria Began to Reign.*

Lambert, S., *The Railway King.*

Lanchester, E., *On Food* (1861).

Leveson-Gower, The Hon. F., *Letters of Harriet, Countess Granville.*

Longford, Lady, *Victoria, R.I.*

Longmate, N., *King Cholera.*

Loudon, J. C., *Encyclopaedia of Cottage, Farm and Villa Architecture.*

— *Encyclopaedia of Gardening.*

— *The Suburban Horticulturist.*

Loudon, Mrs, *Instructions in Gardening for Ladies.*

Martin, Sir T., *Life of H.R.H. The Prince Consort,* 5 vols.

Bibliography

Mayhew, H., *London Labour and the London Poor* (1851), 2 vols.
Maxwell, H., ed., *The Creevey Papers*.
Mitchell, B. R. and Dean, P., *Abstract of Historical Statistics*.
Morris, M., *The Story of English Public Health*.

Neville, R., *Memoirs and Letters of Lady Dorothy Neville*.
Newman, G., *The Rise of Preventive Medicine*.
Niell, The Rt Rev. S., *Anglicanism*.

Owen, R., *Life of Robert Owen*.

Pevsner, Sir N., *The Sources of Modern Architecture*.
Pereira, J., *On Food and Diet* (1843).

H.M. Queen Victoria, ed., Benson and Esher, *Letters*, vols. II, III.
— *Leaves from a Journal of our Life in the Highlands*, ed., A. Helps, vol. I.

Robinson, H. Crabb, *Diary and Letters*, ed., Thomas Sadler, 3 vols.
Robinson, V., *The Story of Medicine*.
Rogers, T., *Six Centuries of Work and Wages*, ed., G. D. H. Cole.
Rohde, E. S., *The Story of the Garden*.
Rowell, G., *The Victorian Theatre*.
Ruskin, J., *The Seven Lamps of Architecture*.
— *Praeterita*.

Sanger, G., *Seventy Years a Showman*.
Singer, C. and Ackworth, E., *A Short History of Medicine*.
Smiles, S., *Self Help*.
Summerson, Sir J., *Victorian Architecture*.

Taine, H. A., *Notes on England*, trans. Edward Hyams.
Thompson, D., *England in the Nineteenth Century*.
Timbs, J., *Hints for the Table* (1859).
Toynbee, A., *The Industrial Revolution*.
Trevelyan, G. M., *Social History of England*.
— *British History in the Nineteenth Century*.

Wans, J., *A Short History of Scarisbrick Hall*.

Williams, E. N., *A Documentary History of England*, vol. II.

Wilson, H., *Memoirs*, ed., Laver and Davis.

Wise, D. and Cox Johnson, A., eds., *Diary of William Taylor, Footman* (1837).

Wyndham, The Hon. Mrs H., ed., *Correspondence of Sarah, Lady Lyttelton.*

Young, G. M., *Victorian England.*

SOURCES

CHAPTER I

1 M. Hopkirk, *Queen Adelaide.*
2 *Ibid.*
3 R. Huish, *The Life and Reign of King William the Fourth* (1837).
4 C. Greville, *Memoirs*, pt. II, vol. I (entry June 25th 1837).
5 The Hon. F. Leveson-Gower, *Letters of Harriet, Countess Granville* (letter, November 21st 1837).
6 The Hon. Mrs H. Wyndham, *Correspondence of Sarah Spencer, Lady Lyttelton* (letter, February 28th 1839).
7 G. M. Young, *Victorian England.*
8 *Ibid.*
9 M. Clive, ed., *Caroline Clive* (Journal of Archer Clive, June 1st 1838).
10 A. G. Temple, *The Art of Painting in the Queen's Reign.*
11 Mrs Hemans, *The Homes of England.*
12 W. Cobbett, *Rural Rides* (entry November 14th 1821).
13 C. Greville, *op. cit.* (entry March 2nd 1839).
14 *Ibid.* (entry May 12th 1839).
15 Clive, *op. cit.* (letter, January 1840).
16 Leveson-Gower, *op. cit.* (letter October 10th 1839).
17 Lord Broughton, *Recollections of a Long Life* (entry, February 10th 1840).
18 *Ibid.*
19 Greville, *op. cit.* (entry February 13th 1840).
20 Exhibition Catalogue, *The Queen's Stamps* (1965).
21 G. M. Trevelyan, *History of England.*
22 Benson, A. C. and Viscount Esher, *The Letters of Queen Victoria*, vol. II (to the King of the Belgians, July 7th 1846).

23 Sir T. Martin, *Life of H.R.H. the Prince Consort*, vol. I (May 18th 1847).
24 N. Hawthorne, *English Note Books* (entry, July 30th 1857).
25 R. W. Emerson, *English Traits*.
26 Anonymous, *An Outline of English History in Verse*, n.d. (author's copy inscribed 1859).
27 Martin, *op. cit.*, vol. II (memorandum 1849).
28 G. Faber, *Oxford Apostles* (quoting N. P. Liddon's *Life of Pusey*).
29 Hawthorne, *op. cit.* (entry, February 23rd 1854).
30 *Ibid.* (entry, August 12th 1855).
31 Martin, *op. cit.*, vol. II (letter, December 1853).
32 *Ibid.* (letter, January 11th 1854).
33 H.M. Queen Victoria, *Leaves from the Journal of our Life in the Highlands* (1848–1861), ed., A. Helps (entry, September 8th 1848).
34 *Ibid.* (entry, October 13th 1856).
35 *Ibid.* (entry, September 2nd 1842).
36 *Ibid.* (entry, September 4th 1842).
37 C. Gray, *The Early Years of the Prince Consort* (completed for and annotated by Queen Victoria).
38 Leveson-Gower, *op. cit.* (letter, October 20th 1840).
39 Martin, *op. cit.*, vol. II (letter, April 19th 1849).
40 Emerson, *op. cit.*

CHAPTER II

1 R. Adam, *Works*, vol. I, Preface.
2 J. Wans, *A Short History of Scarisbrick Hall* (quoting F. H. Cheetham).
3 *Ibid.* (quoting M. Trappes-Lomax).
4 A. W. N. Pugin, *Contrasts*.
5 N. Hawthorne, *English Note Books* (entry, December 31st 1856).
6 A. Pope, *Eloisa to Abelard* ll. 1–2; 140–4; 155–6; 163–6; 169–70.
7 J. Thomson, *The Seasons—Winter*, l. 5.
8 E. Young, *Night Thoughts*, Night IV.
9 Horace Walpole, *The Castle of Otranto*, Preface, 2nd edition.
10 H. Repton, *Design for the Pavilion at Brighton*.

11 R. W. Emerson, *English Traits.*
12 Hawthorne, *op. cit.* (entry, March 13th 1854).
13 Sir J. Summerson, *Victorian Architecture.*
14 H. G. Schenk, *The Mind of the European Romantics.*
15 T. Fuller, *The History of the Worthies of England*, vol. II.
16 *Ibid.*, vol. I.
17 K. Clark, *The Gothic Revival.*
18 *Ibid.*
19 H. C. Robinson, *Diary*, vol. II (entry, May 21st 1823).
20 E. Halévy, *A History of the English People in the Nineteenth Century*, vol. II.
21 E. Burton, *The Jacobeans at Home.*
22 *Ibid., The Elizabethans at Home.*
23 Hawthorne, *op. cit.* (entry, September 26th 1855).
24 C. Greville, *Memoirs*, pt. II, vol. III (entry, March 8th 1847).
25 G. G. Scott, *Remarks on Secular and Domestic Architecture, etc.*
26 J. Ruskin, *The Seven Lamps of Architecture.*
27 *Ibid.*
28 *Ibid.*
29 *Ibid.*
30 Hawthorne, *op. cit.* (entry, August 25th 1855).
31 F. Engels, *The Condition of the Working Class in England in 1844.*
32 *Ibid.* (quoting *The Artisan*, October 1842).
33 *Ibid.*
34 S. Bamford, *Passages in the Life of a Radical*, vol. I.
35 E. Jones, *Song of the Lower Classes.*

CHAPTER III

1 A. Trollope, *Barchester Towers*, vol. I.
2 *Ibid.*
3 Victoria and Albert Museum Album, *The Great Exhibition of 1851* (as quoted by C. H. Gibbs-Smith).
4 E. Burton, *The Elizabethans at Home.*
5 C. Dickens, *Our Mutual Friend*
6 Mrs Gaskell, *Cranford.*
7 J. Gloag, *The English Tradition in Design.*

8 W. M. Thackeray, *The Book of Snobs.*
9 M. R. Mitford, *Recollections of a Literary Life.*
10 R. W. Emerson, *English Traits.*
11 E. Burton, *The Georgians at Home.*
12 D. Marshall, *The English Domestic Servant in History* (Historical Association).
13 Dickens, *Our Mutual Friend.*
14 L. Wright, *Home Fires Burning.*
15 Mrs I. Beeton, *Beeton's Book of Household Management* (1859–61).
16 Emerson, *op. cit.*
17 Beeton, *op. cit.*
18 H. Mayhew, *London Labour and the London Poor* (1851 edition).
19 *Ibid.*
20 *Ibid.*
21 N. Hawthorne, *English Note Books* (entry, August 20th 1853).
22 A. Trollope, *The Last Chronicle of Barset.*

CHAPTER IV

1 Mrs I. Beeton, *Household Management.*
2 R. Burton, *The Anatomy of Melancholy*, pt. III; sect. 3; memb. 1; subsect. 2.
3 *Ibid.*, pt. I; sect. 2; memb. 2; subsect. 2.
4 H. Misson, *Memoirs and Observations in his Travels over England* (trans. Ozell).
5 E. Acton, *Modern Cookery for Private Families* (preface, 1856 edition).
6 E. Burton, *The Georgians at Home.*
7 J. Drummond and A. Wilbraham, *The Englishman's Food.*
8 *Ibid.*
9 *Punch*, vol. xx, 1851.
10 G. K. Chesterton, The Song against Grocers.
11 J. Timbs, *Hints for the Table.*
12 *Ibid.*
13 D. Wise, ed., *Diary of William Taylor, Footman* (entry, May 14th 1837).

14 *Ibid.*
15 J. Pereira, *A Treatise on Food and Diet.*
16 Lady Burton, *Life of Sir R. F. Burton*, vol. I.
17 N. Hawthorne, *English Note Books* (entry, February 19th 1855).
18 *Ibid.* (entry, July 30th 1855).
19 Timbs, *op. cit.*
20 P. L. Simmonds, *The Curiosities of Food.*
21 Sir F. Bacon, *The New Atlantis* (trans. 1620).
22 E. Burton, *The Jacobeans at Home.*
23 Anonymous, *London at Table* (1858 edition).
24 *Ibid.*
25 A. Hayward, *The Art of Dining*, vol. II.
26 B. E. Hill, *The Epicurean's Almanac.*
27 J. Burnett, *Plenty and Want.*
28 The Hon. Mrs H. Wyndham, *Correspondence of Sarah Spencer, Lady Lyttelton.*
29 Timbs, *op. cit.*
30 Αγωγὸς, *Hints on Etiquette* (1834).
31 Pereira, *op. cit.*
32 Hawthorne, *op. cit.* (entry, August 4th 1853).
33 *Ibid.* (entry, September 24th 1853).
34 *The Times,* November 16th 1864.
35 T. Carlyle, *Past and Present.*
36 F. Engels, *The Condition of the Working Class in England in 1844.*
37 *Ibid.*
38 H. Mayhew, *London Labour and the London Poor*, vol. II.
39 *Ibid.*, vol. II.
40 Engels, *op. cit.*
41 Mrs Gaskell, *Cranford.*
42 J. L. Hammond and B. Hammond, *The Life of Lord Shaftesbury.*
43 *The Times,* October 12th 1843.

CHAPTER V

1 Lady Longford, *Victoria R.I.*
2 H. Graham, *Surgeons All.*
3 V. Robinson, *The Story of Medicine.*

4 T. Hood, *Mary's Ghost—A Pathetic Ballad,* V vi; V vii; V ix; V xi.
5 J. Müller, Preface to *The Letters of Sir Charles Bell* (ed. Lady Bell).
6 Sir C. Bell, *Letters.*
7 D. Guthrie, *A History of Medicine.*
8 A. E. Owen, quoting *Records of Commissions of Sewers,* history, vol. LII, no. 174, H.A. Pub.
9 V. Dickenson, ed., *Miss Eden's Letters* (to Lady Theresa Lewis, August 1859).
10 C. Woodham-Smith, *Florence Nightingale.*
11 C. Dickens, *Martin Chuzzlewit.*
12 C. Greville, *Memoirs* (entry, November 11th 1830).
13 *Ibid.* (September 17th 1831).
14 J. Hogg, *Domestic and Surgical Guide.*
15 T. J. Graham, *Modern Domestic Medicine.*
16 F. Engels, *Condition of the Working Class.*
17 Dickinson, *op. cit.*
18 Graham, *op. cit.*
19 Hogg, *op. cit.*

CHAPTER VI

1 M. Clive, ed., *Caroline Clive (Diary and Family Papers).*
2 Lord Broughton, *Recollections of a Long Life* (entry, May 3rd 1847).
3 A. C. Benson and Viscount Esher, *The Letters of Queen Victoria,* vol. II (to the King of the Belgians, June 12th 1847).
4 H. Mayhew, *London Labour and the London Poor,* vol. I.
5 N. Hawthorne, *English Note Books* (entry, August 17th 1855).
6 Mayhew, *op. cit.,* vol. II
7 *Ibid.*
8 Hawthorne, *op. cit.* (entry, September 13th 1854).
9 H. A. Taine, *Notes on England.*
10 *Ibid.*
11 Broughton, *op. cit.,* vol. v (entry, n.d. January 1839).
12 *Ibid.,* vol. VI (entry, February 6th 1852).
13 Mayhew, *op. cit.,* vol. I.
14 *Ibid.*

15 C. Dickens, *Nicholas Nickleby.*
16 E. Ollier and R. Wilson, *Life and Times of Queen Victoria.*
17 Clive, *op. cit.* (entry, April 1st 1847).
18 Sir T. Martin, *The Life of the Prince Consort,* vol. v.
19 Hawthorne, *op. cit.* (entry, April 1st 1856).
20 Mrs Gaskell, *Cranford.*
21 The Hon. Mrs H. Wyndham, *Correspondence of Sarah Spencer, Lady Lyttelton* (letter, September 30th 1841).
22 J. Aston, *Gossip in the First Decade of Victoria's Reign.*
23 Wyndham, *op. cit.* (letter, October 5th 1849).
24 C. Cotton? *The Compleat Gamester.*
25 The Hon. F. Leveson-Gower, *Letters of Harriet, Countess Granville,* vol. ii (letter, November 29th 1844).
26 *Ibid.* (letter, n.d. August 1837).
27 W. Acton, as quoted by Steven Marcus in *The Other Victorians.*
28 Broughton, *op. cit.,* vol. i (entry, June 3rd, 1840).
29 Clive, *op. cit.* (July 11th 1844).
30 Broughton, *op. cit.,* vol. vi (entry, May 1st 1851).
31 C. Greville, *Memoirs,* pt. ii; vol. iii (entry, May 10th 1851).

CHAPTER VII

1 The Hon. Mrs H. Wyndham, *Correspondence of Sarah Spencer, Lady Lyttelton* (letter, October 14th 1840).
2 Sir T. Martin, *The Life of the Prince Consort,* vol. i.
3 J. C. Loudon, *An Encyclopaedia of Gardening.*
4 *Ibid.*
5 J. Austen, *Sense and Sensibility.*
6 H. Repton, *Observations on the Theory and Practice of Landscape Gardening,* ed., J. C. Loudon.
7 Loudon, *op. cit.* (preface).
8 *Ibid.*
9 *Ibid.*
10 B. Disraeli, *Henrietta Temple.*
11 W. Cobbett, *The English Garden.*
12 Loudon, *op. cit.*
13 Mrs Loudon, *Instructions in Gardening for Ladies* (1841).
14 *Ibid.*
15 *Ibid.*

16 J. Parkinson, *Paradisi in Sole Paridisus Terrestris.*

17 Loudon, *op. cit.*

18 G. F. Chadwick, *The Works of Joseph Paxton.*

19 Loudon, *op. cit.*

20 Mrs Loudon, *op. cit.*

21 J. W. Croker, *The Croker Papers*, ed., L. J. Jennings (letter from Sir Robert Peel to J. W. Croker, October 29th 1838).

22 Loudon, *op. cit.*

23 H. Ward, Letter to author, July 18th 1968, quoting *East London Observer*, September 30th 1911.

24 Mrs Loudon, *op. cit.*

25 *Ibid.*

26 N. Hawthorne, *English Note Books* (March 13th 1854).

27 W. Irving, *The Sketch Book of Geoffrey Crayon, Gent. (Rural Life in England.)*

28 Hawthorne, *op. cit.* (entry, March 13th 1854).

29 M. Clive, *Caroline Clive—(Diary and Family Papers)* (entry, July 23rd 1844).

30 M. R. Mitford, *Recollections of a Literary Life.*

31 Irving, *op. cit.*

CHAPTER VIII

1 A. C. Benson and Viscount Esher, eds., *The Letters of Queen Victoria*, vol. III (to the King of the Belgians, August 26th 1861).

2 *Ibid.*

3 *Ibid.* (to the King of the Belgians, October 21st 1861).

4 *Ibid.* (to the King of the Belgians, November 26th 1861).

5 Sir T. Martin, *Life of H.R.H. the Prince Consort*, vol. v.

6 *Ibid.* (letter to Baron von Stockmar, November 14th 1861).

7 Benson and Esher, *op. cit.*, vol. III (letter to the King of the Belgians, November 26th 1861).

8 R. Wilson and E. Ollier, *The Life and Times of Queen Victoria*, vol. II (quoting Count Vitzthum).

9 Martin, *op. cit.*, vol. v.

10 *Ibid.*

11 Benson and Esher, *op. cit.*, vol. III (letter to the King of the Belgians, December 12th 1861).

12 Martin, *op. cit.*, vol. v.

INDEX

Where significant information is given in an illustration, the page reference is italicised.

Abbotsford, 50
Aberdeen, George Hamilton Gordon, 4th Earl of, 27–8, 38, 39, 44
Accum, Friedrich Christian, 132–3
Acton, Eliza, 107, 154; quoted, 130–31
Acton, Dr William, quoted, 256–7
actors, 236–7
Adam, Robert, 45
Addison, Thomas, 187
Adelaide, Queen of England, 6, 22, 214, 226, 283n.
agricultural labourers, 15, 131, 167–70
agriculture, 15
Ainsworth, Harrison, 234
air pollution, 284
Albert, Prince Consort: birth, 2; early life, 20–1; character and attributes, 21, 40–3; marriage: planned, 3, 19, takes place, 21–3, ballads on, 226; personal unpopularity, 38–9, 41; loves Scotland, 40; designs Osborne House, 71–2; designs Kennington flats, 83; enjoys billiards, 250, gardening, 266–7, music, 96, 213–14, 218, novels, 242, Tennyson's poems, 245, theatre, 231; exhausted by overwork, 302–3, 304–5; deals with Prince's escapade, 305–6, with *Trent* affair, 308–9; last illness, 306–7, 308–12; death, 312; *other mentions*, 31, 32, 36, 94, 137, 277

letters: on forthcoming Crimean war, 39; to Victoria, when absent on business, 43; on gardening, 267
Albert Edward, Prince of Wales, 43–4, 300–1, 305–6, 312
Alexandra, Princess, 305–6
Alice, Princess, 242, 312
All England Cricket Club, 253
All England Croquet Club, 252n.
Allingham, William, 245
Allsop and Sons, 136
Amberg, Isaac van, 230
anaesthesia, 172–3, 174–8
Anatomy Act (1832), 183–4, 194
Anderson, Lucy, 217
Anson, George, 250
Anti-Corn Law League, 26–7
aphids, 284–5
appendicitis, 187
Appert, Nicholas, 149
archery, 252
Armitage, Edwin, 30
Armstrong, Dr George, 191
army, medical services in, 196–7, 198
Arne, Dr Thomas, 219
Arnold, Matthew, 243
Arnold, Samuel, 219
Arnott, Neil, 194
Aspidin, Joseph, 74
Attwood, Thomas, 220
Ayrton, W. E., 243n.

badger baiting, 254–5
badminton, 253

Bailey, Philip James, 243
baking powder, 147
Balfe, Michael, 220
ballad-operas, 219–20
ballads, 224–6
Balmoral Castle, 40, 303, *304*
balustrades, 103
Bamford, Samuel, quoted, 81
Banks, Sir Joseph, 267
Barber-Surgeons Company, 178, 179
Barlow, W. H., 75n.
Barrett, Edward, 59
Barrett, Elizabeth, 7, 244–5
Barry, Charles, 29, 49, 68, 70
Basevi, George, 64
bathing, 259–60
baths, 109–12
Battley's Sedative, 209
bear baiting, 254
Beard (*photographer*), 29
Beckford, William, 55, 56, 57
'Bedchamber Crisis', 18–19
bedding plants, 279–80
bed-making, 119–20
bedroom, 115–23
beds, 115–19, *117*
beer, 136
Beeton, Isabella, 128, 129, 131;
    quoted, 108, 120, 128, 145, 159
Bell, Sir Charles, 185–6, 196
Bentham, Jeremy, 194
bentwood furniture, 91
Berlioz, Hector, 218
billiards, 250–1
Birkenhead, 289, 297
Birmingham, 79, 218, 290m.
Bishop, Henry, 219
Bishop and Williams case, 183
Black Drops, 209
Blackwell, Dr Elizabeth, 198
bleeding, 187
Blenheim Palace, 295
Blessington, Marguerite, Lady, 116,
    249
Blomfield, Bishop Charles James,
    203, 204
body-snatchers, 178–84, *181*

Borden, Gail, 151
bottled food, 149–50
botulism, 136
Boucicault, Dion, 233, 235
boxing, 44, 255
'Bozomania', 238
Bramah, Joseph, 113
bread, 135, 147; price of, 26–7, 28,
    132
breakfast, 139
Brewster, Sir David, 246, 247
bricks, 73–4
Bright, John, 26
Brighton, 259, 260
Brinton, Dr William, 140
Bristol, 79
Brodie, Sir Benjamin, 184–5
Brontë sisters, 241
Brooke, G. V., 237
brothels, 228
Broughton de Gyfford, Lord, quoted,
    22, 214, 222, 234, 262
Brown (*Royal Apothecary*), 311–12
Brown, Lancelot ('Capability'), 270
Browning, Robert, 234, 244
Buchanan, James, 44, 71
Budding, Edwin, 293
building materials, 72–5, 76
bull baiting, 254
Bulwer-Lytton, Edward (Lord Lyt-
    ton, Lytton Bulwer), 234, 240,
    249
Bunning, J. B., 75
Burke and Hare case, 183
burletta, 232
Burton, Decimus, 277
Burton, James, 64
Burton, Richard, 139–40
Burton, Robert, quoted, 128–9
Butterfield, William, 63

Cadogan, William, 191
Callcott, John, 220–21
Canada, 43
canals, *13*, 73
candelabra, 100–101
candles, 99–100, 157

Candy, Joseph, 65
card games, 247–8
Carlyle, Thomas, 95; quoted, 162
Carpenter, Richard Cromwell, 67
Carré, Edmund, 149
carriages, 30–1
castles, 57
caterpillars, 286
Chadwick, Edwin, 194–5, 202, 203
chairs, 90–1, *91*
chamber pots, 114
charities, 93
Chartists, 16
Chatsworth, 278, 287, 295; Great
  Conservatory, 45, 275–7
children, 164–6; as labourers, 11n.,
  163–4; *see also* paediatrics
chloroform, 172, 176–8
cholera, 200–201, 203–5
Clanny, Dr W. Reid, 201
Christian Socialism, 36–7
Church Building Act (1818), 61–3
Church Building Society, 61
churches, 60–63
Clark, Sir James, 17, 172, 306, 309
Clarke, Sir Charles Mansfield, 17
classical style, 63, 64, 68
Clementi, Muzio, 215
Clive, Rev. Archer, 213; quoted, 14,
  19–20
Clive, Caroline, quoted, 213, 244,
  259
clock garden, 282
Clough, Arthur Hugh, 212, 243
coal, 284
Cobbett, William, 15, 273n.
Cobden, Richard, 26
cock-fighting, 254
Cole, Henry, 94
Collins, Sam, 238
colour theory (in gardening), 281–2
comic songs, 225
concerts, 215, 219
cone flower-bed, 282
Conroy, Sir John, 3, 8
Conyngham, Lord, 8
Cook, Thomas, 260–1

Cooke, James, 220
cookery books, 130–1, 154
Cooper, Sir Astley Paston, 182–3, **184**
Cope, C. W., 30
Corn Laws, 26, 27–8, 132
Costerton, Charles, 189
costume: men's, 31–2, 33–4;
  women's, 32–3, effect on furni-
  ture style of, 89–90, in histori-
  cal plays, 233
cottage gardens, 297–8
Coventry, 289n.
Cramer, J. B., 215–16
Cremorne pleasure gardens, 256,
  257
cricket, 253–4
Crimean War, 37–8, 39, 141–2; *see
  also* Nightingale, Florence
Crockfords, 249–50
Croker, John Wilson, 23
croquet, 252–3
Crystal Palace, 45, *46*, 75
Cubitt, Lewis, 65
Cubitt, Thomas, 64–6, 71
Cubitt, William, 64
Cumming, Alexander, 112
Curtis, John Harrison, 189

Daffy's Elixir, 208
dancing, 222–3
Davis, Jefferson, 307
Davis, John Bunnell, 191
Davy, Humphry, 174
Delafosse, Rev. Charles, 140
Derby, 274n.
Derby, Edward Stanley, 14th Earl
  of, 42
Derby Day, 258
dermatology, 188
diabetes, 207–8
diagnostics, 186–7
dial garden, 282
Dibdin, Charles, 219
Dickens, Charles, 219–20, 225, 234,
  238
dinner, 130, 138–9
dinner parties, 153–61

diphtheria, 208
Disraeli, Benjamin, 240, 249, 250
Donkin, Bryan, 150
door-knocker thefts, 255–6
door-stops, 105
d'Orsay, Count, 249
Dover's Powders, 208
drama, 233–5
Dubosq, J., 247
Dudley, Lord, 153
Dumas, M. J., 176
Duncan, Dr W. H., 196

ear diseases, 187–8, 189
earth closets, 113–14
Eastlake, Charles Lock, 241n.
Eastnor Castle, 63
Ecclesiastical Movement, 77
Eden, Hon. Emily, quoted, 197, 210
Edinburgh, 218
Egan, Pierce, 234
Elgin, Lady, 253
Eliot, George, 242
Elizabethan style, 68–9, 86–7
Ellis, William Webb, 254
Elmes, Harvey Lonsdale, 68
Emerson, R. W., quoted 33–4, 44, 57, 97, 112, 287n.
enclosures, 15, 168
Engels, Friedrich, quoted, 79, 80, 208
envelopes, pictorial, 24–6
epergnes, 156–7, *158*
Epicure's Almanac, 154
Ernest, Prince of Leningen, 306
Ernest II, Duke of Saxe-Coburg and Gotha, 19, 42
ether, 175–6
European travel, 39–40
Evangelicalism, 35
Evans, Mary Anne, *see* Eliot, George
Evelyn, John, 268
excursions, 260–61

Factory Acts, 163–4
Fairfax, Lieutenant Macneil, 307

fairs, 229–30, 265
family prayers, 34, 78–9
Ferdinand, Prince of Portugal, 305
Ferrabee, John, 293
Field, John, 217
finger glasses, 159–60
fireplaces, 102, 122–3
Fitzgerald, Edward, 95, 243
Fliedner, Theodor, 199
florist's flowers, defined, 283n.
flour, 147
flower-gardens, 272–3, 279–84
Fonthill Abbey, 51, 55, 56–7
food, adulterated, 132–6; preserved, 149–51
Food and Drug Act (1860), 44, 136
football, 254
Forrest, Edwin, 237
Foster, Myles Birket, 15
Fry, Elizabeth, 199, 200
Fuller, Dr T., 60–1
furniture, 85–97

gaming houses, 248–9
garden furniture, 291
garden houses, 291–2
gas lighting, 99, 157, 159
General Board of Health, 195, 204
Glasgow, 218
glasshouses, 274–8, *276,* 279
glees, 220–1
Gore, Mrs Charles, 240
Gothic revival, 46–7, 50–7, 58, 62–3, 66–7, 75–6
gout, 210
Granville, Harriet, Countess of, quoted, 8–9, 43, 251
Gray, Euphemia (Mrs John Ruskin), 241
Gray, Henry, 189
Great Exhibition, 28, 85, 110, 144, 152, 261–5, 293; *see also* Crystal Palace
Greville, Charles, quoted, 6, 17–18, 72, 201, 262
Grimwade, F. S., 151
Grisi, Giulia, 214

grottoes, 294–5
Guthrie, Samuel, 176

Halifax, 289n.
Hall, Marshall, 110, 186–7
Hallé, Charles, 215
hangover, 160–1
Harington, Henry, 219
Harlaxton Manor, 69–70
Harris, Walter, 190–1
Harrison, James, 149
Harrison Apparatus, 107–8
Hastings, Lady Flora, 17–18
Hawthorne, Nathaniel, quoted, 32,
  37, 38, 50, 58, 78–9, 126, 141–2,
  161, 223–4, 227, 297
hearth furniture, 101
Heaton, Sir John Henniker, 25n.
Heller, Stephen, 217
Hemans, Felicia Dorothea, 15
Herbert, Sidney, 116, 197
Hickman, Henry Hill, 174
High Church movement, 35
Highclere Castle, 70
Hill, Rowland, 23
Hinton, James, 188
Hobhouse, Sir John Cam, *see* Brough-
  ton de Gyfford, Lord
Hogg, Dr Jabez, 206–7
Holloway's Pills, 209
Holmes, Oliver Wendell, 175
Hood, Thomas, quoted, 184
Hook, Theodore, 240
Holland, Sir Henry, 311
Hooker, Sir Joseph Dalton, 288n.
Hooker, Sir William Jackson, 288
Hoole, The, 295–7
Hope End, 59
Horsley, Charles, E., 220
Horsley, William, 220
hospitals, 189, 192, 199, 200
hotels, 152–3
houses, 11, 67, 79–83, 115; rural, 15–
  16, 168, 298; Ruskin on, 78
Hullah, John, 219–20
Hundred Guinea Dish, 142

ice-houses, 148
Ingram, Herbert, 209
Inwood, Henry William, 63
Inwood, William, 63
Irish labour, 12
Irish potato famine, 27, 132
iron, as structural material, 71, 74–
  5, 77–8, 277; for furniture, 103,
  104–5, 291
Irving, Washington, quoted, 299
Italianate style, 58, 65, *66*, 71–2

jacks (kitchen), 106–7
James's Powders, 208, 211
Jekyll, Gertrude, 273n.
jelly, 144–5, 146
Jenner, Dr William, 211, 306, 309,
  311

Kaiserswerth, 199–200
kaleidoscope, 246
Kean, Charles, 233, 234
Kemble, Charles, 233
Kenilworth Buffet, 86–7
Kent, Edward Augustus, Duke of, 1,
  2
Kent, Mary Louisa Victoria, Duchess
  of, 1, 3–4, 8, 9, 17, 22, 248,
  301–2
Kentfield, Jonathan (Edwin), 251
Kew Gardens, 288
Kingsley, Charles, 36, 37
kitchen, 105–8, 110
kitchener, 108
Kitchiner, Dr William, 130
Knight, Richard Payne, 270

lamps, *88, 91*
Lancet, 134–5, 172
Landseer, Sir Edwin, 230n.
Latitudinarians, 35–6
laughing gas, 174
lawn mowers, 293–4
lawn tennis, 252n.
League Bread Company, 135
Lear, Edward, 247
Lee Priory, 55

Leeds, 203–4
Lehzen, Baroness, 10
Leopold, King of the Belgians, 2, 3, 19
Leopold, Prince, birth of, 172
Lever, Sir Ashton, 252
Liebig, J. von, 176
Lincoln, Abraham, 44n.
Lind, Jenny, 214–15
Lister, Joseph, 175, 177n.
Liston, Robert, 173, 174, 178
Liszt, Ferencz, 218
Little, William John, 192
Liverpool, 68, 79, 126, 141, 196, 218, 289
London, 28–31; children, 164–5; epidemics, 201, 203, 205; filth, 12; gaming houses, 248–50; hotels and restaurants, 152–3; milk supplies, 137; medical officer of health appointed, 195–6; music-halls, 237–8; pleasure gardens, 256, 257; poverty, 82–3, 124–6; sight-seeing, 263; theatres, 231–3
districts, streets and buildings: All Saints church, Camden Town, 63; Belgravia, 65–6; Bridge-water House, 70n.; British Museum, 63; Buckingham Palace, 48, 65, 213, 266; Chelsea church, 62; Cleopatra's Needle, 188–9; Coal Exchange, 75; Enon Chapel, Clement's Lane, 223; Houses of Parliament, 29–30; Hyde Park, *138*, 229; Kennington flats, 83; Kensington Palace, 2; Lonsdale Square, Islington, 66–7; Paddington Station, 277n.; Porchester Terrace (J. C. Loudon's villa), 277–8, 290–91; Reform Club, 70; St Pancras church, 63; St Pancras Hotel, 75n.; South Kensington, 264; Trafalgar Square, 29, 68; Westminster, 193; *see also* Great Exhibition; Thames, River

London Working Men's Association, 16
Lonsdale, Lord, 252
looking-glasses, 92
Loudon, John Claudius, 267–9, 274, 277, 279, 280, 284, 286, 289–90; London home, 277–8, 290–1
Lovett, William, 16
Lowther Castle, 63
Lyttelton, Lady, quoted, 10, 20, 248
Lytton, Lord, *see* Bulwer-Lytton, Edward

Macaulay, Thomas Babington, 234
Macready, William Charles, 234, 237
magazines, gardeners', 286–7
malnutrition, 165–6
Manchester, 68, 79–81, 215, 218, 289n.
marriage settlement, 116
Marylebone Cricket Club, 253
Maurice, Frederick Denison, 36–7
Mayhew, Henry, 124–6; quoted, 163, 223, 226–7, 236, 248
meat, tinned, 150–51
medical books, 188, 206–8
medical officers of health, 196
Melbourne, William Lamb, 2nd Viscount, 9, 10, 18, 116
melodrama, 235
menageries, 230
Mendelssohn, Felix, 214, 218
Meredith, George, 241–2
Metropolitan Society of Florists and Amateurs, 283n.
milk, 137, 151
mines, 11n.
Misson, Henri, quoted, 129
mistresses, 228
Mitchell, John, 135
Mitford, Mary Russell, 15, 96, 234, 244, 298
Moore, Tom, 220
Morgan, Joseph, 100
Morrison's Universal Pill, 208–9
Morton, Charles, 238
Morton, William, 175

moss houses, 292
Moule, Rev. Henry, 113
mudlarks, 165
Müller, Johannes, quoted, 185
Mulready, William, 25
Muntz metal, 100
museums, 264
music, 213–21, 224–7
musical evenings, 213–14, 218–19
music-halls, 237–8

Nightingale, Florence, 196, 197–8, 200, 205
nitrous oxide, 174
Normanby, Lord, 203
Norris's Drops, 209
Norton, Caroline, 116
nouveaux riches, 93
novels, 238–42
nursing, 198–200

Old Price riots, 231
ophthalmia, 207
orchids, 278, 279
orthopaedics, 192
Osborne House, 21, 71–2, 96, 111, 250, 251, 260n., 266–7
ottoman, 90
over-eating, 161–2
Owen, Robert, 166–7

paediatrics, 190–92
Paget, James, 189–90
Palmerston, Henry Temple, 3rd Viscount, 38, 309, 311
papier-mâché, 90–91, 98–9
Parian ware, 102
Parkinson, John, quoted, 284
parlour, 97–102
Parr's Life Pills, 208, 209
Partridge, Dr Richard, 183
patriotic songs, 225
Patti, Adelina, 218
Paxton, Joseph, 45, 75, 261, 275, 277, 286–89, 296
Pedro V, King of Portugal, 305

Peel, Sir Robert, 18, 27–8, 41, 71, 95; quoted, 293
penny post, 23–4, 25n., 27
Pereira, Dr Jonathan, 139
Perkins, Jacob, 149
pest control, 284–5
Petit, Jean Louis, 188
Phelps, Samuel, 234
photography, 29, *38*
physiology, 190
piano-playing, 215–17, 219
pianos, 95–7, *216*
picturesque style, 270–71
piers, 260
Place, Francis, 16
pleasure gardens, 273; public, 256, *257*
poets, 243–6
poor relief, 194–5, 202–3
Pope, Alexander, 53–4
Portland cement, 74
postage stamps, 23–4
potato famine, 27, 132
Pott, Dr Percivall, 192
poverty, 79–83, 124–7, 162–70, 298; *see also* poor relief
Price, Sir Uvedale, 270
prostitutes, 228, 256–7
public health, 195–6, 203, 204
puddings, 145
Pugin, A. W. N., 29, 45, 47–9, 75–6; house at Ramsgate, *76*
Pugin, C. A., 48
Punch, 25, 135–6
purl, 208

quack medicine, 208–10

racing, 258
railways, 10–11, 12–14, *13*, 73, 146; excursions, 260–61; station, *24*
Ransome, James, 293
rat catching, 255
Reed, Priscilla, 237
Reed, Thomas German, 237
refrigeration, 148–9

religion, 34–7, 60, 61
Repton, Humphry, 269–70, 271–3, 277; quoted, 57
restaurants, 152–3
resurrection-men, *see* body-snatchers
Rickman, Thomas, 50n.
ridge and furrow roof, 277, 278
riding, 253
Rigby, Elizabeth, 241
Ripon, Lord, 214
Roberts, John, 251
Robinson, Henry Crabb, quoted, 62–3, 159n.
Robinson, Robert ('Long Bob'), 253–4
Robinson, William, 273
Rochefoucauld, François de la, 130
rock-work, 295–7, *296*
Roman Catholic Church, 49–50
Rosenau, 1, *4*
roses, 283–4, 286
Rossetti, Dante Gabriel, 243
Royal College of Surgeons, 178n.
Royal Toxophilite Society, 252
Rubinstein, Anton, 218
Rugby football, 254
rural life, 15–16, 168, 297–8; *see also* agricultural labourers
Ruskin, John, 75, 241, 289n.; quoted, 77–8
Russell, Lord John, 27, 39, 203
Russell, William, 37

Saddington, Thomas, 149, 150
St Leonards, Edward Burtenshaw Sugden, Baron, 42
Salt, Sir Titus, 83, 166
Saltaire, 166
Salvin, Anthony, 69
Sanger, James, 229–30
Sanger, 'Lord' George, 229–30
Sanitary Commission, 195
sanitation, 194, 204
Saunders, John Cunningham, 189
Scarisbrick, Charles, 49–50, 52
Scarisbrick Hall, 45–6, 47, *49*, 51–3
scarlet fever, 208

scavenger's budget, 167
Schlomburgk, Robert, 287
schools, 109, 139–40, 254
Schumann, Clara, 218
Schumann, Robert, 217
science, degrees in, 44
Scott, Sir Giles Gilbert, 75
Scott, Sir Walter, 50, 234
Scribe, Eugène, 234–5
sea chanties, 221
seaside resorts, 259–60
'select' flower gardens, 282–3
servants, 104, 120–1; rooms for, 123–4
service à la Française, 154–6
service à la Russe, 159
sewers, 192–3
Shaftesbury, Anthony Ashley Cooper, 7th Earl of, 16, 169–70
Shield, William, 219
shops, 29
shower baths, 111–12
sideboards, 87–9, *88*
Siebold, Marianne, 1
Simon, Sir John, 196
Simpson, Professor James Young, 174, 175–7
skittles, 255
Slough, 289
Smirke, Sir Robert, 63
Smith, Thomas Southward, 194
Smith, William, 40
Snow, Dr John, 172, 204–5
soap tax, 285
Society for Improving the Conditions of the Labouring Classes, 16
sofas, 89–90
songs, 219–21, 224–7
Souberain, Eugène, 176
Soyer, Alexis Benoît, 142, 144n.
Speenhamland system, 202
Squire, Dr Peter, 175
staircase, 103
Stalybridge, 80
Stanley, Henry, 249
steamer trips, 258–9, *264*
stereoscope, 247

Sterndale Bennett, Sir William, 217–18

Stockmar, Christian Friedrich, Baron von, 19, 305, 306

Strauss, Johann (*elder*), 222

Strawberry Hill, 51, 54–5

street musicians, 224

Stromeyer, G. F. L., 192

Strutt, Sir Joseph, 174n.

Sullivan, Barry, 237

Summerly, Felix, *see* Cole, Henry

Sunderland, 201

sunlight, fear of, 92

Sydenham, Dr Thomas, 187

Sylvester Apparatus, 107

Syme, James, 173

Syon House, 295

table manners, 159–60

table silver, *143*, 156n.

tables, *91*, 98–9

Taine, Hippolyte, quoted, 227, 228, 257, 267

Talbot, William Henry Fox, 29

Taylor, Professor Tom, 235

Tennyson, Alfred, 32, 94–5, 245

terrace, 272

Terry, Ellen, 233

Tew Park, 268

textile industry, 163–4

Thackeray, William Makepeace, 240; quoted, 95

Thames, River, 28, 194, *195,* 258–9, *264*

theatres, 231–3; audiences, 235–6; *see also* drama

Thomson, James, 54

Thornet, Michael, 91

Thurston, John, 251

Timbs, J., quoted, 137, 148

Times, The, quoted, 161–2

tinned food, 149, 150–1

tommy-shops, 166

toothache, 207

towns, 11, 59–60, 79–83, 193

Toynbee, Joseph, 187–8

traffic, 30–31

Tree, Ellen (Mrs Charles Kean), 233, 234

Trent affair, 307–9

trichinosis, 190

truck payments, 166, 169

Tupper, Martin, 245–6

Turkish style, 59

twopenny hops, 223

typhoid fever, 210–12

'typhus fever', 210

umbrella stands, 104–5

Underwood, Michael, 191

unemployment, 163

United States of America, 44, 307–8

Vauxhall pleasure gardens, 256

Victoria, Princess (Princess Royal), 266n., 303

Victoria, Queen of England: birth, 1; character, 19–20, 21; comes of age, 3; succeeds, 7; early years of reign, 8–10; Hastings scandal, 17–18; 'Bedchamber Crisis', 18–19; marriage planned, 3, 19; falls in love, 20; marriage, 21–3, ballads on, 226; religious faith, 36; Albert's influence on, 41–2; builds Osborne House, 71–2; approves chloroform in childbirth, 172; at races, 258; bathes at Osborne, 259–60; visits Great Exhibition, 262, 264; enjoys archery, 252, dancing, 222, drawing and painting, 247, gardening, 266, music, 213–14, 218, novels, 241, parlour games, 248, theatre, 230, 231, 233, Tupper's verses, 245, 246; grief at mother's death, 301, 302–3; in Albert's last illness, 306, 311, 312; *other mentions,* 96, 211, 242, 277, 303

journal: on Balmoral Castle, 40; on Pedro V's death, 305

letters: on Peel's resignation, 27–8; on food prices, 28; on Prince of Wales, 300; on mother's death, 301; on Pedro V's death, 305; on Albert's illness and death, 306, 311, 312
Victoria regia lily, 287–8
villas, 58, 80, 290, 297

Wagner, Richard, 218
Wakley, Thomas, 135
Wales, Prince of, *see* Albert Edward, Prince of Wales
walking, 253
Walpole, Horace, 51, 54, 55, 57
Ward, Nathaniel Bagshaw, 278
Ward, Robert, 240
Wardian Case, 278–9
wardrobes, 121–2
wash stands, 109
water closets, 112–13
water supply, 193–4
Waterford, Marquis of, 256
watering machines, *285*
Watson, Dr Thomas, 311
Watts, G. F., 30
Webb, Jane (Mrs J. C. Loudon), 269, 280–1, 286, 295
Webster, Daniel, 298–9

Wellington, Arthur Wellesley, 1st Duke of, 14, 18, 153, 249, 262
West, Charles, 190, 191–2
Weymouth, 259
Wheatstone, Sir Charles, 246
White Conduit House, 256
Wilkes, Captain Charles, 307–9
Wilkins, William, 68
Willan, Robert, 188
William IV, King of England, 3, 4–5
Wilson, Sir Erasmus, 188–9
Wilson, Professor George, 173–4
Wimbledon, 252n.
Windsor Castle, 48, 57, 111, 213, 234, 266, 289, 306–7, 310
Wordsworth, Bishop Christopher, 244
Wordsworth, William, 243–4
workhouses, 202; food in, 140–1
working hours, 11–12, 163–4
Wyatt, James, 54, 55–6, 57
Wyatville, Sir Jeffry, 48, 57

Yearsley, James, 189
yeast, 147
Young, Edward, 54
Young, Thomas, 189

zoetrope, 246